John Rutledge

The Dialogue of the Dead
in Eighteenth-Century Germany

German Studies in America

Edited by Heinrich Meyer

No. 17

John Rutledge

The Dialogue of the Dead
in Eighteenth-Century Germany

Herbert Lang
Bern and Frankfurt/M.
1974

The Dialogue of the Dead
in Eighteenth-Century Germany

by

John Rutledge

Herbert Lang
Bern and Frankfurt/M.
1974

ISBN 3 261 01324 9

©

Herbert Lang & Co. Ltd., Bern (Switzerland)
Peter Lang Ltd., Frankfurt/M. (West-Germany)
1974. All rights reserved.

Printed by Lang Druck Ltd., Liebefeld/Berne (Switzerland)

PREFACE

I wish to express my gratitude to the Deutsche Akademische Austausch-dienst, whose generous fellowship made possible a year of research in Germany. Many thanks are due to Dr. Lieselotte E. Kurth, my Doktormutter who first brought the Totengespräch to my attention, for her encouragement and for the many hours she spent reading the work. I am also grateful to Dr. Harold Jantz for his helpful suggestions, for the use of materials in his library and for his careful examination of my text. Lastly I thank my wife Joyce for her understanding companionship during the writing, for her gentle critiques, and for proofreading the manuscript in all its stages.

September 4, 1972
Fall River, Massachusetts

CONTENTS

I have a clearer idea of the Elysian
fields than I have of heaven . . . .

— Yorick, in Sterne's Sentimental Journey

CHAPTER I

INTRODUCTION

A remarkable phenomenon of German literature is the large number of dialogues of the dead which were produced between 1680 and 1810. During this time the Totengespräch flourished as it had not since Lucian, the originator of the genre; literally hundreds of Totengespräche, Entrevuen or Gespräche im Reiche der Todten, as they were variously called, were written for the most divergent of reasons. There were dialogues of the dead which reported political manoeuverings and those which discussed philosophical matters, and just as the subject matter ranged from journalistic controversy to philosophy, so the dialogues varied widely in quality.

To date no one has investigated this literary genre thoroughly. A few general studies, and several dissertations on David Faßmann (1683-1744) — the name hitherto most closely associated with German dialogues of the dead — have been written, but the existing secondary literature gives only an inaccurate picture of the role of the dialogue of the dead in eighteenth-century German literature.

Given the nature of German literary activity in this period, the dialogue of the dead found fertile soil in a number of areas, each of which produced its particular kind of Totengespräch. This investigation, then, examines Totengespräche in these "fields of endeavour" as they develope in what seems to be a natural order and attempts to present a general outline; at the same time it emphasizes the relation of the Totengespräch to German literature and literary criticism. A preliminary step in this process will be an analysis of the nature of the dialogue of the dead as a genre.

The acknowledged father of the genre is Lucian (born about A. D. 120) of the Syrian town Samosata. Of dialogues of the dead before Lucian very little is known. Although there exist examples of voyages to the nether world in literature preceding Lucian, notably in the eleventh book of the Odyssey and the sixth part of the Aeneid, Lucian seems to have been the first to produce independent dialogues taking place in the subterranean realms.

Two formative events in the history of the genre were the publication of series of dialogues des morts by Bernard Le Bouyer de Fontenelle (1683)[1] and by François de Salignac de La Mothe-Fénelon (1712).[2] These collections did much to revivify the genre and enjoyed great respect in Germany.

Perhaps the most important device in the dialogue of the dead is the "realm of the dead" fiction, the setting of the scene in the world beneath this one. The device is a venerable one, having been employed in several genres from ancient times to the present. In the early eighteenth century Johann George Neukirch commended the fiction in his Anfangs=Gründe zur reinen teutschen Poesie Itziger Zeit:

Welches sind nun die <u>Fontes</u> zu den <u>Fictionibus Poeticis</u>?
. . . Die zur Zeit im Schwange gehende Schrifften und
paßirende Dinge, als die Europäische <u>Fama</u>, Gespräche
im Reiche der Todten, . . . so könte man eben dergleichen <u>fingi</u>ren und poetisch vorstellen. [3]

Neukirch is not praising the <u>Totengespräche</u> of his own day, but rather recognizing
the legitimacy of the fictive device, which was a popular motif in the eighteenth century, so popular, in fact, that it became an object of satire and parody. Some authors simultaneously diverged from as well as benefited from the custom by styling
their dialogues "Gespräche im Reiche der Lebendigen". Conversations in fictive
realms such as a "neutrales Reich", or a "Reich der Geister" or limbo also were
published in the eighteenth century. Few, if any, of these other fictive realms allow the variety of satiric and humourous possibilities that the realm of the dead
provides, and by sheer number no other fictive realm persisted so long, nor provided the setting for so many dialogues as did the "realm of the dead".

Most of the German writers of dialogues of the dead draw heavily on
the mythological heritage of the Greeks and expect the reader to be familiar with
the nature, the personalities and the geography of the Greek nether world. In this
they follow Lucian himself, who took a knowledge of Hades and its regions for
granted.

Since the Greek conception of the afterlife included a number of locali-
ties, a dialogue of the dead could theoretically take place in a variety of netherworldly sites. In practice, however, the geographic area is often not specified, or
is mentioned obliquely. Yet there are a number of traditional settings for these
dialogues.

A writer may choose to set his dialogue on the shores of the river Styx.
This arrangement permits the contrast between earthly and netherworldly life,
upon which the moral of the dialogue is often drawn. Lucian's tenth dialogue of the
dead serves as the prototype for this usage. [4] Here several shades are made to
leave their worldly goods on the bank before they embark for the crossing. A sol-
dier must leave his medals behind; a philosopher is stripped of boastfulness and
fancifulness.

The author may elect to have the dialogue take place in Charon's bark.
Here, too, contrasts between this boat and an actual ship provide an absurd kind
of humour and a gentle playing with tradition. Frequent motifs are overcrowding,
difficulties of rowing the boat, and irregularity of schedule. Such burlesque plays
a part in the most humourous of Lucian's <u>Totengespräche</u>. An excellent example
from German literature is Georg Karl Claudius' "Die Schatten, erster und zweyter
Transport."

A favourite scene of the dialogue of the dead is the netherworldly court
or hall of judgement. That the scene is to be so construed is often indicated merely
by the presence of one of the judges of the underworld, Minos, Rhadamanthus or
Pluto. A few eighteenth-century <u>Totengespräche</u> contain lavish descriptions of the
splendours of the court, but simplicity of description is the general rule. Judgement scenes also appear in Lucian's dialogues of the dead. [5]

A large number of dialogues take place in the Elysian fields, that select

12

area where only the noble dead are allowed to wander. By selecting Elysium as the scene the author grants his characters an added air of sublimity, but he also limits his choice of speakers: the ignoble dead may not inhabit the Elysian fields, nor appear in dialogues enacted there. Elysium is particularly well suited for the highest level of discourse, since it represents a realm of truth and wisdom.

The existence presented in the dialogue of the dead never resembles the Christian heaven. Only a few writers of Totengespräche (among them, however, David Faßmann) make an attempt to reconcile the two views of the afterlife. In Faß- mann's interpretation, Elysium is the place where the dead await the day of judgement. Although a sizable number of dialogues of the dead deal with religious questions, even the writers of theologically-oriented dialogues do not feel compelled to revise Greek mythology to fit Christian eschatology.

The element of time has its particular use in the realm of the dead just as it does in the realm of the living. Tradition allows the author various possibilities for the arrangement of time. He may dissolve time altogether and thus free himself from it by setting his scene in a realm beyond time. The effect is to re- open the past to the reader's inspection; the great men of history stroll and converse in the environs of Hades, irrespective of their specific eras and nationalities. This allows for a great degree of directness, and thus promotes a concise and clear presentation of ideas. Often the author chooses to present the realm of the dead as a situation in which time is of no immediate concern. Although the author himself still labours under the burden of the flesh, his fictive shades discourse until they exhaust the topic, seemingly unhindered by the limitations which time places on earthly discussion.

Yet as time is a flexible thing, some writers bend it towards the other extreme, using paucity of time as an excuse to break off the discourse; or, if time is limited, regular meetings in the realm of the dead may be arranged. The latter usage was favoured by writers of historical or journalistic Totengespräche.

Normally time in the nether world flows parallel to earthly time: the dialogue of the dead may be netherworldly, but it is rarely otherworldly. It must correspond to this world if its satire and criticism are to be effective, or if its value as news carrier or curiosity piece is to sell it. A misanthropic, nether- worldly "Tymon" may still claim, "Der Tod hat mir nichts geraubt: ich rede hier mit eben dem Nachdrucke, wie ich in der Oberwelt redete, und ich hasse die Schat- ten eben so sehr, als ich die Menschen hassete."[6] Further testimony on this matter is given by Johann Heinrich Merck in his dialogue "Die schöne und die häßliche Seele"; at one point one of Merck's shades states: "Diese Unterwelt ist der Ober- welt in vielen Stücken so ähnlich, daß man zuweilen irre wird."[7]

Biographical and political dialogues of the dead were often written just a few months or a few years after the death of a statesman. In fact, they some- times appeared indecorously soon after the death of a famous man. David Faßmann saw this fault in his "imitators" and was moved to comment on the abuse in the "Vorbericht" to his Neu=entdeckten Elisäischen Felder.[8] Often the entrance of a shade into the subterranean realm links the chronology of the Oberwelt with that of the Unterwelt. Such arrival scenes, in which the newly-arrived shade is be- sought by those gone before him for news of the world above, were devices fre- quently employed to introduce new topics to the discussion.

As a rule the dialogue of the dead has two speakers. Occasionally a dialogue features several speakers or consecutive pairs of speakers. There seem to be few restrictions as to who may appear conversing in the realm of the dead. Even the requirement of respectability that they be dead has been violated by several writers, notably by Frederick II, King of Prussia. Most often, however, the characters are famous historical figures, or they are anonymous and archetypical. The two speakers must relate to one another in some important way, either by past personal relationship (e.g., Lucian's "Phillip and Alexander"), similarity of accomplishments (two "gelehrte Frauenzimmer" such as Wilhelm Ehrenfried Neugebauer's Elephantis and Anne Dacier) or mutual antagonism as seen in Lucian's "Alexander, Hannibal, Minos and Scipio" (Dialogue XII). Nameless shades must represent some group of human endeavour, virtue or vice. The selection of the speakers determines to a large degree how well the dialogue will cohere. If the speakers have neither mutual interests nor shared history to discuss, then the level of the conversation often suffers.

Although a great diversity of speakers appears in dialogues of the dead, certain conditions and characteristics of the dead remain static. The dead are remarkably unphysical. The change from life to death, and the consequent loss of the body often prove to be an experience of enlightenment; Christoph Martin Wieland stresses this theme in his "Dialogen im Elysium". Relieved of the necessities of the body, the shades can pursue intellectual occupations with the greater vigour. Indeed, intellectual change is the only kind now possible, since according to custom the dead are physically powerless. One particular tradition of netherworldly mythology appears only rarely in eighteenth-century Totengespräche: the drinking of water from the Lethe. Absence of memory would inhibit the conversation of the shades, and for this reason the banishment of memory is omitted from most dialogues of the dead.

The great number of eighteenth-century Totengespräche – more than 500 were produced in Germany alone – invites some explanation. What are the inherent characteristics of the genre that made it attractive to so diverse a group of writers? A partial answer is that the dialogue of the dead has many qualities, not all of them useful to any one author. The writer must choose which of many aspects he wishes to emphasize.

Simplicity of form is a quality which the dialogue of the dead must have; compactness lies at the core of the Totengespräch. Extraneous matters fall away, leaving the dialogue pure and reduced to the essentials. Through the mouths of his characters the author may present whatever ideas he wishes, while the simplicity of the form allows for their expression in a straightforward manner.

The Totengespräch is ideally suited to the eighteenth-century passion for expressing multiple points of view. It is a form that allows the great men of the past to speak again with a directness possible in few other genres. The value of the Totengespräch for presenting multiple perspectives is confirmed by the Swiss historian, pastor and author of Totengespräche, Johann Konrad Fäsi, in the introduction to his collection Unterredungen Verstorbener Personen:

> Schriften dieser Art, da verstorbene Personen redend vorge-
> stellt werden, gestatten es, Wahrheiten in ein so helles Licht

zu setzen, als durch einen andern Weg nicht leicht so gut,
auch nicht so einleuchtend, geschehen möchte. Es lassen
sich auch die Folgen der Ursachen und der Begebenheiten,
aus mehrern Gesichtspunkten übersehen und beurtheilen,
als der eigentliche Geschichtsschreiber, ohne auszuschwei-
fen, thun kann. [9]

Another important aspect of the Totengespräch is its ability to pass
judgement. In this genre it is possible for the writer to administer "poetic" justice. Since the dialogue form itself is dramatic, the writer need only set the scene
in the presence of one of the judges of the nether world and swift "justice" may
soon be delivered. Yet not Rhadamanthus, nor Minos, nor Aeacus is indispensible
for judgement; it may be passed by shades themselves, in their refusal to talk or
associate with the shades of their social or moral inferiors. Of course the author
himself shapes the dialogue; he determines which ideas or persons are favourably
presented, thereby passing "judgement". By skillful arrangement of the dialogue
the author may allow the shade unintentionally to condemn himself.

The "Reich der Toten", the realm of the dead, presents in itself an
ideal realm with which this imperfect sublunary sphere may be well compared for
satiric and moralistic purposes. Lucian himself often uses the contrast between
the inequatitity of this world and the absolute equality of the next to warn his hearers
against pursuing vain things. The nether world as it is often depicted has many Utopi-
an characteristics. Thus the shade of "Olivier Cromwel" states: "Jeder Unter-
schied höret hienieden auf, und meine reformirte Religion soll mich nicht mehr
von einem Fürsten der römischen Kirche entfernen . . . ". [10]

Because the Totengespräch does present problems from several perspectives, because it is able to pass judgement, it was all too frequently used for
didactic purposes. Didacticism is a part of the Totengespräch from its Lucianic
beginnings, of course; but later dialogues of the dead often increased the quantity
of instructive material without a compensatory increase in grace, charm or humour. Faßmann himself intended his interviews in the realm of the dead partially
as instruction, and their value as a preceptive device is attested by several writers.

Christian Adolf Klotz reviewed two dramatic fragments set in the nether
world, Johann Georg Jacobi's "Elysium" and Johann Benjamin Michaelis' "Die
Schatten". In writing the notice for the Deutsche Bibliothek der schönen Wissenschaften he comments on the dramatic properties of Elysium:

> Handlungen kann es in Elysium wenig geben. Die Schatten
> bringen zwar die nemlichen Leidenschaften mit dahin, die
> sie auf Erden hatten, allein die Gegenstände fehlen, sich
> thätig zu zeigen. Ihre Leidenschaften äussern sich nur in
> Unterredungen. Sie unterreden sich entweder über Empfin-
> dungen oder über Handlungen. In der ersten Art Gespräche
> äussern sich die Leidenschaften lebhafter, als in den letz-
> tern. [11]

Klotz's comments hold true for many dialogues of the dead, but fail to include some of the more elaborate variations such as were used for literary satires. Most shades do speak either of their perceptions or of (past) actions. However, those Totengespräche which take the form of judgement scenes often involve a dramatic development which leads to the condemnation of a particular shade or an idea.

Normally the dialogue of the dead allows for no psychological developement. There is no chance for further personal accomplishment after one has crossed the Styx. It is, of course, possible — indeed, it frequently occurs — that shades gain new knowledge after death, in the sense that death is an unburdening; but the psychological developement of the shade cannot play a large role in the dialogue of the dead. Without physical bodies, they remain mere shades of themselves, and cannot receive new sensations for growth. The effect of this incorporeality is to increase the importance of the intellect and wit. The dialogue of the dead is a form in which both must excel: lack of either results in impoverishment.

In only a few Totengespräche is any attempt made to explain how knowledge of conversations in the underworld was obtained. It was part of the reader's duty not to ask embarrassing epistemological questions. Occasionally, however, a writer introduces his dialogue by means of an explanatory framework. Such frames often involve the fiction of a dream (Traumfiktion). The dream fiction may result in a lengthy sojourn in the realm of the dead, such as Fielding's Journey from this World to the Next, or Seybold's Lucians neueste Reise. [12]

Only a small percentage of eighteenth-century Totengespräche are intentionally humourous. Despite the ability of the genre to produce comic effects, the dialogue of the dead is basically serious, as witness Lucian's own moralistic carpings. Yet since humour plays a part in many dialogues of the dead it is necessary to investigate some of its peculiarities.

The dialogue form permits the writer to display the graces of badinage which often contribute greatly to a dialogue of the dead; however, the Totengespräch possesses inherent characteristics which provide bases for humour not possible in many other dialogue forms. One precondition for humour in the Totengespräch must be met: the audience must be sufficiently detached from fear of the afterlife to view the situation disinterestedly. Thus satirical dialogues in the style of Lucian's dialogues of the dead occurred only when popular religious literalism was losing its grasp on many minds. (Herein lies a possible explanation for the paucity of Totengespräche set in the Christian heaven or hell.)

Only when this prerequisite is present can the subtle humour of playing with the tradition itself arise. Of this technique Lucian is unquestionably the master. Relatively few of the eighteenth-century writers approach Lucian's twisting of tradition. In his tenth dialogue Lucian presents Charon's bark as "small . . . and unsound, and [it] leaks almost all over . . .".[13] Lucian's twenty-fourth dialogue calls into question the entire operation of netherworldly justice. Eighteenth-century writers find it more difficult to tamper with the traditions, partially because the audience for whom they wrote no longer had so complete a knowledge of the Greek understanding of the afterlife. Some writers provided footnotes explaining the particulars of the nether world and its dramatis personae.

As a fictive device the realm of the dead offers great opportunity for absurd humour. Not surprisingly, Lucian used this to advantage, particularly in his tenth dialogue in which shades of the dead fear drowning when crossing the

Styx. [14] George Lord Lyttleton, an English author of dialogues of the dead, allows one shade to threaten another physically, only to be reminded by Charon that shades, after all, are powerless. [15] Such absurd humour often borders on burlesque.

Reduction or degradation is one of the most frequently employed kinds of humour in the dialogue of the dead. Lucian often stated the theme of the democracy of death; in his dialogues the beautiful of earth, the athlete and the philosopher are alike reduced to a pile of bones. This reduction often functions as an implied judgement, for if a shade's reputation and stature in the nether world varies greatly from his earthly fame, there can be no doubt but that the latter was an incorrect assessment.

Not all the devices, techniques and purposes discussed above find application in every dialogue; rather as the various themes and means are employed, great variety is produced by their interaction. Still a certain inheritance from Lucian, whose dialogues are a continuing source of inspiration for later writers, remains in all the permutations of the later use of the genre.

NOTES

1 Nouveaux dialogues des morts. Paris. 1683. A translation of these dialogues was published by Johann Christoph Gottsched in 1727.

2 Dialogues des morts composez pour l'education d'un prince. Paris, 1712. Fénelon's dialogues were translated into German by Johann Michael von Loen (1745).

3 Halle, 1724, p. 780.

4 Lucian, transl. M. D. Macleod (Cambridge, Mass., 1961), VII, 101-118. The traditional order of the dialogues has been retained in this study. This volume of the "Loeb Classical Library" is a standard text; citations to it are hereafter given as "Lucian".

5 An ancestor of the form may be seen in Plato's dialogue Gorgias.

6 "Gespräch im Reich der Todten zwischen Alcibiades und Tymon, dem Menschenfeinde", Abendstunden in lehrreichen und anmuthigen Erzählungen. XIV (Breslau, 1776), 117.

7 Teutscher Merkur (Jan. 1783), p. 48.

8 Die Neu=entdeckten Elisäischen Felder und was sich in denenselben sonderbares zugetragen (Frankfurt and Leipzig, 1735), p. 8.

9 Johann Konrad Fäsi, Unterredungen Verstorbener Personen (Halle, 1777). p. [1]. Fäsi's Totengespräche are dealt with in Chapter VI.

10 "Gespräch im Reich der Todten zwischen Olivier Cromwel und dem Cardinal Richelieu", Abendstunden in lehrreichen und anmuthigen Erzählungen. XIV (Breslau, 1776), 141.

11 Christian Adolf Klotz, Deutsche Bibliothek der schönen Wissenschaften, V (Halle, 1771), 96.

12 Such works have been included in this study only if the first person narrator does not intrude upon the dialogue form. A particularly interesting example of the Unterweltwanderung in German literature is Friedrich Freiherr von der Trenck's "Pater Pavian, Voltaire und Ich in der Unterwelt" (Berlin and Leipzig, 1784). The work preaches anticlericalism and reasonable Christianity with much humour.

13 Lucian, VII, 101.

14 Lucian, VII, 101-119.

15 George Lord Lyttleton. Dialogues of the Dead (London, 1760), p. 45.

18

CHAPTER II

THE PREVIOUS STUDIES: A REVIEW AND AMPLIFICATION

The previous work on the subject of German dialogues of the dead has
been neither intensive nor extensive, despite the frequency and variety of dialogues
in the eighteenth century.[1] The Merker-Stammler Reallexikon[2] is one of the standard reference works that could be consulted for preliminary information on the Totengespräch. The article there by C. Kaulfuß-Diesch not only fails to give an adequate picture of the form in eighteenth-century Germany — the satiric tradition is
hardly touched upon — but is also misleading in its emphases, particularly in the
amount of space devoted to Frederick the Great and Grillparzer. The dialogues of
the dead by these two men can only be considered an interesting sidelight in the
history of the genre. In stating that the dialogue of the dead rises and falls with
the spirit of the Enlightenment, Kaulfuß-Diesch overlooks important aspects of
the tradition of the genre. Yet despite inadequacies the article in the Reallexikon
is the best short summary presently available.
    Much more inadequate than Merker-Stammler is the short paragraph
in Kosch's Deutsches Literatur-Lexikon.[3] The article relates little more than that
Lucian wrote dialogues of the dead and that such dialogues were popular in the
eighteenth century. Kosch's reference to a study by Johannes Rentsch is its most
valuable service.
    Rudolf Hirzel's two-volume history of the dialogue published in 1895
devotes considerable attention to Lucian and takes some note of the eighteenth-
century revival of Lucian's form. However, in the short space accorded these
later dialogues he can only list the most important authors. Hirzel's chief concern
is the origin and developement of the dialogue, for which he constructed a theory.
Tersely formulated, it states that dialogues appear in revolutionary periods of the
world's history; they are signs of inward spiritual convulsions. Later writers on
the dialogue of the dead, Johan S. Egilsrud especially, have accepted this theory.
    One of the first scholars to examine the dialogue of the dead as a genre
was Johannes Rentsch, writing in the same year as Rudolf Hirzel. The title of
Rentsch's study, "Das Totengespräch in der Litteratur",[4] indicates the wide scope
of the work. After preliminary discussion of Lucian himself, Rentsch treats of the
Totengespräch in the Middle Ages and the Renaissance — perhaps his most valuable
contribution. Especial emphasis is given to dialogues of the dead in eighteenth-
century France and Germany.
    While Rentsch does give some idea of the variety of uses for which the
form was employed in the eighteenth century, much is ignored. Many of the fore-
most German writers of Totengespräche are either omitted or treated in all too
summary a fashion. To Wieland, translator of Lucian and author of dialogues of
the dead, Rentsch devotes only eight lines; furthermore, Rentsch is aware of only

three of Wieland's five Totengespräche. While literary traits are ignored, another tradition of the genre — the journalistic aspect — is overly emphasized, and the lack of a consistent literary focus aggravates the tendency of the work toward superficiality. For several reasons, chief among them lack of chronology. Rentsch's study fails to provide an adequate picture of the genre and its developement in eighteenth-century Germany. However, it does tell enough to excite curiosity, and, to this end Rentsch's bibliographic footnotes are helpful, if at times incomplete.

A rather thorough review of Rentsch's study appeared in an early issue of Euphorion.[5] Its author, Richard Rosenbaum, discovers a number of lacunae in Rentsch's work, and points to Rentsch's cursory treatment of the developement of the Totengespräch until the end of the seventeenth century. For Rosenbaum David Faßmann is a more positive figure than for Rentsch; the Entrevuen in dem Reiche derer Todten are for him "ein Magazin der damaligen Volksbildung".[6] Rentsch's treatment of Faßmann's "imitators" Rosenbaum finds too abridged and he adds a few titles to the bibliography. Rosenbaum's critique serves mainly as a supplement to the study reviewed. He adds many titles and authors to Rentsch's list, the names Fäsi and Seybold in particular. Rosenbaum's article helps to make clear what further work on the genre is needed.

The most complete study of German dialogues of the dead to date is that of Johan S. Egilsrud, Les dialogues des morts dans les littératures française, allemande et anglaise (1644-1789).[7] Interested evidently in comparative literature, Egilsrud attempts the large task of examining the traditions of the dialogue of the dead in three major languages. The work suffers from inadequacies of several types, the most serious perhaps a case of ideological myopia. The restricted scope of the study limits its usefulness: only the period 1644 to 1789 is covered, while the dialogue of the dead continues beyond the turn of the century in Germany.[8] A recent writer on English dialogues of the dead finds Egilsrud's treatment of English works able, if unsympathetic.[9] Unfortunately only the second adjective may be applied to Egilsrud's survey of German uses of the form. At times it seems that he stubbornly refuses to look for examples of German dialogues, and while he places too much emphasis on those Totengespräche surrounding the life and career of David Faßmann, under whom, in Egilsrud's words, the genre is "metamorphosed",[10] large areas of literary activity (including the moral weeklies and the literary journals) are inadequately treated. Furthermore, Egilsrud, who bases his chronological understanding of the genre strongly on Rentsch, like Rentsch fails to provide a balanced picture of the multifarious embellishments upon the form in Germany.

Egilsrud's inability to examine objectively the German dialogue of the dead results in part from ideological fetters. The outcome of his investigation seems to be determined by several prejudices on which the study operates. His acceptance of Hirzel's theory contributes to the problem. In his treatment of German dialogues he is generally unappreciative and seemingly unwilling to consider dialogues by German authors — with few exceptions — true dialogues. Obviously if one allows only the dialogues of Lucian, Fontenelle and Fénelon as legitimate, one will indeed find few true dialogues in Germany. Too often Egilsrud claims French influence without sufficiently supporting his claim as is seen in his treatment of David Christoph Seybold.[11] German dialogues of the dead in periodicals "suivent presque tous la tradition française et ont une saveur française. Ils sont relativement peu nombreux, comparés aux excellent dialogues alors constamment publiés dans les périodiques français."[12] Yet Egilsrud has overlooked numerous German periodical publications.

Another example of unfortunate bias occurs near the end of his study. There he makes the following observations:

> La littérature allemande a toujours penché vers l'expression des sentiments, mais, au moment où paraissaient les meilleurs dialogues des morts, la pendule atteignait son point extrême du côte de l'intelligence et se préparait déjà à revenir vers l'extrême opposé. C'est alors que la forme connut son court moment d'épanouissement, puis ce fut le violent et rapide retour à la sensibilité avec le Sturm Und Drang et le romantisme. Durant cette ère nouvelle vouée aux émotions intenses, la forme, bien entendu, ne présenta aucun intérêt. Sa réserve, sa passivité réflective, son bon sens, autant de qualités que trouvait glaçantes la ferveur romantique.[13]

Even if one chooses to accept Egilsrud's statement about the tendency of German literature to express emotions, one cannot accept the implications of his statements concerning the historical developement of the genre, for the effects of a "violent et rapide retour" cannot be demonstrated in actuality. The production of dialogues of the dead in the 1770's equalled that of the 1760's in Germany. And if one will have a sensibilité without interest in dialogues of the dead, as Egilsrud implies, one must explain away Goethe's farce in Elysium (1773), Göckingk's "Demokrit und Heraklit" (1773), Kretschmann's "Gellert und Rabener" (1772) and several dialogues by Schubart (1787-1789). The dialogue of the dead is not, as Egilsrud says, reserved, passively reflective, but rather inclines toward the dramatic. A number of satirical scenes in the nether world illustrate this point.

Missing also in Egilsrud is any discussion of the particular fictional devices of German Totengespräche. Form is almost completely neglected. Yet despite its flaws Egilsrud's study furnishes the most complete survey of the genre.

Partially because of his importance to the history of journalism David Faßmann has been the subject of no fewer than four dissertations. An early biography by Hanns Stain in manuscript at the University of Vienna was not accessible.[14] Käthe Kaschmieder's David Faßmanns "Gespräche im Reiche der Todten" (1718-1740). Ein Beitrag zur deutschen Geistes- und Kulturgeschichte des 18. Jahrhunderts[15] also did preliminary work on the Leipzig journalist. Although Kaschmieder's work did help refurbish Faßmann's reputation, it has largely been superseded by the scholarly studies by Ludwig Lindenberg[16] and Wilhelm Damberg.[17] These two studies have proved useful for their analyses of Faßmann's style and methods. By their very nature, however, they do not attempt a detailed and complete view of the dialogue of the dead in Germany. Both studies provide useful bibliographies of related secondary materials.

A study by Karl d'Ester of Moritz Flavius Trenk von Tonder's journal of political dialogues of the dead is also of some benefit.[18] D'Ester's brief attempts at a history of the _Totengespräch_ are helpful, despite the strong inclination of the study toward the politics of the right.

Finally two English-language studies should be mentioned. "News from Hell"[19] by Benjamin Boyce contains provocative discussion of the traditions of literature which deal with the nether world. Boyce points out some of the advantages an author may derive from the fictional conventions of the various "deadly" genres. A recent dissertation by Frederick Michael Keener, cited earlier, on British dialogues of the dead continues what Egilsrud began.

Before examining the dialogues of the dead of the eighteenth century, some indication of their earlier ancestors should be given. Egilsrud excludes most of the earlier periods from his study. Although Rentsch's five pages on the _Totengespräch_ of the Renaissance and Baroque stand in need of some amplification, they are still the most thorough work available on the subject, and frequent reference shall be made to them.

A great proliferation of dialogues is found at the time of the Reformation. Many of these are lively broadsides against the opposing religious or political party. Surprisingly, however, not many of these dialogues — Goedeke alone lists several hundred — take place in the realm of the dead. There are dialogues which approach the genre under consideration, such as the dialogue between Franz von Sickingen and Saint Peter at the gates of heaven. A number of conversations between various popes and the devil have been found as well.[20]

Lucian attracted a number of translators in the Renaissance, perhaps the most famous of whom was Erasmus.[21] German translators of Lucian include Jacob Schwenck, Hieronymus Ziegler, Jacob Vielfeld and Johann Galinarius. Rentsch names Dietrich von Plenningen and Reuchlin.[22] At least eleven translators were drawn to Lucian during the period 1450 to 1550 in Germany.[23] Lucian's twelfth dialogue of the dead, the verbal battle between Alexander, Scipio and Hannibal, underwent at least four German reworkings in the Renaissance.[24] Lucian's influence on the dialogues of Hutten and on Hans Sach's play "Der Caron mit den abgeschiedenen Geisten" has been noted.[25]

Rentsch describes an original dialogue of the dead translated from the Italian into German in 1538. The dialogue entitled "Ein kleglich gesprech babsts Leonis und babsts Clementen mit erem Kemmerer, Cardinaln Spinola, in der helle gehalten . . ." ironically praises the unscrupulous avarice and cunning politics of the popes.[26] Another _Totengespräch_ on this topic is Johann Schradin's "Gründlich ursach der jetz schwebenden Kriegsleuff . . ." (1546),[27] which is set in the nether world with Ariovistus, Arminius, "Kaiser Rotbart" and George of Frundsberg.

Several other dialogues from the time of the Reformation, none of which are known to Rentsch, deserve mention here since they present interesting variations on the form, especially in their mixture of classical and Christian traditions. The "Pasquillus vom salzburgischen Baurngjait",[28] a short, rhymed dialogue of 1542, contains Lucianic elements. In this dialogue the devil fetches a "Pfaffen" from earth. Back in the nether world he bids Charon, who speaks only once in the work, take the pastor across the "hellischen Stix".[29]

The "lustig Gespräch der Teufel und etlicher Kriegsleute"[30] is, like most others of the period, rhymed. Participating in the dialogue are Lucifer, Pluto, Belial, "kleine teuflin" and various representatives of the military.

The "drei neue und lustige gespreche" of 1542 – all are Totengespräche in Knittelvers – claim to be translated from the Latin. The three dialogues form a unified whole. These early judgement scenes in the nether world are the ancestors of a popular eighteenth-century form. The work presents the condemnation of Heinz of Wolfenbüttel,[31] although Heinz himself does not appear in the dialogues. Instead, his place is taken by Lycaon, the tyrannical king of Arcadia, whose name superficially cloaks the person of Heinz. The author of the dialogue had a fairly extensive knowledge of classical mythology, which is revealed in his setting of the scene in a hell of component Christian and classical parts. The dialogue delights in the description of the inferno: no fewer than ten punishments are meted out to the tyrant.

The Erinyes (die hellwütrin) have speaking parts in the dialogue; they function as the expositors of the action. The scene is set by their discussion of Lycaon-Heinz's crossing of the Styx. Heinz, it is reported, embarked armed with an explosive device to blow up Charon's ship. Charon notices the plot and take his revenge on Heinz, as "Megera" reports: "Ein dapfern kampf du hetst gesehn, / Wie frei zusamen trafn die zwen."[32] Despite Charon's advanced age he defeats the villain after a two-hour battle.

Lycaon stands accused of the most abject wickedness, spelled out in the dialogue in earthy language – as are the punishments. To all the charges Lycaon pleads guilty and throws himself upon the mercy of the hellish court, claiming that all he did was for Pluto's greater glory. The nether-worldly court inclines toward leniency but is hindered in its desires by the presence of a "Genius", representative of the heavenly powers, who demand the harshest of retributions.

The punishments, too, are of both Christian and classical inspiration. No hell is complete without its snakes and worms which devour the flesh, and they are present in this fictional hell, too. Another punishment imposed upon Lycaon-Heinz is like that of Tityus, whose liver was devoured by two vultures. Other classical references occur in the tortures as well. Such mixing of traditions was not a characteristic of later dialogues but is peculiar to these which stand so close to the events of the Reformation.

On the topic of dialogues during the Baroque period Rentsch is able only to mention related genres. Certainly there are dialogues in this period. Perhaps the best known are Georg Philipp Harsdörffer's Frauenzimmer Gesprechspiele of 1644. Indeed there are examples of the use of hell for satirical purposes. Rentsch himself lists the sixth "Gesicht" ("Höllenkinder") of Moscherosch's Wunderliche und Wahrhaftige Gesichten Philanders von Sittewald (Straßburg, 1650) and describes the scene as a "Strafgericht über die verderbte Zeit".[33] However, Moscherosch's satire is more specifically a Höllenwanderung than a Totengespräch.

To Rentsch's findings could be added several other scenes in hell, among them Bartholomäus Ringwaldt's (1530-1599) "Neue zeitung, so Hanns Fromman mit sich auß der Hellen und dem Himmel bracht hat" (1582), reissued in 1588 as "Christliche warnung des Trewen Eckharts" and in 1597 as "Zustandt des Himmels, vnd der Hellen . . .". Here as in the "drei neue und lustige gespreche" the author luxuriates in the description of hell, where he naturally finds various of his contemporaries. Yet, as the title indicates, the work is not strictly a dialogue of the dead. Another visionary scene in hell is related by Balthasar Kindermann in

Kurandors Schoristen-Teuffel (1661), which Faber du Faur describes as a "nether-world fantasy in the style of Dante."[34] The work is divided into a first and second "Gesicht" and Faber du Faur notes the influence of Moscherosch.[35]

Moscherosch (then still alive) appears as a speaking character in the anonymous Güldner-Zanck-Apfel of 1666 as do recently deceased persons. Yet the work is modeled not on Lucian, but on Trajano Boccalini's Ragguagli di Parnasso.[36] Although the mountain Parnassus does provide a fictional realm, it lies in the opposite direction from the realm of the dead.

In 1609 a translation of Alfonso de Valdés' "Dialogo de Mercurio y Caron" appeared in Germany.[37] Although the title has been amplified to emphasize the political aspects, the translation is nevertheless a faithful one.

Valdés claims Lucian, Giovanni Pontano and Erasmus as his models. This dialogue with its mixture of history and moralizing is prophetic of a trend to be seen later in eighteenth-century dialogues. The setting of the dialogue is still polemically Christian; in the German title the name Charon is explained as a poetic convention.

Charon and Mercury discuss the war of 1522 and 1523 and as they converse, they are sporadically interrupted by arriving souls (not shades!). Ten souls arrive and are damned; among them are a "Prediger Mönch", a "Königlicher Raht" a "Secretarius" and a hypocrite (Gleißner). The parade of souls, frequently found in eighteenth-century dialogues of the dead, continues with the arrival of eight saved souls as examples of positive behaviour. A modern editor of Valdés maintains that Valdés tried to represent all the estates impartially and without anti-clericalism.[38]

The dialogue discussed above is a true dialogue of the dead. However, the seventeenth-century dialogue of the dead must be accounted a relative rarity when compared with the enormous production of Totengespräche in the eighteenth century. The question of Lucian's influence in the Baroque has not been adequately investigated to date and could well stand some clarification. By the end of the Baroque period, however, David Faßmann had begun to issue his monthly Entre-vuen in dem Reiche derer Todten. These, and a few dialogues of the dead of the late seventeenth century, are discussed in subsequent chapters.

NOTES

1   In the course of the present study, reference will be made to other scholars
     at the point where their work clarifies the particular topic under considera-
     tion.
2   Paul Merker and Wolfgang Stammler, Reallexikon der deutschen Literatur-
     geschichte, III (Berlin, 1928-29), 379-380.
3   Wilhelm Kosch, Deutsches Literatur-Lexikon, IV (Bern, ²1958), 3030-3031.
4   Lucianstudien II. (Wissenschaftliche Beilage zu dem Programme des König-
     lichen Gymnasiums zu Plauen, 1895), pp. 15-44.
5   V (1898), 126-134.
6   Euphorion, V (1898), 129.
7   Paris, 1934.
8   Indeed, examples are found in the nineteenth century and in the twentieth as
     well.
9   Frederick Michael Keener, Shades of Lucian: British Dialogues of the Dead
     in the 18th Century. Dissertation Columbia University, 1965.
10   Egilsrud, p. 119.
11   Egilsrud, pp. 134-135.
12   Egilsrud, p. 129.
13   Egilsrud, p. 143.
14   Das Leben David Fassmanns, 1908.
15   Breslau, 1934.
16   Ludwig Lindenberg, Leben und Schriften David Fassmanns (1683-1766) mit
     besonderer Berücksichtigung seiner Totengespräche, (Berlin, 1937).
17   Wilhelm Damberg, Die politische Aussage in den Totengesprächen David
     Fassmanns, ein Beitrag zur Frühgeschichte der politischen Zeitschrift.
     Dissertation Münster, 1952.
18   Das politische Elysium oder die Gespräche der Todten am Rhein, (Neuwied,
     1936).
19   "News from Hell, Satiric Communications with the Nether World in English
     Writing of the Seventeenth and Eighteenth Centuries", PMLA, LVIII (1943),
     402-437.
20   Max Osborn presents an interesting study of the devil in the literature of the
     Reformation in his Die Teufelliteratur des XVI. Jahrhunderts (Berlin, 1893,
     facsimile reproduction, Hildesheim, 1965).
21   See Richard Förster, Lucian in der Renaissance (Leipzig, 1886).
22   Rentsch, p. 23.
23   L. S. Thompson, "German Translations of the Classics between 1450 and
     1550", JEGP, XLII (1943), 343-363.
24   Rentsch, p. 23.
25   Rentsch, p. 24-25.
26   Rentsch, p. 24.

27 Rentsch, pp. 24 and 42.
    Goedeke, however, designates the work as anonymous (Grundrisz, II [Dresden, [2]1886], 300).

28 Satiren und Pasquille aus der Reformationszeit, ed. Oskar Schade, I (Hannover, 1856), 145-153.

29 Satiren und Pasquille, p. 153.

30 "Ein lustig Gespräch der Teufel und etlicher Kriegsleute von der Flucht des großen Scherrhansen Herzogen Heinrichs von Braunschweig", Satiren und Pasquille, I, 54-67.

31 Duke Henry the Younger of Braunschweig and Lüneburg (1489-1568) was an opponent of the Reformation.

32 Satiren und Pasquille, I, 102.

33 Rentsch, p. 27.

34 Curt von Faber du Faur, German Baroque Literature, A Catalogue of the Collection in the Yale University Library (New Haven, 1958), p. 110.

35 Faber du Faur, p. 110.

36 Faber du Faur, pp. 116-117.

37 "Discours Über Kayser Carolen den Fünfften mit dem König aus Franckreich Francisco Valesio gehaltener Schlacht vor Pavien / . . .", (Amberg, 1609).

38 Alfonso de Valdés, Dialogo de Mercurio y Caron, ed. Jose F. Montesinos (Madrid, 1929), p. 2.

CHAPTER III

DAVID FASSMANN AND THE POLITICAL-BIOGRAPHICAL

DIALOGUE OF THE DEAD

The present chapter undertakes the study of what has been heretofore considered the most important aspect of the Totengespräch in eighteenth-century Germany. It is true that Totengespräche dealing with history, politics, and biography over shadowed the more belletristic form, if only by sheer bulk. From the worst examples of the political and biographical writers the dialogue of the dead acquired a bad reputation. Yet despite occasional attacks from moral and literary guardians, these writers enjoyed a close relationship with their public; they wrote, as it were, by public demand, supplying the curious world with ever-loquacious heroes, people of quality, "high government officials" and even criminals, who in the world beyond recounted their lives and exploits with seeming gusto.

The master of this style, David Faßmann, private tutor to the Cowper family and later journalist, merits serious attention, before a general survey of the developements in the historical-political-biographical Totengespräch is made. Faßmann (1683-1744), whose lengthy Totengespräche appeared monthly in Leipzig from 1718 to 1739, is usually credited with being the originator of the genre "Totengespräch" in Germany.

This chapter has set itself the task of exploring Faßmann's "influence" — a topic not adequately treated previously — and the further developement of the historical-political-biographical Totengespräch in eighteenth-century Germany. This undertaking is made more difficult by several factors: the materials themselves, usually available only in the original edition, are often rare or not available; even when obtainable, dialogues of this type are frequently unrelated to literary topics, and hence, are not the primary objects of literary investigations. [1]

An examination of the many Totengespräche in the tradition of Faß-mann is necessarily preceded by a brief look at some possible sources of Faß-mann's own inspiration and an analysis of Faßmann's own work. Although he claimed Lucian and Fontenelle as his literary forebears, his dialogues are quite unlike theirs. Faßmann refers to Fontenelle and Fénelon on several occasions and attempts to justify his own use of the form by pointing to the dialogues of these masters. In the "Vorbericht" to the Neu=entdeckten Elisäischen Felder, the continuation of the Leipzig Entrevuen in dem Reiche derer Todten, Faßmann names Fontenelle specifically as his inspiration in the writing of the "Todten=Gespräche". [2]

The influence of Lucian and Fontenelle on Faßmann has been dealt with by Egilsrud, Kaschmieder and Lindenberg and needs only to be briefly summarized here. Despite Faßmann's claim of intellectual relationship to Fontenelle, and although Faßmann went so far as to appropriate material from Fontenelle's dialogues des morts, there are but few similarities between their works, while there are major differences in purpose and techniques. These are well summarized by Lindenberg:

Ein Vergleich läßt erkennen, daß Fontenelle Lucians Schöpfung
nachgeahmt hat. Faßmanns Werk dagegen hat mit dem Fon-
tenelles kaum eine Aehnlichkeit. Ein kleiner Oktavband gibt
den 36 französischen Gesprächen in geräumigem Druck 243
Seiten. Die Unterredner sind zwar hier wie dort historische
Personen, aber während Faßmann in Entrevuen von der drei-
ßig- oder vierzigfachen Länge der Dialoge seines Vorgängers
Lebensschicksale und sonstige Begebenheiten breit erzählen
läßt, deutet Fontenelle diese nur eben soweit an, wie sein ab-
seits davon liegender Zweck es erfordert. Er will keine Sach-
verhalte mitteilen, sondern zu Werturteilen über solche führen
und erreicht sein Ziel in meist kurzer Rede und Gegenrede. [3]

Lindenberg further and justly concludes that neither Fénelon nor Lucian exerted
essential influence on Faßmann. [4]

One impetus to Faßmann may have been the existence of dialogues of
the dead in French between heads of state on political matters. A number of such
publications (some of them listed by Rentsch) were printed — some in Cologne —
between 1680 and 1710. [5] Faßmann of course knew French and had visited Paris
while in the service of the Cowper family. His first work, in fact, is a translation
from the French. [6] The titles of such discourses as "Entretien dans la royaume
des tenebres sur les affaires du temps ENTRE Mahomet et Colbert . . ."[7] indicate a purpose similar to Faßmann's. This dialogue is much more speculative
than purely historical, however, and its style is far from Faßmann's own. Nevertheless, it did relate news items of current and popular interest, and thus anticipated one of Faßmann's purposes.

Another possible source for Faßmann's "inspiration" is a group of
anonymous Totengespräche published monthly in 1683 entitled "Historische / Politische und Philosophische Krieg= und Friedens=Gespräche / Auf das 1683. Jahr".
This publication bears many similarities to Faßmann's Totengespräche, but in
contrast to the Faßmann dialogues, the "Historische / Politische Krieg= und Frie-
dens=Gespräche" have a personal narrator who enlivens each dialogue with gossip
and talk on subjects of an entertaining nature. This personal narrator, called Herr
Simplex, is summoned on the last day of each month by Mercury, who transports
him to the Elysian fields by his hair. There he is to put onto paper all that is said
in the discourses conducted there

> damit der erbahren Welt / zu ihrem frommen und besten /
> als welche immer zu derer Sachen zu wissen sehr begierig
> ist / auch möchte hierdurch kund und zuwisen gethan
> werden. [8]

Participating in the discourses are various personifications of European countries,
anagrammatically construed; thus Frau Argemina is Germania, Alitia, Italy, etc.
Also present are Christusio (Historicus), Pholisophus (Philosophus) and Topilicus
(Politicus).

In addition to Simplex's discussion on the care of apple and pear trees

(184-186) and the side effects of smoking tobacco, the magazine presents news of the Austro-Turkish war as well as theoretical discussions such as the question raised by Topilicus "Ob es nutzlicher wäre / daß man entweder mit dem Türken einen vorgeschlagenen Frieden eingehen / oder mit ihme den Krieg fortsetzen sollte?" (200).

Whether Faßmann knew this publication is largely a matter of speculation. However, the "Historische / Politische Krieg= und Friedens=Gespräche" anticipate much of the style of the publications which were to become famous through Faßmann. Egilsrud points to the existence of these pre-Faßmann Totengespräche and claims that they were to be the model for the genre in Germany.[9] Other studies make no mention of these dialogues.

A number of precedents which may have contributed to Faßmann's format may be found in Germany. The first German monthly periodical, Christian Thomasius' Monaths=Gespräche, employed the dialogue form. Faßmann's affection for Thomasius has been noted.[10] Wilhelm Ernst Tentzel's Monatliche Unterredungen einiger guten Freunde von Allerhand Büchern would also have familiarized some of Faßmann's future readers with a periodical in dialogue form.

Whatever Faßmann's sources of inspiration, he exerted strong influence in the world of German journalism during his own lifetime and for many years afterwards, as some of the dialogues discussed later in this chapter will show. Faber du Faur's estimation of Faßmann is a useful one: Faßmann was a "capable news gatherer" whose skillfully written dialogues filled the "noticeable need for the orientation and information of the public" at a time when "there were as yet no opposition parties and no political press in the modern sense".[11]

In his study of Totengespräche Johannes Rentsch uses Heinsius[12] as his main source for knowledge of the further developement of the genre. The fifty Totengespräche which Heinsius lists Rentsch considers to be imitations of Faßmann. However, Heinsius' titles are incomplete and most often do not reveal whether the particular dialogue was written in the manner of Faßmann or not. After pointing to the triviality of Faßmann and his imitators, Rentsch states that Totengespräche lost their appeal at the market; he does not make clear, however, at which time period the loss is supposed to have occurred. The genre does not disappear entirely, he maintains, but recaptures its stature by returning to the Lucianic form; the Totengespräche "ziehen sich auf die Höhen der Litteratur zurück".[13]

There are two oversights in Rentsch's analysis. First, dialogues of the dead with political-biographical content did not disappear; rather they continued to be published until after 1800 (admittedly the production in the 1790's did not match that of the middle decades of the century). Secondly, the dialogue of the dead never really regained the "heights of literature", but remained for the most part a minor genre for the experimentation of satirists, moralists and scholars, although the dialogues by Goethe and Wieland are certainly highly literary examples.

In her study of Faßmann, Kaschmieder devotes only the last three pages to the influence and effect of the Entrevuen in dem Reiche derer Todten. She takes over Rentsch's analysis of the post-Faßmann developement practically verbatim. According to Rentsch and Kaschmieder, then, the essence of the Faßmann inheritance is historical, political and biographical content. The later course of the genre is seen to fall into three categories, the necrologue, the journal for current events and a form for academic feuds. Neither Rentsch nor Kaschmieder provides an adequate investigation of the genre after Faßmann, nor is great or more extensive knowledge of this topic to be obtained from the studies of Lindenberg and Damberg.

The categorization of dialogues by their tendency to contain historical-political-biographical information seems a useful one. However, to investigate all such dialogues would have been impossible, and as suggested earlier, unrewarding. In many cases the sole information available was the title and only from it could one surmise the nature and intellectual ancestry of the particular dialogue.[14] Yet the great blossoming of Totengespräche during and after Faßmann's time produced variations and ornamentations on form and subject matter. To understand the developement of the Totengespräch in Germany it will be necessary to look at the main trends within the roughly-defined category of political-biographical content from the time of Faßmann's "invention" onward.

It is generally acknowledged that Faßmann set the trend, that his Entrevuen in dem Reiche derer Todten established a fashion that endured for decades. However, several problems arise in trying to determine influence by Faßmann. Chief of these is the fact that other writers of dialogues of the dead could have availed themselves of the same sources which Faßmann had. Any writer of Totengespräche could claim, as Faßmann himself claimed, that his inspiration had come directly from Lucian and Fontenelle. Before going into the later history of the Totengespräch this study presents an examination of the structure and technique of Faßmann's dialogues to provide a point of reference. An understanding of Faßmann's unchanging formula supplies a standard with which all Totengespräche thought to be in imitation of Faßmann may be compared.

All of the Entrevuen are proceeded by an engraving which depicts the two persons in the dialogue. These persons are always of high social standing (or are at least famous), and there is usually some point of similarity between them, however ephemeral that point may be. Usually some mention is made of the scene of the discourse; this Schauplatz matches the person's rank on earth and is in accordance with the probity which the person maintained on earth.[15] (This feature Faßmann probably did take over from Fontenelle.)

Most of the dialogues begin with a Vorspiel, in which one of the conversants discusses some important aspect or significant moment of his life. This often has the form of a monologue of some length which is delivered in the unsuspected presence of the other partner of the dialogue. After this Vorspiel one of the persons asks a question which somehow concerns both conversants. This question provides a beginning for the major portion of the Entrevue, the life histories of the two speakers.[16]

The lengthy biographies are followed by a Nachspiel, in which the "Secretarius" reads news from the Oberwelt. After this information has been read, the speakers then express their views on the various items. This Nachspiel was considered an important part of the Totengespräch and was always mentioned in one part of the title.[17]

In the course of publication of the Entrevuen Faßmann varied his technique very little — so little, in fact, that Kaschmieder can state that the 240th dialogue is constructed like the first one.[18] Although Damberg detects a lessening in quality from 1730 to 1733 and the inclusion of more documents in the text,[19] Faßmann's principles and procedures remained practically unchanged throughout more than 20 years of publication.

Faßmann himself was aware of the imitations of his dialogues and spoke out about various aspects of such publications. His criticism of them he included in his own editions of Totengespräche. As early as the twelfth Entrevue Faßmann warns also of pirated editions from Frankfurt, Nuremberg, Leipzig and Hamburg, which could easily be identified by the poor quality of the engravings. The motivation for his objections could well have been financial[20]; a further admonition against them comes at the end of the sixteenth Entrevue: there Faßmann warns that the index to the first sixteen dialogues will not correspond to the pagination of the pirated editions.

After only a few years of publication Faßmann's dialogues drew forth both criticism and satire. In 1721 there appeared an "Abgenöthigte Critique der sogenannten Gespräche in dem Reiche derer Todten".[21] Luckily, the card catalogue of the Preußische Staatsbibliothek in East Berlin indicates that the "Abgenöthigte Critique" consists of four parts, three of which relate directly to the dialogue of the dead. Part I would seem to be a Totengespräch itself; part II, a defense of the fictional convention "Reich der Todten"; part III, a reply to Faßmann's thirtieth interview. Johann Christoph Gottsched in his essay on the dialogue (which served as an introduction to the translation of Fontenelle's dialogues of the dead) calls the author of the "Abgenöthigte Critique" "ein gelehrter Mann" and rejects as he did elsewhere the "beruffenen Gespräche im Reiche der Todten die eine Nachahmung der Lucianischen Todten=Gespräche seyn sollen".[22] Faßmann, on the other hand, called the man an "Einfalts-Pinsel", and as late as 1735 Faßmann was still nursing his injuries:

> In Francken haben die Leipziger Todten=Gespräche, denen
> ich, durch meine neu=entdeckten Elisäischen Felder, gar
> keinen Abbruch zu thun gemeynet bin, bis auf diese Stunde
> viele hohe und vornehme Patronen gefunden. Gleichwohl
> sind sie daselbst, vor einiger Zeit, von einem rechten Ein-
> falts=Pinsel, gantz zur Ungebühr angegriffen worden. Die-
> ser hat sich angemasset, eine Critique über das, was man
> vom Reiche derer Todten fingiret, zu machen, meynet auch,
> sie könten von niemand anders als Handwercks=Leuten
> aestimiret werden. Gleichwohl kommet er alsdann selber
> mit Todten=Gesprächen angestochen, verräth mithin sein
> Affen=Spiel, und machet sich des Baders Affen gleich, der
> eine Katze hat barbieren wollen.[23]

A satire of Faßmann's monthly outpourings was published in 1724. Entitled a "Gespräch in dem Reich derer Todten" between the deceased souls of an ox and a swine, the piece attacked Faßmann's pedantry.[24] Further evidence of the extent of Faßmann's influence is vouchsafed by the existence of translations of his

<u>Totengespräche</u> into English. These were published in London about 1722.[25]

Faßmann felt compelled to deny authorship of certain <u>Totengespräche</u> which brought together "Spitzbuben" and thieves.[26] He was probably reacting to the "Gespräche in dem Reiche derer Todten zwischen dem Güldenen Tafel-Dieb Nickel Listen und dem Kirchenräuber Lips Tullian"[27] and the "Gespräche in dem Reiche derer Todten unter den Spitzbuben".[28] The former was popular enough to be reprinted in 1727 (with slightly different title). Faßmann complains that authors have appropriated not only the term "Gespräch in dem Reiche derer Todten" but also "Entrevue". He denies authorship not from any scruples against bringing together disreputable characters (such complaints <u>are</u> found in the moral weeklies), but because he "einem jeden die Ehre gerne gönnet / die er mit seiner Arbeit verdienet / und nicht will, daß man sie ihme beylegen solle . . .". Further, Faßmann disclaims these <u>Totengespräche</u> to avoid the "<u>Censur=</u>Gebühren".[29] In the "Avertissement" following the 24th <u>Entrevue</u> Faßmann repeats that he is not responsible for those <u>Totengespräche</u> which are not part of his series,[30] and reiterates the same message in 1729.[31]

During the year in which David Faßmann was issuing his monthly <u>Entrevuen</u> a great many other <u>Totengespräche</u> were being published for which Faßmann was, indeed, not responsible. Even a casual glance at this production reveals that it differed from Faßmann's in style and method of presentation as well as in subject matter.

<u>Totengespräche</u> concerned with religious subjects were especially prominent during the 1720's and 1730's; Faßmann's dialogues, too, occasionally feature clerics among their speakers. An anonymous <u>Totengespräch</u> of 1720 brought together Gottlieb Wernsdorffer and Gottfried Arnold.[32] Interestingly enough, the setting and fictional devices of this dialogue belong to Christian and not to Greek mythology. The introduction refers to an alleged dialogue of the dead in the Bible, however: "Wer die Beschaffenheit des Reiches der Todten recht verstehet, weiß, daß wenn gleich die grosse Klufft zwey Personen von einander scheidet, sie dennoch zusammen reden können, so wie der Bruder des reichen Mannes mit dem armen Lazaro ein weitläufftig Gespräche hielten." This is one of the few instances in which there is hint of Biblical inspiration for dialogues of the dead.[33]

In this dialogue Wernsdorffer attacks Arnold's <u>Kirchen-</u> und <u>Ketzerhistorie</u>, which Arnold, of course, defends. The discussion of this work leads directly to <u>curriculae vitarum</u>. Later in the dialogue the theologian Edzardus, himself the author of <u>Totengespräche</u>, is sharply criticized. Such polemics seem to be the purpose of the writing, for the author has little interest in the literary possibilities of the <u>Totengespräch</u>. It is likely that the fictional device "Reich der Todten" was employed to promote sales and for few other reasons.

A dialogue of the dead of 1729 united Christian Thomasius and August Hermann Francke.[34] It too concentrates on biographical information and theological issues. The scene is "the heavenly kingdom". The author had stated in the introduction that the purpose of the work was to make known the life of each man. The lack of subtlety in the presentation may be seen by one of the author's transitions: at one point Thomasius says to Francke, "Fangen Sie also, wann Sie belieben, ihre Lebens=Beschreibung an."

While the above two works are in large part biographical, there were from an early date pamphlets dealing with religious matters. Two such were published around 1722 by Sebastian Edzardus, the polemical Hamburg pastor and author of the anti-Patriot papers, Patriot-Schnatriot. Both of these dialogues are quite short and have little in common with the Faßmann-type Entrevue. In the five-page "Unterredung im Reiche der Todten zwischen Cartouche, Zvinglio, und Tossano . . ."[35] Edzardus makes a simple comparison: while Cartouche was a worldly robber, Zwingli was a spiritual thief for robbing the Holy Communion of the Real Presence.

A popular Totengespräch between the Dutch pastor and author of De betooverte Wereld (1691),[36] Balthazar Bekker and the famous theologian Christian Scriver discussed the appearance of ghosts, sorcerers and pacts with the devil.[37] Bekker had attempted to explain supernatural events recorded in Scripture without the necessity of non-human spiritual beings such as devils and angels. He was long censured by the Church and was thus a controversial figure.[38] A dialogue of the dead on the subjects about which Bekker wrote was certain to be a success. In fact, the public reception of the dialogue was so favourable that — so the author explains in the introduction to the second part — a continuation was necessary. This illustrates the close interaction between writers and their readership in the production of dialogues of the dead.

In 1735 there began a series of dialogues between an Old Testament figure and a related figure from the New Testament, of which the first dialogue was an "Ausserordentliches Gespräch im Reiche der Todten zwischen dem ersten Menschen Adam und Joseph dem Pfleg=Vatter des Herrn Christi . . .".[39] There followed dialogues between Eve and Mary, Cain and Judas, Abel and Stephen, and others. In the preface the author proposed to present the history of the Church as well as the lives of various Church fathers. He tries to justify his use of a slightly disreputable form, the Totengespräch:

> Das gute Absehen, welches der Erfinder oder Anfänger
> solcher Todten=Gespräche gehabt, ist nachgehends von
> andern, die nur lauter abgeschmackte Sachen um eines
> schnöden und schlechten Gewinns willen vorgetragen ha-
> ben, sehr gemißbrauchet worden, also, daß manchem
> Gelehrten anjetzo dieser Titel gantz eckel vorkommet.
> Gleichwohl ist es auch gewiß, daß man eines bösen
> Misbrauchs halber einen guten Gebrauch nicht weg-
> werffen / sondern solchen immer mehr und mehr zu
> erheben suchen soll.[40]

The author of these Totengespräche hardly added to the good name of the genre, for the fourteen parts of these dialogues strove to please the less critical segments of public taste. They are packed with information and misinformation on divers subjects.[41] The dialogue between Adam and Joseph, for example, begins with a paraphrase of the Genesis account of creation and attempts a physical and reasonable explanation of its events. Since Adam lived very soon after the establishment of natural laws he is able to answer Joseph's question (e. g., Where do clouds come from?) with some expertise.

33

Although there are many Totengespräche in the 1720's and 1730's on "religious" topics, the trend does not continue through the 1740's and 1750's. A few dialogues of the latter two decades include popes, but most frequently they are in conversation with important political figures. Later in the century dialogues of the dead on religious topics and dialogues between religious figures are seen again. There are a few instances of the use of the form for theological pamphlets.

Faßmann had complained about the "Gespräche im Reiche derer Spitzbuben", and the author of the dialogue between Adam and Joseph speaks of the "abgeschmackte Sachen" with which other writers of Totengespräche filled their pages. During the years of Faßmann's publications numerous Gespräche im Reich der Toten involving criminal figures may be found. Two dialogues by Edzardus which feature the thief Cartouche have been mentioned, as has the dialogue between Nickel List and Lips Tullian, who take part in several dialogues. These Totengespräche between rogues described not the "Helden=Thaten" but the "Uebel=Thaten" of history. Since they contain examples of thieves' jargon they are of linguistic interest.[42]

Between 1722 and 1728 a set of three dialogues of the dead among thieves styled "Curieuse Gespräche im Vorhofe des Reichs der Todten"[43] was published. The title reflected the practice of segregating the dead according to quality, a custom which was followed by most writers of political-biographical Totengespräche, including Faßmann.

In 1729 there appeared the "Besonders=Curieuses Gespräch in dem Reich derer Todten zwischen Zweyen . . . Zigeuner=Spitzbuben Hemperla und Gabriel".[44] Evidently the earlier Spitzbuben had merited an imitation.

A Totengespräch of 1739-40 does its utmost to satisfy human curiosity about torture and death. The "Gespräche im Reiche derer Todten zwischen dem Knees Alexi Dolgorucki, Ehemahligen Rußischen Reichs=Cantzler . . . und seinem Sohne Knees Johann Dolgorucki"[45] describes in bloody detail how the Russian father and his sons were first tortured on the wheel then beheaded for lèse majesté.

Another case of offense against royalty made good material for Totengespräche, namely, the attempted assassination of Louis XV by Robert François Damiens. The notorious cruelty subsequently inflicted upon Damiens must have helped to sell copies of this dialogue between Damiens and the Portuguese rebel, Joseph de Mascarenhas.[46]

The German reformer in the Danish court, Johann Friedrich Struensee, was treated as a common criminal in a Totengespräch of 1773, the year after his cruel execution.[47] The method of presentation in the dialogue resembles Faßmann's somewhat, but is a great deal terser. Some elements of the Greek nether world are present. Charon's bark deposits the unfortunate shades in a place filled with wild snakes and insects, where the two speakers are to be punished by the Furies. After a very brief introduction (even in this horrid place, Count Struensee, upon seeing Cornfitz Ulefeld, wants to strike up a conversation!) the usual exchange of biography takes place; typically the speakers utter not a word in their own defense. Like Gleichmann, this anonymous author condemns La Mettrie as Struensee says: "Die freygeisterischen Schriften eines Voltaire und de la Mettrie erstickten vollends den Saamen des Guten in mir".[48] Like the Faßmann dialogues this one too ends with a report of news from the Oberwelt, which the "Secretair" reads aloud.

The dialogue of the dead which dealt with criminal figures was from the beginning a spurious form, condemned by many. This use of the genre was considered a less than perfect means of presenting the ideal of virtue. [49] Its period of greatest popularity is the 1720's; thereafter it occurs only sporadically, although Rentsch cites a Totengespräch among robbers and thieves as late as 1808.

A Totengespräch interesting for its social critique of the gallant world is the "Andere Assemblee Unglücklicher=Verliebten im Reiche derer Todten", [50] which uses the form to present two versions of a rake's progress. The language of the dialogue is a mixture of French, Latin and German which parodies the polyglot style of the German galant. The dialogue opens with a discussion of prostitution (Hurerey) from historical and practical standpoints. Amaliere then voices the usual plea for exchange of biography: "Woltet ihr nun so gütig seyn, und mir euren gantzen Lebens=Lauff, den ich lange zu wissen begehrt, communiciren, würdet ihr mich zu gleicher revanche verbindlich machen" (53).

The "hero" Melidor relates his amorous adventures to Amaliere (a beautiful coquette) at some length, including the text of the cantata he once sang for "Amara". When sent away to school he spent his time playing the "Viol di Gamba" and attending "Frauenzimmer Assembleen" rather than studying. Unwilling to find an honourable trade or profession, he allows himself to be supported by a 46-year old woman. His mother, shamed by his conduct, dies of chagrin. After a few more unsavoury episodes Melidor is finally despatched to the lower realms by a cuckolded husband. Amaliere next relates her tale, as she had promised.

Although other dialogues can be found between disreputable characters, this one is unusual for several reasons. While in style it resembles the political-biographical Totengespräche, it features fictitious characters — something which the Faßmann Gespräche did only very rarely; and while other Totengespräche offer criticism of individual morality, few attack a whole style of behaviour such as the gallant world. [51]

The religious and criminological Totengespräche constituted only interesting variations on the political-biographical form; most political-biographical dialogues present historical information about famous generals, statesmen and potentates. Throughout the eighteenth-century the great political men of history revealed their lives and activities to each other and to an eargerly awaiting public.

In the "Vorbericht" to his Neu=entdeckten Elisäischen Felder (1735-1742) Faßmann unleashes his most vitriolic criticism against those who wrote Totengespräche in imitation of his own style. [52] Faßmann labels them his "Affen" and decides to drop the name "Todten=Gespräch" so that his work will not be confused with their "läppisches, närrisches und ungegründetes Gewäsche". [53] Hardly is a great man or famous general dead, Faßmann complains, before a certain book printer in Magdeburg has a Totengespräch ready. [54] Although the Elisäischen Felder were explicitly intended as a continuation of the Leipzig Totengespräche, Faßmann completed only five interviews in the new series.

Yet with the cessation of Faßmann's periodicals in 1742 the fashion by no means ended: the year actually produced a bumper crop. While the great bulk of the political-biographical Totengespräche were published in the 1720's and 1730's, the mode continues through the 1740's and 1750's. A testimony to Faßmann's enduring presence is a dialogue between the queens of Poland and Prussia in 1757;

its author styled himself "Faßmann der Jüngere". In 1747 Gleichmann's series was begun and in 1757, Richter's monthly histories. It is to these two men that the study now turns.

A number of Totengespräche were written by Johann Zacharias Gleichmann (1685/90-1758), a "Hof-Advocate" and "Steuereinnehmer" in Gotha, who published under the pseudonyms Johann Sperante and Veramandus, among others.[55] Gleichmann's early Totengespräche, which deal mainly with matters of theology and law, sometimes tend toward sensational topics, such as the dialogue concerning Pope Joan. This dialogue enjoyed a number of continuations and reprintings. Nearly all of these dialogues of the dead and some pamphlets concerning them were published pseudonymously in Frankfurt and Leipzig between 1725 and 1740.[56]

It has been generally maintained that Gleichmann was an imitator of Faßmann.[57] Although Gleichmann did acknowledge a certain indebtedness to Faßmann, the similarity between the works of the two dialogists does not amount to plagiarism. Gleichmann, for example, does not employ Faßmann's typical formula "Entrevue in dem Reiche derer Todten", and Gleichmann often includes two phrases in his titles which Faßmann did not use, namely "Stille Gesellschaft des Reichs der Todten" and "Curiöses Gespräch".

However, it is for his systematic dialogues of the dead that Gleichmann should best be remembered. While Faßmann's speakers had been chosen with little regard for chronology, Gleichmann added a novum to the genre by producing pairs of speakers in their historical sequence. This he did in the Merkwürdige Staats- und Kaysergespräche im Reiche der Todten, which were published from 1747 to 1751.[58] In this series emperors from Caesar to Charles VII are paired in conversation.

The Kaysergespräche were followed a few years later by the Ertzbischöffliche und Churfürstliche Gespräche in der stillen Gesellschaft des Reichs der Todten. The complete title may serve here as an indication of the contents:

> Merckwürdige und in der historischen Wahrheit gegründete
> Ertzbischöffliche und Churfürstliche Gespräche in der stillen
> Gesellschaft des Reichs der Todten, in welchen zuerst die
> Erzbischöffe und Churfürsten zu Maynz, Trier und Cölln, wie
> sie in ihren Regirungen auf einander gefolget, auch alle welt-
> liche Churfürsten, nach der Successions- und Juris publici
> Ordnung aufgeführet werden, Und von ihnen alles Notable, so
> unter ihren Regirungen vorgefallen, erzehlet wird; wobey zu
> Ende eines jeden Stückes auch das remarquableste aus denen
> Reichen und Staaten der Welt mit vorkommet, und mit einem
> vollständigen Register versehen.[59]

Contrary to his earlier practice Gleichmann identifies himself in the first volume of this series. Among the "remarkable" things which Gleichmann promised in the title were comments on and references to various aspects of literature.

One of the first of these literary references draws attention to "Herr[n] Professor Gellert in Leipzig", whose "Fabeln und Erzehlungen" are praised. To illustrate the point the Secretarius of the "quiet realm of the dead" reads Gellert's

"Der Fuchs und die Elster" to the assembled group. [60] On another occasion also Gleichmann quotes from Gellert and includes one of his poems. [61] Gleichmann evidently favoured the fable in general for he recommends those of Hagedorn and Holberg as well; Hagedorn's, he finds, are as deserving as Gellert's.

For the author of the Ertzbischöffliche- und Churfürstliche Gespräche poetry exists for the glory of God and for Christian edification. At one point in the dialogues the poem "Zufriedenheit" from Proben poetischer Übungen eines Frauen-zimmers[62] is read aloud and commended. Brockes and "Herr Hofrath Triller"[63] are favourably mentioned. Six odes by "Silvander" (Heinrich Christian von Brocke?) gain the approval of the Secretarius:

> In der ersten findet man erhabene und geistreiche Gedanken
> so wohl ausgedrucket, daß man nichts von übertriebenen
> Klopfstockischen Erdichtungen; sondern eine reine Ehr-
> furcht für Gott und seiner höchsten Majestät, wahrnimmt. [64]

Such opposition to Klopstock is consistently maintained throughout the Gespräche. Elsewhere Gleichmann speaks disdainfully of the "Klopfstockianer" whom he defines as "solche Leute, welche an denen ungereimten oder ohne Reimen abgefassten Hexa-metern des Herrn Klopfstocks einen besondern Geschmack finden". [65] At other points in the dialogues Gleichmann indicates his high estimation of rhyme in poetry.

Nor is the novel neglected. Following the practice of including criti-cism of the novel in works which were not specifically intended as vehicles for liter-ary criticism, Gleichmann speaks well of Johann Michael von Loen's Der red-liche Mann am Hofe, and especially of its fifteenth book, the "Leben des Ritters von Castagnetta", which Gleichmann considers "mit vieler Anmuth beschrieben". [66] His opinion of the novel is high enough to warrant his quoting an excerpt.

Although the second volume displays far less concern with literary mat-ters than the first, it nevertheless contains a commendation of satire as a moral tool. Rabener's satirical works in particular are lauded. [67] In Volume I Gleichmann had complimented Hagedorn for his satire Der Poet. [68]

It is true that Gleichmann's Totengespräche dealt at times in sensational-ism and controversy: these aspects of journalism were explicitly advertised on the title pages. The volumes of historical dialogues did, however, provide a compen-dium of historical information which the readers (Gleichmann's readership was probably similar to that of Faßmann) could put to use. From a literary point of view their greatest usefulness was their dissemination of sections, if not complete works, of more important writers.

Few of the previous studies of dialogues of the dead have investigated with any thoroughness those by Christoph Gottlieb Richter (1717-1774), a Nurem-berg lawyer. Both Kaschmieder and d'Ester list Richter as an imitator of Faß-mann. Egilsrud knows Richter's "Die Geschichte des jetzigen Kriegs zu unpar-theyischer Erkenntniß seines Anfangs und Fortgangs in Gesprächen im Reiche der Todten vorgestellt"[69] well enough to state that Richter's style is simpler and less affected than Faßmann's although it still lacks elegance and clarity. Egilsrud fur-ther notes that Richter has benefited from the advances made in the writing of his-tory and that Richter makes an effort to report impartially. [70]

Richter himself took sharp issue with Faßmann in the preface to his
own historical dialogues of the dead. Faßmann, according to Richter, ruined his
Totengespräche by not choosing his conversants carefully enough. Richter also
objects to the large number of excurses in Faßmann's texts. Nor were Faßmann's
sources for his facts adequate. Richter blames Faßmann's lack of ability for the
bad reputation which haunts the genre, but this he sees as only a whim of fashion.
Just as Faßmann had done, Richter likewise grounds his own dialogues on the ones
of Lucian and Fontenelle, at the same time acknowledging that their purposes were
not strictly historical. Perhaps Richter anticipated Egilsrud's charge of lack of
elegance when he stated that dialogues of the dead in the style of Lucian and Fontenelle often remain nothing more than "Saillies d'Esprit" ([9]).

Compared with Faßmann's dialogues, Richter's are much more purely
historical. Many of the volumes provide the reader with detailed maps and charts
of the battle strategies under discussion in the text. Richter avoids unpertinent
topics and sheer Klatsch. There are no references to literary topics or literary
criticism in his five volumes of dialogues. In view of Richter's criticism of Faßmann and the essential differences in their dialogues, it would be unwarranted to
label him an imitator of Faßmann.

Richter provides an explanation as to why the writer of history prefers
the dialogue form and the dialogue of the dead in particular. Among the excellences
of the dialogue Richter lists the following: 1) it allows the author to maintain his
impartiality; 2) it permits the omission of "forced turns of phrase" (gezwungene
Wendungen) and "vexatious repetitions" (verdrüßliche Wiederhohlungen) ([7]);
3) it enables one to think in a more orderly fashion and 4) it works for the ex-
clusion of inessentials. A chief virtue of the dialogue is its characteristic por-
trayal of multiple points of view: "Wie kan ich aber die Urtheile über eine Sache,
die verschieden sind, und die Art, wie einerley Sache auf zweyerley Weise betrachtet wird, besser darlegen, als wenn ich in einem Gespräche zween reden,
und jeden seine Meynung verfechten lasse?" ([9]). Allowing the dead to speak
also has advantages: the dead can no longer complain about the words which the
author attributes to them; furthermore, the dead may speak more freely than the
living.

Richter's series continued into the early 1760's, but that decade saw
comparatively fewer Totengespräche on topics of a political-biographical nature.
Although there were two in 1764 involving the controversial Count Brühl, a Saxon
soldier-statesman who had died the year before, it was generally a period of
quietude — a quietude which contrasted squarely with the concomittant developements in a more literary sphere of endeavour.

The 1770's, however, saw more political-biographical Totengespräche
than had the 1760's. Between 1772 and 1773 Frederick the Great himself wrote two
dialogues of the dead; they were of course written in French. [71]

The suppression of the Jesuit order brought forth several dialogues of
the dead. [72] At least eleven on this topic were written by Christoph Heinrich Korn
(1726-1783) of Tübingen. In 1774 Korn brought together "Pater Angelo", a Jesuit,
and a "Ritter von Moncada" of the Knights Templar. Together the two discussed
the history of their suppressed orders in a series of five dialogues. [73] The following year Korn produced an appendix (Anhang) to the dialogues which contained

"noch mehrere Merkwürdigkeiten"[74]; within the same year a continuation in two parts of the same Totengespräch was forthcoming.[75] Korn's three-part dialogue between Clement XIV — Ganganelli, who dissolved the order — and Loyola its founder, at last revealed major historical figures of the dispute in conversation.[76]

The dialogue between Loyola and Clement XIV takes place in an "Aufenthalt der Ruhe und des Friedens".[77] It displays some traits of the Faßmann style, although the language of Korn's work — separated in time by 30 years from Faßmann's — is simpler and less weighted with French and Latin phrases. Individual speeches are generally shorter, monologues few. Like Faßmann's dialogues this one too speculates on political matters and includes texts of documents for the readers' information; but it does not end with a review of the latest news from the world above.

For the loyal reader of political-biographical Totengespräche the 1780's must have been a period of comparative uneventfulness. Two phenomena, however, brighten that otherwise doleful epoch: the dialogues of Johann Ferdinand Gaum and the Neuwieder Gespräche der Todten am Rhein.

Although Johann Ferdinand Gaum (1738-1814) was not as prolific in his production as were Faßmann, Gleichmann and Richter, he nevertheless produced several volumes of conversations between political and religious figures. These include a five-part dialogue between Frederick II and Maria Theresia (1787),[78] a three-part dialogue between Gregory VII, Clement XIV and Luther (1783), an exchange of letters between Clement XIV and Luther (1782), and dialogues between Mary Stuart and Marie Antoinette (1793), and Brutus and Charlotte Corday (1794).

Gaum acknowledged his indebtedness to Faßmann as had other writers of Totengespräche: in the Briefwechsel aus Elysium (1782) Gaum praises "Faßmann, den unerschöpflichen Schreiber der Gespräche im Reich der Todten, glorwürdigen Andenkens, deßen zahlreichen Quartanten mancher ehrliche Handwerker seine zeitkürzende erbauliche Lust, und manche wißbegierige Seele Meere von historischen Kenntnißen noch bis auf diese Stunde demüthig verdankt."[79]

Evidently Gaum saw the chief use of the dialogue of the dead to lie in the presentation of historical information. He makes practically no use of the inherent possibilities of the genre; the dialogue between Maria Theresia and Frederick, for example, has no frame to explain the setting of the dialogue in the "Reich der Todten". In the "Vorbericht" to this dialogue Gaum notes that his purpose in writing was to present the most essential elements of Frederick's biography for those who do not own a particular recently-published biography of him.[80] Thus Gaum's Totengespräche are more purely historical than Faßmann's; despite Gaum's obvious admiration for Faßmann, his procedures bear little resemblance to Faßmann's.

One of the last series of Totengespräche to appear periodically was Moriz Flavius Trenk von Tonder's (1746-1810) Politische Gespräche der Todten. The periodical appeared in Neuwied between 1786 and 1810 and is sometimes called the "Neuwieder Zeitung" or the "Neuwieder Gespräche". This publication underwent several reprintings and pirated editions — just as Faßmann's Gespräche had done — and was even translated into several languages, including Latin in Vienna.[81] This is surely strong attestation to the popularity of Totengespräche in the late eighteenth century. The dialogue form continued to be used in the "Neuwieder Gespräche" until just after 1810 when it was found to be no longer in accordance with the taste of most readers. [82]

The "Neuwieder Gespräche" consisted not only of dialogues of the dead, but also of letters between the living and the dead as well as documents. The dialogues are short (rarely longer than eight pages) and tend to be true Wechselreden rather then mutual monologues. As in Faßmann's Totengespräche the dialogue form is used for political raisonnements and for reportage. The first dialogue of the series confronts Adam with Charlemagne. After a very brief introductory greeting, Adam suggests, "Lasset uns beim Anfang dieses Jahres die wichtigste Begebenheiten jener Welt durchgehen. "[83] On other occasions Mercury reports the latest events or newly-arrived shades (e.g., a Dane, a Russian) may be called upon to report. These dialogues often feature several conversants, an aspect which these dialogues share with other political Totengespräche of the later years of the eighteenth century.

Tonder claimed Lucian as his master and model; d'Ester, however, suggests that the French encyclopaedists also exerted influence on his dialogues.[84] In structure and length these Totengespräche by Tonder are unlike those of Faßmann. The biographical details, which played such an important role in Faßmann's Entrevuen, Tonder relegates in summary style to footnotes to his dialogues. Nor does Tonder's style display great similarity to Faßmann's. Rather it resembles Rabener's and C. F. D. Schubart's. [85]

Christian Friedrich Daniel Schubart's four dialogues of the dead, which were published in the Vaterlands-Chronik between 1787 and 1789, unite felicitously several traditions of the Totengespräch. First, the dialogues are lively, genuinely dramatic and conversational; secondly, they participate in the general glorification of Frederick the Great — he speaks in all four dialogues — which takes place after his death; thirdly, two of the dialogues offer criticism of two biographies of Frederick which were published soon after his death. The dialogues are strongly nationalistic. While two of them survey Frederick's biographers, another informs the great ruler of his successor's deeds, and a fourth laments the bloodiness of the French Revolution.

Schubart is aware of the traditions behind his chosen genre, the dialogue of the dead: Faßmann speaks in one of the dialogues, Lucian in another! Schubart identifies Faßmann thus:

> [Faßmann's] Todtengespräche waren die Lieblingsleserei
> der deutschen Fürsten, Minister, Generale, rumoren auch
> noch in den Wachtstuben. Sie las der Prälat und der Dorf-
> schulmeister und die Matrone und das Nähermädel mit glei-
> chem Entzücken. Auch stifteten sie wirklich ungemein viel
> Gutes. [86]

These sentiments recall Gaum's estimation of Faßmann of five years earlier. Faßmann should have been pleased to find himself so eulogized.

After the turn of the century it is difficult fo find Totengespräche of the political-biographical type in the old style. The dialogues written after 1800 tend to be shorter; frequently they gather several crowned heads into one short dialogue. The tradition of including news reports for the readers had been made obsolete by the advent of daily or semi-weekly newspapers on a popular basis. The political-biographical Totengespräche fulfilled their function of presenting historical information for those hungry for knowledge, and odd facts and ideas for the curious; this use of the form does not survive in the nineteenth century. Subsequent chapters will show how the other modes of publication and other uses of the dialogue of the dead came to terms with this persistent tradition.

NOTES

1 Those dialogues which were either not available or not of sufficient literary interest to warrant discussion will be found in the chronological list of dialogues at the end of this study.

2 Frankfurt and Leipzig, 1735, p. 9.

3 Lindenberg, p. 90.

4 Lindenberg, pp. 93-94.

5 Rentsch, p. 29, footnote.

6 Lindenberg, p. 15.

7 Cologne, 1683.

8 "Historische / Politische und Philosophische Krieg= und Friedens=Gespräch / Auf das jetz neu=eingehende 1683. Jahr. Worinnen auch allerley leß= und merckwürdige Discursen, unter dem so genannten frantzösischen Kriegs= Simplicissimo, in den Elisäischen Feldern / Aller Monatlich deß gantzen Jahrs / ab gehandelt werden", (Jan., 1683), s. l. [Vienna?], p. 8. Subsequent references to this text are given in parentheses.

9 Egilsrud, p. 120.

10 Curt von Faber du Faur, German Baroque Literature, A Catalogue of the Collection in the Yale University Library (New Haven, 1958), p. 444.

11 Faber du Faur, p. 444.

12 Wilhelm Heinsius, Allgemeines Bücher-Lexikon oder Vollständiges alphabetisches Verzeichnis aller von 1700-1892 erschienenen Bücher. 19 vols. Leipzig, 1812-1894.

13 Rentsch, p. 36.

14 The appendix to this study contains titles of many such dialogues.

15 The previous work on Faßmann has fairly thoroughly investigated this procedure. The analysis in this study of Faßmann's technique is based on Lindenberg (pp. 94-119) and Damberg (pp. 68-70) as well as personal observation.

16 Lindenberg, p. 103; Damberg, p. 69.

17 Lindenberg, p. 119; Damberg, p. 70.

18 p. 13.

19 p. 68.

20 Kaschmieder, p. 64.

21 Halle, Frankfurt and Leipzig, 1721. Rentsch speculates that the work is that of a student in Leipzig (p. 36). Egilsrud reports that the work attacks Faß-mann for his ostentatious manner and for the presumptuousness of his attempt to educate others (p. 129). One copy of the work has been located in the Stiftsbibliothek Zeitz, DDR.

22 "Discurs des Uebersetzers an statt einer Vorrede, darinnen von Gesprächen überhaupt gehandelt wird", (Leipzig, 1727), sig. c3^r.

23 David Faßmann, Die neu=entdeckten Elisäischen Felder (Frankfurt and Leipzig, 1735), "Vorbericht", p. 8.

24 Rentsch, p. 36. Search for this work showed it to be unavailable in West German public libraries and it is unknown to standard reference works.

25 The title "Interviews in the Realms of Death: or, Dialogues of the dead: between several great personages deceas'd . . . Written originally in High Dutch" appears in the Ten-Year Supplement to the British Museum Catalogue of Printed Books, XV (London, 1968), Column 178.

26 Faßmann, III, "Avertissement" after the 41st Entrevue; cited by Kaschmieder, p. 65.

27 Frankfurt, Hamburg and Leipzig, 1722. Entrevue 1.

28 Frankfurt and Leipzig, 1722.

29 III, 686.

30 III, 844.

31 IX, 546.

32 Freystadt, 1720.

33 See Luke xvi, 19. The anonymous author's paraphrase of Scripture is inexact. The rich man talks with Abraham, not with Lazarus.

34 s. l., 1729.

35 s. l., 1722.

36 About the popularity of De betooverte Wereld Herbert Schöffler says, "Das Buch hatte in zwei Monaten viertausend Exemplare abgesetzt, ein für 1691 ungeheurer Erfolg eines nicht zur Unterhaltung geschriebenen Werkes" (Das literarische Zürich 1700-1750, Frauenfeld and Leipzig, 1925, p. 60).

37 "Curieuse Gespräche im Reiche derer Todten zwischen . . . dem Auctore der bezauberten Welt . . . Bal. Beckern . . . und . . . dem Theologo Chr. Scrivern . . .", (Frankfurt and Leipzig, 1730). Also, s. l., 1732, 1737; Leipzig and Braunschweig, 1731-34. Faber du Faur attributes the dialogues to David Faßmann, as no other source does. The full title does not suggest the typical Faßmann method.

38 Paul Hazard, La crise de la conscience européene (1680-1715). I (Paris, 1935), 226-230.

39 "Erster Theil", (Frankfurt and Leipzig, 1735).

40 "Ausserordentliches Gespräch . . . zwischen . . . Adam und Joseph . . .", "Vorbericht" to the "Erster Theil", (Frankfurt and Leipzig, 1735).

41 A curious example of this misinformation is Eve's explanation of the determination of human gender: ". . . wenn semen viri in der rechten Seite matris liege, so werde alsdenn ein Knäbgen gezeugt, lieget er aber in der linken, so werde ein Mädgen daraus formiert" ("Vierter Theil", "Ausserordentliches Gespräch im Reiche der Todten zwischen der ersten Mutter . . . Eva und Maria . . .", [Frankfurt and Leipzig, 1735], p. 181). This odd bit of knowledge has held a fascination for several other writers on the subject of German dialogues of the dead.

42 Rosenberg, p. 131.

43 Leipzig and Nuremberg.

44 Hamburg, 1729.

45 s. l.

46 "Gespräch im Reich der Todten zwischen dem Urheber der Zusammenverschwörung wider den König in Portugall Joseph de Mascarenhas, ehemaligen

Herzog von Aveiro und Robert Franz Damieno . . .", (Frankfurt and Leipzig, 1759); also (Ulm and Stettin, 1759).

47 "Gespräch in dem Reiche der Todten, zwischen den beyden ehemaligen Grafen, . . . Struensee und . . . Brand, und zwischen dem . . . Reichshofmeister Cornifitz Ulefeld . . .", (Copenhagen, 1773).

48 "Gespräch . . . zwischen . . . Struensee und . . . Brand", (Copenhagen, 1773), p. 35.

49 Vociferous opposition came from editors of moral weeklies. See in particular Der Einsiedler, No. 27 (July 6, 1740), pp. 209-210.

50 Frankfurt and Leipzig, 1725. Subsequent references to this text are given in parentheses.

51 One other possible example of this would be a "Gespräch im Reiche der Todten . . . zwischen Adam und Eva . . . und einem neumodischen Galanthomme" probably published in Leipzig in the 1750's. The dialogue was unfortunately unavailable for this study.

52 Frankfurt, Leipzig and Rudolstadt, 1735-1742.

53 Neu=entdeckte Elisäische Felder, p. 7.

54 Neu=entdeckte Elisäische Felder, p. 8.

55 Gleichmann's pseudonyms include Clarus Michael Hellmond, Puramandus, Sinceramandus, Claramandus, Miramandus, Fridemandus and Justamandus.

56 Johann Georg Meusel, Lexikon der vom Jahr 1750 bis 1800 verstorbenen teutschen Schriftsteller, IV (Leipzig, 1804 Facsimile reproduction Hildesheim, 1967), 219-220.

57 Rentsch does not indicate that Gleichmann's Totengespräche differ from Faßmann's, while Egilsrud states that Gleichmann is among the most typical of the plagiarists.

58 3 vols., Erfurt.

59 Erfurt, 1754. Title page.

60 Johann Zacharias Gleichmann, Ertzbischöffliche- und Churfürstliche Gespräche, I (October, 1752), 473-475.

61 Gleichmann, I (November, 1752), 522.

62 P. C. A. Dilthey, (Altona, 1751).

63 Daniel Wilhelm Triller (1695-1782) was the author of Neue äsopische Fabeln (1740).

64 Gleichmann, I (December, 1752), 575.

65 Gleichmann, I (Dec., 1753), 1109-1110.

66 Gleichmann, I (Dec., 1752), 561.

67 Gleichmann, II (Nov., 1755), 774.

68 Gleichmann, I (Jan., 1753), 583.

69 Frankfurt and Leipzig, 1756-1763. Subsequent references to this source are given in parentheses in the text.

70 Egilsrud, p. 127.

71 For a translation see Friedrich II, King of Prussia, Werke, ed. G. B. Volz, transl. Friedrich von Oppeln-Bronikowski, V (Berlin, 1913), "Totengespräch zwischen dem Herzog von Choiseul, Graf Struensee und Sokrates (Februar 1772)", 234-240; "Totengespräch zwischen Prinz Eugen, Lord Marlborough und Fürst Liechtenstein (1773)", 241-248.

72 Probably Georg Wilhelm Zapf's "Zusammenkunft im Reiche der Todten zwischen Maximilian III. Churfürsten von Bayern und Ganganelli unter dem Namen Clemens XIV römischen Pabste" (Augsburg, 1778) belongs in this category also.

73 "Gespräch im Reiche der Todten, zwischen dem Pater Angelo, einem Jesuiten, und dem Ritter von Moncada, einem ehemaligen Tempelherrn; worinn die Geschichte dieser beeden berühmten Orden, und die Aufhebung derselben, nebst andern merkwürdigen Dingen kurz und unpartheyisch erzehlet wird", (s. l., 1774).

74 "Anhang zu dem Gespräch im Reiche der Todten, zwischen dem Pater Angelo . . . ." (s. l., 1775).

75 C. H. Korn, "Neue Nachrichten aus dem Reiche der Todten. Oder Fortsetzung der Gespräche zwischen dem Pater Angelo . . . ." (s. l., 1775).

76 "Gespräch im Reiche der Todten zwischen dem Stifter des Jesuiten=Ordens Ignatius Lojola und dem letztverstorbenen Pabst Clemens XIV", (s. l., 1775).

77 "Gespräch . . . zwischen . . . Lojola und . . . Clemens XIV", p. 3.

78 The death of Frederick the Great sparked, as might be expercted, a plethora of dialogues of the dead, and after 1787 (the year of his death) the grand monarch appeared very frequently in Totengespräche. Some of these are discussed in Chapter VII. On Frederick's death Goethe wrote from Rome: "So hat denn der große König, dessen Ruhm die Welt erfüllte, dessen Thaten ihn sogar des Katholischen Paradieses werth machten, endlich auch das Zeitliche gesegnet, um sich mit den Heroen Seinesgleichen im Schattenreiche zu unterhalten. Wie gern ist man still, wenn man einen solchen zur Ruh gebracht hat." (Werke [Weimar, 1903], XXXVI, 256-57.)

79 Cited by Rentsch, p. 34.

80 Johann Ferdinand Gaum, "Gespräch im Reiche der Todten zwischen Maria Theresia und Friedrich . . . Erstes und zweytes Stück", (Mexico [Ulm], 1787).

81 Karl d'Ester, Das politische Elysium oder die Gespräche der Toten am Rhein (Neuwied, 1936), p. 79. D'Ester has published two lengthy and thorough studies of Tonder and his journal. Rather than repeat what d'Ester has said, the present study will treat Tonder only summarily.

82 D'Ester, p. 135.

83 "Politische Gespräche der Todten über die Begebenheiten des 1786ten Jahres", No. 1 (January 11, 1786).

84 D'Ester, p. 130.

85 D'Ester, pp. 300-301.

86 Christian Friedrich Daniel Schubart, Vermischte Schriften, VIII (Stuttgart, 1840), 23. This particular dialogue appeared in der Vaterlands-Chronik of 1787.

CHAPTER IV

DIALOGUES OF THE DEAD IN THE MORAL WEEKLIES

David Faßmann was not the only writer to employ the dialogue of the dead in periodical publications. There were not only those writers who imitated and modified his style, but also those who opposed and vilified him in their journals. This the moral weeklies did energetically and produced original Totengespräche of their own as well. The contributors to the moral weeklies re-introduced a classical flavour to the life of the nether world as it was fictively portrayed in eighteenth-century Germany.

The moral weekly possesses several properties, which together help define the genre. Among these are 1) a fictive authorship, 2) a strong fictive central personality who edits the papers and whose name appears in the title (e.g., Der Bürger, Der Jüngling), 3) periodic publication and 4) organic unity of the single issue.[1] The approach and purpose of the moral weeklies was at variance with that of Faßmann and his "imitators". Rather than detailed accounts of historical and political affairs and compendious biographical recounting, the moral weeklies chose to offer shorter dialogues, wittier and more barbed, which heightened the effect of that property which the dialogue of the dead possesses characteristically: the opportunity for passing judgement. In this respect dialogues of the dead in the moral weeklies return to their intellectual ancestor, Lucian. Moral judgements are found in Faßmann and others, but such judgements are not the primary purpose of such discourses,[2] as is the case in a great number of Totengespräche in the moral weeklies.

Length of dialogue has to be "sacrificed" in the moral weekly. Thus, a Totengespräch in a moral journal will have only five to ten percent of the length of a dialogue in the Entrevue style. It would have been visually undesirable to accommodate a complete Entrevue to the independent unit of the moral weekly. Occasionally, however, one dialogue of the dead may fill the entire weekly publication of a moral journal; but in general, voluminous dialogues did not suit the journalistic aims of the moral weekly. As a consequence of the shortening of the whole, duration of individual responses within a dialogue is also reduced; thus the occurrence of arid monologues (a frequent fault of the Entrevuen) declines in favour of more dramatic conversation.

The choice of characters in dialogues of the dead found in moral weeklies reflects the different purpose of the writing. While the Totengespräche by Faßmann and his "school" tended to concentrate on political figures of European history after 1500, the moral weeklies present such personages only infrequently. Since the judgement scene was a prominent form of the Totengespräch in the moral weeklies, figures from antiquity such as Diogenes, Democritus, Rhadamanthus, Pluto or Minos were often called up to examine the shades. Individual shades in such scenes often remain anonymous. In this respect also the moral weeklies are closer to the dialogues of Lucian, whose characters occasionally have no more identification than "an old man" or "a philosopher". Since the audience of the moral weeklies was in large part female,[3] it is quite natural to find that women — both named and unnamed — play a significant number of roles in the dialogues of the dead which appeared in these journals.

The frequent use of the dialogue of the dead and of the dialogue form in general by German moral weeklies must be considered a trait peculiar to the German periodicals. Even if the greatest inspiration for the German moral weeklies came from their English predecessors, it cannot be said that the concern of the German moral weeklies with dialogues of the dead is also of English derivation. An inspection of those English moral weeklies usually held to be the most significant for the developement of the German moral weeklies — The Tatler, The Spectator, The Guardian and others — shows that while they do evince an interest in concepts and descriptions of the Greek afterlife, they make practically no use of the dialogue of the dead as a form of presentation.

Yet the German moral weeklies did not accept the dialogue of the dead unquestioningly. Practically from the earliest appearance of Totengespräche in Germany the editors of the moral weeklies perceived the potential uses and abuses of the form. The attitude adopted by the moral weeklies towards the dialogues vary from editor to editor, and while they appreciate the didactic advantages which the form offers, many editors warn against the then most prevalent form of the Totengespräch in Germany, the Entrevue im Reich der Toten. These interviews offered to the curious reader a view into the world of politics and the court, subject matter which the moral weeklies found at best uninteresting and at worst morally reprehensible. As early as 1721 criticism of such dialogues of the dead may be found in Die Discourse der Mahler, a moral weekly published in Zürich by Johann Jakob Bodmer and his associates; this periodical views the dialogue of the interview type disdainfully:

> . . . [G]emeine Leute halten auf den Entre-Vûes im Reiche
> der Todten und andern Büchern / die mit seltsamen Historien /
> mit neuen Zeitungen / mit Mord= Brand= und Diebs=Geschichten
> angefüllet sind / unendlich mehr als auf einem raisonnirenden
> Buche / weil dieselben ihnen Materie vollauf weisen / das
> Magazin ihres Gedächtnisses zu provisioniren / und sie in den
> Stand zu setzen / daß sie in einer Gesellschaft ihre Portion
> zuschwatzen mit milder Hand abtragen können.[4]

Die Discourse der Mahler further reveals its negative estimation of the Entrevuen in a lengthy soliloquy of self-examination signed by "die Gesellschaft der Mahlern".[5] The discourse is an interior dialogue between the author's reproachful self and his own understanding (Sinn). The accusing voice reprimands the author for being arrogant enough to imitate the English writers poorly and makes this suggestion:

Wenn denn meine Remonstrationen nicht vermögend sind /

> dich von dieser Kranckheit zu schreiben gesund wieder
> herzustellen / so folge meinem Rathe / und schreibe
> Entrevües im Reiche der Todten / oder mache Romane /
> die biß auf zehen Tome anwachsen / das sind Bücher in
> welchen du deinen capricieusen Geist alle Freyheit hast
> herauszulassen; da kanst du eine Once Witz um Golde
> verkauffen.

Thus, the implied faults of the <u>Entrevuen</u> are lack of "serious" purpose, of discipline and of wit or <u>esprit</u>. The accusing voice then anticipates what the <u>Sinn</u> will next reply:

> Aber / wirst du sagen / es ist schwerer $^+$F** [$^+$F**
> nennet sich der deutsche Autor der Entrevües im Reiche
> der Todten] nachzuahmen / als den Zuschauer; *die
> Todten [*Dies ist die Meinung des Herren Fontenelle /
> der selbst seine Todten vortrefflich moralisieren läßt;
> in der Dedication seiner Gesprächen der Todten an
> Lucian / in die Elysische Felder.] müssen besser
> moralisieren als die Sterblichen / sonsten würde es
> sich nicht der Mühe lohnen / sie reden zu machen. Es
> wären schon gnung Lebende vorhanden / unnützliche
> Sachen zu sagen. Und nicht ein jeder ist geschickt zehen
> Theile von eines grossen Helden hohen Thaten auf den
> Thon einer Scudery voll zu liegen . . . . Ein solches
> vornehmen ist mir zu schwer.

Nor is this imagined defense accepted by the accusing voice; it is seen rather as a result of fear which attempts to cover malicious satire (<u>satyrische Boßheit</u>) with affected modesty. The reproachful voice then turns to the topic of public opinion of the authors of moral weeklies:

> . . . Sie sagen ins gemein / . . . daß du glaubest . . .
> daß du ein Singularist seyest / der die Welt nach seiner
> Fantasey regieren wolle / daß die auch die Entrevües
> im Reiche der Todten nicht gefallen / die jederman mit
> Ergetzen lißt . . . .

The understanding argues that he is forced to write when he sees so much foolishness abroad in the world; he cannot accommodate himself to the fashions of the world, he cannot write his <u>Sittenschriften</u> in the style of Hofmannswaldau. The author can neither change himself, nor accept the critique of the accusing conscience. Yet the author (<u>Sinn</u>) is prepared to compromise:

> Jedennoch / wenn es je seyn muß / und sich die Klägden
> der Leuten nicht anderst wollen stillen lassen / will ich
> den Stylum ändern; ich erkläre mich demnach / daß der

Autor der Entrevües im Reiche der Todten ein Lucianus
und ein Fontenelle / daß Menantes die Sonne der Poeten
[sei] . . . .

The understanding (Sinn), to which the accusing voice addresses its remonstrances
in this discourse, is in harmony with opinion found elsewhere in the Discourse der
Mahler. It is clear that Lucian and Fontenelle are found acceptable while Faßmann
is found wanting. Fontenelle receives further recognition in the form of inclusion
in a list of prescribed readings for ladies. Bodmer also includes Lucian's works
as translated by d'Ablancourt.[6] Even more positively the Discourse der Mahler
printed original dialogues of the dead.

The first edition of Gottsched's Die vernünftigen Tadlerinnen (1725-
1726) takes notice of the popularity of the dialogue of the dead and includes some
original examples of the form. That the Tadlerinnen presents Totengespräche at
all, however, is considered by its author to be a concession to the taste of the
times. The 26th Stück of the Tadlerinnen, a fictive letter to the fictive authoresses,
accuses them in short of being arrogant busybodies. That the Tadlerinnen was opposed to the Entrevuen im Reiche der Todten in particular and to the galant and
courtly world in general may be seen from the objection raised here by the fictive
author of the letter:

> Tadelt auch die Nachtigall den Kuckuck, daß er nur immer
> bey seiner alten Leyer bleibet? Und was gehen euch [die
> Tadlerinnen] alle Entrevües im Reiche der Todten, was
> gehen euch Melisso, Celander, Behmeno die unsterblichen
> Geister an? lasset die Eulen, die Raben, die Spechte und
> Fledermäuse, pfeifen, schreyen, zwitschern und krähen.
> Ein jeder Vogel singt wie ihm der Schnabel gewachsen ist.[7]

The choice of birds and noises in the metaphor does not flatter the Entrevuen.

Further evidence of the Tadlerinnen's opposition to the historical-
political Totengespräche is seen in a fictive dialogue between "Deutschlieb" and
"Herr[n] Mischmasch". The topic of conversation is the cultivation of an acceptable style in German, free from the polyglot admixture of French and Latin
phrases. Deutschlieb maintains:

> . . . Im Schreiben ist es noch leichter, das Fremde zu
> vermeiden, als in Reden.
> Mischm[asch]. Morbleu! Es ist ja kein einziges Buch so
> geschrieben. Ich lese Talanders und Menantes Sachen,
> sowohl Romaines als Briefe. Ich lese die Entrevues im
> Reich der Todten, imgleichen der curieusen Eva Staats=
> Assembléen, und dergleichen von unsern besten pieçen
> mehr, und finde par tout solche melanges von Sprachen.[8]

Mischmasch's use of French is almost as reprehensible as his choice of literature.
The citation of the Entrevuen here and in the 26th Stück — and it is important that

they are mentioned as <u>Entrevües</u> — points to the conclusion that a major criticism of the moral weeklies against them was their impure use of the language. The style of the famous <u>Entrevües im Reiche der Todten</u> was full of <u>galant</u> compliments and inflated Baroque phrases. The struggle for purity in the mother tongue was carried on not only by Gottsched, but also by most of the editors of moral weeklies.

<u>Der Patriot</u>, a moral weekly published in Hamburg from 1724 to 1726, makes no use of the dialogue of the dead for the presentation of its moral advice. However, the inclusion of "les Dialogues des morts par Fontenelle" in a recommended reading list (under the category "Zur Klugheit zu Leben") shows that the editor approved of that famous divine's <u>Totengespräche</u>.[9]

The elder Johann Georg Hamann's <u>Der alte Deutsche</u>, published in Hamburg in 1730, finds little to praise in contemporary <u>Totengespräche</u>. In a fictive letter to the editor signed "Ernst Ehrlich"[10] the author praises Lucian and Fontenelle and regrets that so few Germans have been able to follow in their footsteps. Indeed, the acclaim which contemporary <u>Totengespräche</u> receive in Germany is only a sign of the poor taste of the times. The author of the letter satirizes the then fashionable formula for writing dialogues by suggesting that one may soon expect "Gespräche im Reiche der Kirch=Thürme, Gespräche im Reiche der Leichen= Steine; Gespräche im Reiche der Schnupff=Tücher; Gespräche im Reiche der Thee= Tassen; Gespräche im Reiche der Tobacks=Pfeiffen, und dergleichen mehr . . .".[11] "Ernst Ehrlich" sees a danger in the form and present usage of the dialogue of the dead and criticizes those authors who use the <u>Totengespräch</u> to calumniate men who should rather be praised. Although <u>Der alte Deutsche</u> does not itself make use of the <u>Totengespräch</u>, this weekly does include several fictive dialogues among characters of the author's acquaintance.

Similar negative criticism is found in Friedrich Samuel Bock's <u>Der Einsiedler</u> (1740-1741). Bock points out the pervasiveness of the genre:

> Die Gespräche der Todten haben zu unsern Zeiten fast
> nicht wenigere Liebhaber und Leser, als Nachahmer ge-
> funden. . . . Nunmehr scheint es, daß die Welt sich
> ganz in die Todtengespräche verliebt; diejenige sind
> kaum zu zählen, die ihren Büchern diese Aufschrift vor-
> gesetzt.[12]

The editor agrees that the <u>Totengespräch</u> is a good method of presentation; he accepts the <u>Lebensbeschreibung</u> as a literary means of making virtue desirable and vice repugnant; he is prepared to tolerate dialogues between persons, "die vielleicht in ihrem Leben wenig nützliches und erbauliches geredet haben",[13] but finds this — as did Faßmann himself — a falling short of the goal. Bock further criticizes those <u>Totengespräche</u> which rely too heavily on "heydnischen Erdichtungen" and "kaum einen Satz schreiben können, ohne des Pluto und der Proserpina, des Styx und Läthe, des Charon und Minos, Cerberus und Aeacus, u. d. gl. zu gedenken".[14] Although no dialogues of the dead are found in Bock's publication, he does employ fictive dialogues as did <u>Der alte Deutsche</u>. Bock's conservative position on the subject of <u>Totengespräche</u> stems perhaps from the abuses of the <u>Entrevue</u> writers. Yet his religious objections to the form would show that the satirists who employed the realm of the dead as a fictive device in the eighteenth century risked touching a nerve still sensitive to the conservative Christian.

After the middle of the eighteenth century, the moral weeklies express less opposition to the Entrevuen and to Totengespräche in general. When in 1746 Bodmer revised and reissued the Discourse der Mahler as Der Mahler der Sitten, the new journal was enlarged by three new Totengespräche, and all of those found in Die Discourse reappear in Der Mahler. In the third edition of the Vernünftigen Tadlerinnen, published in 1748, Gottsched retained all the dialogues of the dead from the first edition, with no important changes.

It is not surprising that the authors of moral weeklies and Sittenschriften seize on a particular kind of Totengespräch which allows for a passing of judgement. This form, the judgement scene in the nether world, has its origin in Lucian's dialogues. At least half of all dialogues of the dead in moral weeklies take this form. The Discourse der Mahler twice employs the device; two examples are also found in the Tadlerinnen. An indication of the popularity of such judgement scenes in the nether world is the fact that the editor of Der Bienenstock (1755-1757) reprints the dialogue between Diogenes and the ten shades from Die Discourse der Mahler. [15] The second volume of Der Bienenstock contains two such judgement scenes. [16]

Another similar periodical, Das allegorische Bildercabinet oder anmuthige Sittenlehre, published by Johann Peter Willebrandt in Lübeck (1750), purports to be a collection of moral writings drawn from German and foreign sources. These pieces, the publisher maintains in the "Vorbericht", are taken from "bekannten, beliebten . . . Sittenschriften". Reprinted in this collection is "Rhadamanthus: Oder Abbildung des Richterstuhls im Reiche der Todten." [17] The popularity of the judgement scene persists until the latter years of the moral weeklies. Sonnenfels and the Austrian moral weeklies — among the latest of that species of periodical — use the form not at all.

The dialogue of the dead in whatever form it appeared is used by the moral weeklies from the earlies for purposes of literary criticism. One of the first moral weeklies to present literary criticism in the form of a Totengespräch was Die Discourse der Mahler. [18] This is a true judgement scene in the nether world. The "Gespräche des Pluto, und des Diogenes, mit zween deutschen Romanhelden" [19] is described as a supplement to Boileau's "Les Héros de romans". In this Totengespräch [20] charges are leveled at the novels of Bucholtz and Lohenstein in particular, on the counts of manneristic stylization, falsification of history and improbability of plot. A chorus is formed by the humiliated heroes of the novels, who cry woefully to their creators. Because Heidegger is thought to be the author of this dialogue, it is therefore not surprising that criticism of the same type as "Wer Romanen list, der list Lügen" [21] is found here too. [22]

The fourth volume of Die Discourse der Mahler contains another judgement scene in the nether world. The judge in this dialogue is no longer Pluto, as in the work discussed above, but Diogenes himself. Before him are brought ten shades, who represent various kinds of human folly (and an occasional virtue). Among them are such characters as a man who spoke many languages but had learned nothing, a book collector who did not read his books (the ignorant book collector is of course a Lucianic theme), and a galant poet. Whereas in the first edition of Die Discourse the poet is identified only by a snippet of his verse, in the third edition he is designated as a poet of the Hofmannswaldau school. [23] The galant poet's folly was frivolousness, lack of seriousness; in his poetry he was often killed by the glance of one mistress only to be resurrected by that of another. The poet explains that he was never in better form than when he died "in der Metapher" (240). In response to one of the poet's poems, Diogenes exclaims: "Welch klingendes Bombast! Rede etwas natürlicher" (240). The literary preferences here are in harmony with those opinions in the dialogue of the heroes of novels: both urge a more direct and natural literature.

Gottsched's Die vernünftigen Tadlerinnen also criticizes literature by means of a dialogue of the dead. Here seven shades, all feminine, are brought before Proserpine. (Proserpine has been called to the bench, it is explained, because Minos has too many other cases on his hands.) The fifth shade brought before her is that of a "gelehrtes Frauenzimmer", who explains how she spent her time on earth:

> Ich habe gewust, wer Octavia und Clelia,
> Cyrus und Argenis, Hercules und Herculisca,
> die getreue Schäferin Doris und Aramene,
> der Pastor Fido und rasende Roland, die
> himmlische Banise und der Printz Telemaque,
> Arminius und Thusnelda etc. gewesen.
> Pros[erpine].:
> Genug, genug. Das sind lauter Historien,
> davon ich die wenigsten weiß.
> Mercur, sind sie dir bekannt?
> Merc.
> Ach es sind lauter Fabeln, die nirgends
> als in dem Gehirne einiger Romanschreiber
> entstanden sind.

The opposition of the Tadlerinnen to pseudo-historical and pastoral novels is made clear by the punishment inflicted upon this benighted shade:

> Pros.
> Du hast also sehr schlechte Bücher gelesen.
> Fort mit ihr, laß sie ihre himmlische Banise,
> Doris, Aramene etc. hie unter den Todten
> suchen: und wenn sie dieselbige nicht finden
> wird; so übergib sie den Furien zu züchtigen. [24]

Criticism of the novel is also found in a judgement scene in Die mühsame Bemerckerin derer Menschlichen Handlungen. [25] Here a personification of Virtue (Tugend) ascends the judge's bench and is even addressed as "grosse Göttin". One of the shades brought before Virtue is a "gelehrtes Frauenzimmer", who has read all the German and French novels and knows them so well that she is able to discern whether a particular phrase comes from Asiatische Banise or

Bellarmine or Römische Octavia. She has helped her friends write galant love letters and has even published a book of useful phrases on the subject. Her reward, rather than admission to the Elysian fields, is immersion in the Lethe so that she may be "unburdened" of these "vain concepts". Virtue then allows herself a digression from the bench on the vanity of writing galant letters and of making money from lending novels.

Criticism of the theater is also to be found in this dialogue of the dead. After condemning an actor (Comödiant) to forgetful oblivion, Virtue surveys the state of the contemporary theater.

> Die Schauspiele der jetzigen Zeiten sind von schlechter
> Erheblichkeit. Man hat nicht den Endzweck Leute zu bes-
> sern, sondern man tritt etliche Stunden auf den Platz, um
> einen Gewinnst zu erhalten. Wenige sogenanten Banden,
> haben wohl ausgearbeitete Stücke. Die meisten verstossen
> wieder die Regeln eines Gedichtes. Den Endzweck will ich
> gantz und gar nich berühren. Es ist zu leicht zu begreifen.
> Leute, denen es an Vermögen fehlt ihr liederlich Leben
> fortzusetzen, fallen auf den Entschluß, eine solche ver-
> kleidete Puppe um das Geld vorzustellen. Wann die weni-
> gen Stunden, welche sie zum auswendig lernen anwenden
> müssen verflossen sind, haben sie viel andre, ihren alten
> Treiben den Lauff wieder zu lassen. Doch dieses Volck
> ist nicht die eintzige Ursache verderbter Schauspiele. Die
> meiste Schuld muß ich denen Zuschauern beymessen. Vie-
> le gehen deßwegen an diesen Ort, damit die durch eine
> Veränderung die Zeit hinbringen. Bey diesen findet man
> nur so viel Auffmercksamkeit, daß sie eine neue verklei-
> dete Persohn betrachten. Andere besuchen diesen Platz,
> weil man es nicht alle Tage in der Stadt siehet, und die
> meisten deßwegen, Harleqvin macht etwas zu lachen,
> wenn es auch ein unflätiger Ausdruck seyn solte. Kennte
> man das Wesen eines Schauspielers, so würde man ver-
> besserte Comödianten haben. . . .

Certainly the depiction of the condition of the stage in Germany points to certain truths, although one might wish for a kinder attitude towards human nature. Nevertheless, the moral weeklies could not be expected to tolerate the indecencies of a Hans Wurst.

In this same Totengespräch from Die mühsame Bemerckerin an opera singer is condemned to the place of lamentation. Opera singers, Virtue maintains, must be placed one notch below Comödianten:

> Erstlich ist das Singen bey einem Schauspiel nicht
> natürlich, sondern etwas gezwungenes. Denn hat die
> Ausarbeitung eines solchen Stückes keine andere Ab-
> sicht, als die Ohren derer Zuhörer zu kützeln. Deß-

wegen findet man mehr verliebte Arien, als Text von der
Geschichte.

Opposition to the opera, as part of the diversions of the galant and noble world,
are to be expected from most moral weeklies. Gottsched's Der Biedermann criticizes the opera for many of the same reasons as those in Die mühsame Bemerk-
kerin, especially for improbability and diversionary nature.[26] References to the
opera in moral weeklies are, however, infrequent.[27]

Comedies as well as novels are condemned in a judgement scene from
Der Bienenstock. In "Die Urtheile des Rhadamanthus über die Beschäftigungen des
Frauenzimmers"[28] a young woman is damned for having spent her life in the pur-
suit of such literature.

The moral weeklies effected criticism of literature both by their explicit statements and by the inclusion of titles in the reading lists which they offered to their readers. Criticism is further seen in their choice of translations
and styles to be presented in the publications.

While some contemporary examples of the dialogue of the dead were
lamentable, if not worse, those of Lucian and his true, latter-day followers were
quite acceptable to the editors of the moral weeklies. The affinity of the moral
weeklies for Lucian is seen in their explicit praise of him, in their willingness
to imitate his style (especially the judgement scene), in a closeness to Lucianic
themes, and in the presentation of translations of the master's dialogues of the
dead.

In presenting its dialogues of the dead, the Vernünftigen Tadlerinnen
lauds Lucian, "der in dieser Art die Sitten der Mensch zu tadeln, ein vollkommener Meister gewesen".[29] This edition of the journal includes translations of three
of Lucian's dialogues of the dead in addition to two original Totengespräche. The
theme of the short dialogue between Lucretia, Cleopatra and Proserpine has a
Lucianic quality to it. Lucretia, who represents chastity and virtue, is preferred
over Cleopatra, whose life has stood for wealth, courtly behaviour and physical
beauty. The unfortunate Cleopatra is delivered up to the Furies, who are to throw
her into a river of burning pitch.

Der nordische Aufseher praises Fénelon's and Fontenelle's writings
for their value in the instruction of youth.[30] However, the Nordische Aufseher
stands closer to the English writers than do many other moral weeklies. It is not
surprising therefore that an English writer such as Matthew Prior (whose works
include dialogues of the dead) is also quoted as a respected authority. Perhaps
the best known of the English writers of dialogues of the dead is George Lord
Lyttleton, whose Dialogues of the Dead were first published in London in 1760.[31]
The Nordische Aufseher presented its German audience with two of Lyttleton's
dialogues in German translation as early as August 21 and 22, 1761. The translations of the dialogue between Circe and Ulysses (although included in Lyttleton's
collection, it is not strictly a dialogue of the dead) and the dialogue between Bayle
and Locke are credited to Cramer in the table of contents.[32]

The moral weekly declined in popularity in the north before it did in
the south, where it had also begun later. The latter half of the 1760's in Vienna
saw several moral weeklies, including Der Mann ohne Vorurtheil and Theresie

und Eleonore, both edited by Joseph von Sonnenfels (1733-1817), a representative
of Enlightenment thought in Vienna, where he was a professor of political science.
These moral weeklies, like their predecessors, contain dialogues of the dead.
Harshness of judgement in the later moral weeklies has been replaced by a willingness to engage in compromising argumentation. Consequently, none of the Totengespräche in these periodicals take the form of a judgement scene. Although these
moral weeklies contain much literary criticism, they rarely use the dialogue of the
dead to present it. Most often they use the form to present social criticism.

Der Mann ohne Vorurtheil, the most important Austrian moral weekly
of the 1760's,[33] brings forth Diogenes to do his usual battle against human folly;
but this time, in an unusual turn of events, Diogenes is silenced by his partner in
conversation, Roger du Rabutin. The dialogue attempts a defense of inherited nobility. As might be expected, virtue (Tugend) is the mark of the aristocrat:

> Die Tugend ist ohne Zweifel das Kennzeichen des wahren
> Adels; . . . Der Adeliche, der seinen Titel würdig führet,
> ist das bereits was der gemeine Tugendhafte zu werden
> suchet.[34]

It is important to note that this dialogue in Der Mann ohne Vorurtheil presents a
reasoning Diogenes and not a sternly judging Diogenes.

The periodical Theresie und Eleonore (1767) unites Ariadne and Sappho
in dialogue in the nether world.[35] The topic of discussion in this Totengespräch is
the conflict between reason and the passions in the suicides of both women.

The Viennese moral weekly Der Verbesserer, which appeared at practically the same time as Theresie und Eleonore, employs the dialogue of the dead
on at least two occasions. In one of the dialogues a figure quite atypical of the usual
characters of dialogues of the dead in moral weeklies, Ninon de Lenclos,[36] gives
advice to a newly-arrived (so accepted was the Totengespräch that the setting is
never mentioned!) German Frauenzimmer.[37] That Ninon de Lenclos is presented
as a wise woman rather than as a shade to be judged by Diogenes, Minos or Rhadamanthus is astonishing, for Ninon's fame did not rest on her virtue.

Phillis, the newly-arrived young lady, confesses that she, indeed, has
read Ninon's letters in a neatly printed German edition published in Leipzig. This
offers Ninon the opportunity to deny the authorship of the letters.[38] Had she written
them, she maintains, she would have expressed her thoughts "leichter, deutlicher,
und weniger philosophisch steif" (90). In the course of the dialogue Ninon discloses
to the young lady (who died at the age of nineteen) the extent to which she had been
deceived by the German Geschmack- und Sittenrichter. Ninon warns of two extremes,
the "teutsche Modegeschmack" on the one hand, and "das Pedantische" on the other.
Explaining the problem, Ninon contrasts the French writers of letters with the German writers:

> Unsre französischen Schriftsteller, besonders, von denen
> wir Briefe und solche Schriften haben, so die Schreibart
> und Sprache bildeten, lebten im Cirkel der großen Welt —
> sie kannten alle Schattierungen des Angenehmen, des

Scherzhaften, des Witzigen, des Lächerlichen, des Abge-
schmackten. [Die deutschen] Briefschreiber sitzen auf ihrer
Stube — sie wollen nachahmen, und treffen unglücklich — der
Cirkel ihrer Gesellschaft sind etwann ein paar adeliche Land-
familien . . . . (92)

Ninon denounces such writers who lack all humour and wit. Their attempts at "das
Natürliche oder Naive" end only in "schmackloseste Tandeley". To avoid the extremes of ridiculousness (Auslachenswürdigkeit) and pedantry, the critic suggests
that the proper goals are "Welt, Freyheit und Ungezwungenheit" (96). It is in this
call for a natural style that the criticism in Der Verbesserer maintains its intellectual heritage with the earlier, North German moral weeklies.

Throughout the developement of the moral weeklies, their editors
championed, with minor exceptions, the classical standards of the dialogue of the
dead, opposing in the early years what they considered to be perversions of the
genre and offering models of their own inspired by Fontenelle and Lucian. Frequently employing the judgement scene, the moral weeklies criticized not only the
mores of their society, but also the important genres of literary production. In
addition, the efforts of the moral weeklies at placing Lucian and Fontenelle on the
citizens' bookshelves must be recognized.

NOTES

1   In this chapter Wolfgang Martens' definition of the moral weekly has been used as a basis for organization. For a more detailed discussion of these periodicals the reader is referred to Martens' Die Botschaft der Tugend (Stuttgart, 1968), the first eight sections of which are devoted to such a definition. Martens is correct in maintaining that previous writers on the subject of moral weeklies have used the term too inclusively to include journals of a very wide variety. Periodicals such as the Belustigungen des Verstandes und des Witzes, which are included by Max Kawczyński in his Moralische Wochenschriften (Leipzig, 1800), are dealt with in a later chapter of this study.

2   Martens, p. 75-76 (footnote).

3   Martens, p. 146.

4   I, Stück 9 (Zürich, 1721).

5   I, Stück 22 (Zürich, 1721). The following four citations refer to this Stück.

6   IV, Stück 15 (Zürich, 1723).

7   I, Stück 25 (Leipzig, 1725), 195.

8   Tadlerinnen, I, Stück 21 (Leipzig, 1725).

9   I, Stück 8, 1724.

10   Der alte Deutsche, Johann Georg Hamann, ed. (Hamburg, 1730), pp. 395-400. Also cited in d'Ester's Das politische Elysium (Neuwied, 1936), p. 134.

11   Der alte Deutsche (Hamburg, 1730), p. 396.

12   Der Einsiedler, Stück 27 (Königsberg, 1740), 208.

13   Der Einsiedler, Stück 27 (Königsberg, 1740), 208.

14   Der Einsiedler, Stück 27 (Königsberg, 1740), 208.

15   II (Hamburg and Leipzig, 1756), 209-216. The dialogue is here entitled "Gericht in dem Felde der Wahrheit".

16   II (Hamburg and Leipzig, 1756).

17   Stücke 14 and 15. However, for several structural reasons neither Der Bienenstock nor Das allegorische Bildercabinet may be considered "pure" moral weeklies. The work is unknown to Holzmann-Bohatta and other reference works.

18   Stücke 13 and 14 (Zürich, 1721).

19   The title is taken from the table of contents of the third revised edition of 1746. Bodmer made significant linguistic and stylistic emendations in the third edition which heighten and focus the criticism of the dialogue.

20   The literary criticism in this two-part dialogue has been discussed by Lieselotte E. Kurth in "Formen der Romankritik im achtzehnten Jahrhundert", MLN, LXXXIII (October, 1968), 676. It is also treated by Wolfgang Martens in his Botschaft der Tugend, p. 504.

21   Gotthard Heidegger, "Mythoscopia Romantica: oder Discours von den so benannten Romans . . ." (Zürich, 1698), p. 71. Cited in Martens' Botschaft, p. 503.

22	The criticism pertains to "romances" or pseudo-historical Baroque and galant novels. By the time of the third edition of the Discourse der Mahler "histories" such as Richardson's Pamela and Marivaux's Marianne were included in reading lists for respectable young ladies.
23	Der Mahler der Sitten, I, Blatt 22 (Zürich, 1746), 233-246. Subsequent references to this text are given parenthetically. The third edition of 1746 has been used in this instance because it expresses the criticism more clearly and retains the essentials of the first edition.
24	I, Stück 26 (Leipzig, 1725).
25	Stück 27 (Danzig, 1736).
26	II, Stück 95 (Leipzig, 1729).
27	Martens, p. 488.
28	II (Hamburg and Leipzig, 1756), 97-102.
29	I, Stück 26 (Leipzig, 1725).
30	I, Stück 1 (Copenhagen and Leipzig, 1759), 11; I, Stück 87, 249.
31	For an estimate of Lyttleton's role in the English tradition of the dialogue of the dead, see F. M. Keener's dissertation Shades of Lucian: British Dialogues of the Dead in the Eighteenth Century, Columbia University, 1965.
32	A translation of Lyttleton's Dialogues of the Dead, edited by J. G. H. Oelrichs, was published in 1761 as Gespräche der Verstorbenen eine Englische Schrift (Berlin, Stettin and Leipzig). Oelrichs would have done well to have consulted the translation of the dialogue between Bayle and Locke found in Der nordische Aufseher.
33	Martens, p. 141.
34	Der Mann ohne Vorurtheil, II, Stück 24, 610.
35	II, Stück 18, 340-344.
36	Ninon de Lenclos (1620-1705), whose salon was frequented by the literati of Paris, was the authoress of letters and memoirs. Rotermund remarks in the continuation of Jöcher's Gelehrten=Lexikon: "Sie dachte wie Epikur, und handelte wie Lais; zu ihrer Vollkommenheit fehlte ihr nichts, als die Tugend." ("Ninon de Lenclos", Christian Gottlieb Jöchers allgemeines Gelehrten=Lexikon, Heinrich Wilhelm Rotermund, ed., II, (Bremen, 1819), Columns 1577-1578.)
37	"Ninon de Lenclos, und Phillis, ein Todtengespräche", Der Verbesserer, II, Stück 12 (Vienna, 1766), 89-96. Subsequent references to this work are given parenthetically.
38	There are several possibilities for the identification of these letters. They could refer to the apocryphal letters written by Damours (or Crébillon), the Briefe der Ninon de Lenclos an den Marquis von Sévigné, published in Leipzig in 1751. They could also refer to Der Ninon von Lenclos Leben und Briefe nebst den Briefen der Babet, also published in Leipzig, 1755.

CHAPTER V

DIALOGUES OF THE DEAD IN MISCELLANY MAGAZINES

Next to be considered as a source for Totengespräche is a group of
magazines, which for convenience shall be called miscellany or "collection" magazines. These periodicals differed in a number of ways from the moral weeklies
discussed in the preceding chapter. Journals of the miscellany type usually feigned
no fictive author or editor such as "Der Bürger" or "Der Patriot". Rather they
featured signed and unsigned articles by writers representing a large cross section of eighteenth-century literary endeavour.

Unlike the moral weeklies, the miscellany magazines did not display
organic unity in the single issue. The monthly or quarterly issue contained articles,
poems, cantatas, dialogues and not infrequently, plays, oratorios, and an occasional article on natural science. The miscellany magazines appeared from the
1740's onward and (with few exceptions) were thus contemporaneous with some of
the moral weeklies.

Although the titles of the miscellany magazines often proclaimed an
edifying purpose, the scope of purpose of such periodicals was wider than that of
the moral weeklies. Frequently the editors aimed at the improvement of taste, as
the title of the Westphälische Bemühungen zur Aufnahme des Geschmaks und der
Sitten (1753-1755) indicates, as well as the simple amusement of the reader, although concern with moral improvement still plays an important part. The editors
of the Westphälische Bemühungen saw morals closely allied with taste:

> Jedoch eben diese Bemühungen sollen sich auser dem
> Geschmak auch auf die Sitten erstrekken; und das ist
> der andre Zwek, welchen unsre Schrift hat, oder viel-
> mehr der vornehmste, . . . Wir haben uns überredet,
> Geschmak und Sitten gehören zusammen, keines könne
> ohne das andere verbessert werden. Ein Mensch von
> Geschmak wird allezeit anständige Sitten zeigen, und
> ein Mensch von gereinigten Sitten wird in seinem ganzen
> Wesen einen feinen Geschmak sehen lassen.[1]

Yet the audience remains much the same as that of the moral weeklies,
the "gehobenes Bürgertum".[2] As the Rostock Abhandlungen phrased it, the appeal
is to people "die die Wissenschaften entweder gar nicht erlernet, oder doch wenigstens dieselben sich nicht zum Hauptvorwurf von ihren Beschäftigungen gesetzet . . .
haben."[3] The editor of the Neues gemeinnütziges Magazin also states specifically
that his efforts are directed at the non-academic reader. Not included in the category of the miscellany magazines are the scholarly journals, which, for the most

part, utilize the dialogue of the dead only rarely.

This chapter examines the Totengespräch in the miscellany magazines, emphasizing the literary uses of the genre, yet trying at the same time to survey the general role of the form in these belletristic and moralizing magazines.[4]

Both the moral weeklies and the miscellany magazines regarded Lucian with affection, but the miscellany magazines placed an even greater emphasis on presenting the actual works to the audience than do the moral weeklies. In 1745 the editors of the Bremen Beyträge published a trimmed and censored version of Lucian's "Philosophies for Sale" under the title "Ausruf der philosophischen Sekten aus dem Lucian".[5] This work of Lucian is much like his dialogues of the dead, but since the scene of the action is unclear, the work cannot be considered a true Totengespräch. The translation which appeared in the Bremen Beyträge was the earliest eighteenth-century German version of the work.

A dialogue of the dead which is found in the sixth number of the Bremen Beyträge displays influence from Lucian, not only in choice of persons, but also in construction. A footnote by the editor refers to Lucian's "Timon" and recalls the story as transmitted by Lucian. The new dialogue between Pylades and Timon champions philanthropy over misanthropy.[6] Rabener's lengthy narrative "Ein Traum von den Beschäftigungen der abgeschiedenen Seelen" also appeared in the Bremen Beyträge[7]; although it employs the realm of the dead as a fictional device, it is not strictly a dialogue of the dead.

In the first year of publication the Neues gemeinnütziges Magazin (1761) contained three dialogues of the dead, and a poem entitled "Lucian". In the second year two dialogues of the dead and a Göttergespräch are included. The choice and pairing of characters in these dialogues suggest strong Lucianic influence.

The Rostock Abhandlungen of 1767 presented its readers with translations of three of Lucian's dialogues of the gods and five of the dialogues of the dead.[8] From the variety and number of dialogues it would seem that a genuine effort was being made to acquaint the readers with Lucian's works. The translations include the dialogue between Alexander and Diogenes, two characters frequently reunited in eighteenth-century dialogues of the dead.

It should not be thought that only those magazines which presented translations of Lucian were concerned with him. Rather his influence is felt in varying degrees of directness. Although Lucian's influence is sometimes less explicitly expressed than at other times, it is nonetheless present, whether through French sources or from acquaintance with the master himself. The miscellany magazines as well as the moral weeklies must be credited for their pioneering work in translating Lucian and spreading his mode of satire during the eighteenth century.

The most important task for which the miscellany magazines use the dialogue of the dead is without doubt for reviewing directly either specific literature or the literary and intellectual life of the times. At least half of all the Totengespräche found in such periodicals include criticism of literary problems.

One of the first journals of the miscellany type was the Belustigungen des Verstandes und des Witzes, published by Johann Joachim Schwabe, a disciple of Gottsched. Already in the first year of publication, 1741, the Belustigungen offered a dialogue of the dead by Johann Elias Schlegel entitled "Demokritus, ein Todtengespräche."[9] This piece brings together Democritus, Aristophanes and

Regnard and serves as a vehicle for criticism of the theater.

By 1741 Schlegel had himself written three dramas and could speak with some authority on the subject. Consequently, the criticism contained in this Totengespräch is more than a series of off-hand and subjective remarks. Rather the dialogue approaches a highly topical issue in a manner that would have provided reader and theater-goer (who might have seen the Leipzig production of Regnard's play) with a critical framework for assessing its worth.

The chief ground for criticism of Regnard's "Democritus" is the lack of historicity, the disregard for the historical facts. Schlegel introduces this topic in a humourous fashion by having Regnard fail to recognize the real Democritus at their first encounter in the underworld. Democritus then takes Regnard to task for having portrayed him inaccurately, for allowing tigers to appear anachoristically in Athens, for clothing the entire play in Parisian dress. [10] In the ensuing discussion of the general improbability of the plot, Democritus challenges Regnard for having the pupil Strabo accompany Democritus in the desert. Regnard can defend himself only from usus: "Und überdieß müßt Ihr wissen, daß es nicht Gebrauch bey uns ist, einen Herrn aufzuführen, der keinen Diener hätte, weil uns allzuviel Gelegenheit aus den Händen gienge, lustige Dinge zu sagen" (186).

Schlegel then introduces a second authority figure, Aristophanes, into the dialogue. Together Aristophanes and Democritus discuss and criticize the structural principles of Regnard's play. Regnard sets his play in the desert and at the court of the King of Athens; he concludes it with no fewer than three marriages. Democritus objects that there was enough material for three plays, and Regnard admits to having added the complications in order to make the play sufficiently long. The theatrical custom of having the play end in several marriages Democritus dismisses as a whim of fashion.

Regnard had attempted to make Democritus, who laughed at human emotions, appear ridiculous by presenting an infatuated philosopher, in order to prove that even those who mock the passions are not themselves free from them. Much of the effect of this message is lost, Aristophanes maintains, because the historical Democritus was not, in fact, in love. The only thing that Regnard has successfully ridiculed is a phantom, his own Hirngespinst. Regnard seeks refuge in the concept of "poetic license". The dialogue ends as Aristophanes urges greater care in choosing figures for a play so that the literary product does not conflict with historical fact.

Schlegel's Totengespräch has not escaped the attention of earlier scholars. [11] Johann Rentsch is, of course, correct when he states that Schlegel, still under the influence of Gottsched's dramaturgical ideas and particularly Gottsched's obsession with historicity, overlooked the charm of anachronism in Regnard. Yet considered from the standpoints of the place of publication and the intended audience, it is excessive to label Schlegel's Totengespräch an "unbehülfliche Jugendarbeit". [12] It is after all a satire, not a philosophical treatise. Schlegel makes use of some of the classic devices of the dialogue of the dead, including the Verkennungstopos in the first few lines and the principle of judgement by an esteemed authority.

The Belustigungen des Verstandes und des Witzes was continued in 1745 under the title Neue Belustigungen des Gemüths with Christian Nikolaus Naumann as its editor. During this year the journal was particularly receptive to the dialogue of the dead, producing two true Totengespräche[13] and two dialogues incorrectly titled "Todtengespräch".[14]

In 1745 the Neue Beyträge zum Vergnügen des Verstandes und Witzes presented a dialogue of the dead between the poet Horace and his former mentor. Orbilius.[15] The choice of persons is intended to contrast a poet's idea of literature with that of a schoolmaster. To Orbilius all of Horace's criticism is simply ingratitude. Horace accuses Orbilius of spending his life in petty argumentation (a charge reminiscent of the diatribes of the moral weeklies against Pedanterei and the Schulfüchse). Orbilius displays his knowledge of poetry by suggesting that Horace should have written in the style of Livius Andronicus, that is, in a dead language, understood only by scholars. This "ideal" Horace ironically contrasts with his own purpose of poesy:

> Denn die Poeten schreiben nicht dazu, daß sie auch Unge-
> lehrten die Wahrheit deutlich und angenehm machen, daß
> sie die verderbten Sitten ihrer Zeit durch Satiren und Lob-
> gedichte bessern wollen. Nein! Dazu schreiben sie, daß
> Leute wie du [Orbilius], sie in ihren Schulen, doch erst
> nach einigen Jahrhunderten, exponiren lassen, und Phrases
> daraus ziehen können.[16]

Such criticism accords with the attempt of the miscellany magazines and of the moral weeklies as well, to appeal to the literate, but non-scholarly segment of the middle class.

Reunion of teacher and pupil in the nether world recurs frequently in eighteenth-century dialogues of the dead. A related combination of speakers shows a major and a minor writer in conversation. This combination is exhibited by a dialogue between Jonathan Swift and David Faßmann, which appeared in the Westphälische Bemühungen.[17] This dialogue is of special importance in that it indicates an attitude of the miscellany magazines towards Faßmann's Totengespräche; significantly the dialogue appeared twelve years after the last of Faßmann's Neu-entdeckten Elisäischen Felder. That "Vasman" is described in the footnote to his name as the author of "der Todtengespräche und verschiedener, unglüklicher Lebensbeschreibungen" (332) gives the reader a clue as to the opinion of the dialogue writer on the subject of Faßmann's works. In the course of the dialogue Faßmann and Swift gradually reveal their personality and history to one another through exchange of opinion on various literary topics. Their discourse turns to the value and effect of satire, whether it is better to ignore minor writers or to silence them by satire. Faßmann disapproves of those who would try to muzzle their supposed inferiors. He adds this dictum:

> Man mus eine jede Handlung nach der Absicht des jenigen,
> der sie verrichtet, beurteilen; und hätten Sie das getan,
> so würden viele ihrer Satiren vielleicht unterblieben sein. (334)

"Vasman" goes on to list several reasons why authors write, giving supplementary examples. "Schwift" cannot accept this heterodox view of literature:

> Ich höre also doch, daß es Teutschland niemals an Dunzen
> und Chapelains gefelet habe, und daß es diesen weder an
> Verteidigern, noch Scheingründen, ihre Raserei zu bemän-
> teln, mangele. Ich lasse keine Entschuldigung für einen
> elenden Autor gelten, es wäre denn, daß er zur erlaubten
> Nohtwehr und Rettung seines Lebens schriebe. (336)

Thus the attitude of regarding the intention of the author himself when criticizing literature — voiced by Faßmann — finds rejection in this dialogue, despite the large role it was to play in later criticism. The criticism in this dialogue, as in so many other Totengespräche, is moralistic in nature and less inclined to be tolerant of such "arcane" points as the "intention of the author".

When Swift learns that his partner in conversation is the author of the Todtengespräche, he rejects him outright. Faßmann belongs to that group of writers against whom Swift's own satires had been directed. The author of the dialogue lets Faßmann confess:

> Denn unter uns gesagt, der Magen war dazu mein Haupt-
> beruf, und der mittelmässige Beifal und Geschmak meiner
> Zeiten trug das seinige zu meinem Unterhalt redlich bei. (336)

Faßmann also comments on the history of the genre Totengespräch in Germany, and notes with pride that German writers still utilize "his" genre (337). Faßmann reasons correctly, of course, in one respect. When the dialogue "Vasman. Schwift" was written, there were still numerous Totengespräche of the Entrevue type. However, the implied evaluation of such works is that they are as much to be pitied as censured. The miscellany magazines did not devote much time to denouncing David Faßmann.

Since the dialogue of the dead allows men of different ages to converse in perfect freedom, this genre was especially well-suited to convey ideas on one important eighteenth-century controversy: the querelle des anciens et des modernes. The relationship between the speakers in the dialogue between Swift and Faßmann finds an approximate parallel in a dialogue of the dead between Horace and a modern scholar. This conversation was printed in the monthly periodical Unterhaltungen in 1766.[18] In the space of eleven pages the author outlines the alleged weaknesses of eighteenth-century intellectual activity. Beginning with an attack on the slavish-ness of contemporary scholars to the ancient writers, he condemns both the pre-ference of Latin over the vernacular as well as the selection of ancient materials for works of literature instead of materials from German history. He laments the absence of the chorus in the theater (now replaced by harlequins and acrobats, the modern-day scholar relates), and exalts the chorus as "die Freundinn und Rath-geberinn der Tugend" (241). The author bewails the decline of philosophy, which has become too abstract and general. History, likewise, is no longer properly used. The point of absurdity for Horace is the use of rhyme in contemporary poetry; here the poet breaks off the conversation. Thus the collection magazines continue the tradition of mocking pedants in much the same way as the moral weeklies had done.

The relationship between Horace and the modern scholar finds a sequel in Wilhelm Ludwig Wekhrlin's dialogue of the dead between Cornelius Tacitus and Magister Schönfleck, a fictive member of several learned societies and a contributor to the Allgemeine Deutsche Bibliothek. [19] (Ebeling also includes this dialogue in his history of comic literature. [20]) The dialogue pretends to discuss the efficacy of improving manners and morals. The modern German attempt at social improvement by means of the stage is contrasted with the Roman prescriptive approach to acceptable speech and behaviour. Tacitus, who has expected the Germans to remain the strong, noble people whom he described, is surprised that contemporary Germans allow the "Götzzitat" on the stage. The dialogue closes with a diatribe against presumptuous critics (Kunstrichter) who tolerate or perpetuate such barbarities.

The dialogue of the dead does not require that one of the characters play the fool, although that is a frequent method for achieving humour. The form may also be used to present persons in a favourable light. The editors of the Deutsches Museum pay tribute to Fénelon by presenting him in a dialogue of the dead with Louis XIV. [21] The topic of the dialogue is the greatness and incomprehensibility of God. In talking on the subject, Fénelon is shown to be wise and witty, able to converse with the king in an audacious manner. The dialogue, signed "Mßr.", is most probably by August Wilhelm Meißner, [22] a frequent contributor to the Deutsches Museum.

Satire is not the only means by which the dialogue of the dead "judges" the poets. Serious discussion of the comparative worth of several poets is found in two dialogues in the Neues deutsches Museum. [23] These dialogues are sequential and bring together Frederick II, King of Prussia, and contemporary philosophers. The two dialogues were probably written by one author, to judge by the style, and by the opinions expressed. The first, a dialogue between Frederick II, Voltaire and "Wolf", is not primarily concerned with literary problems; however, it does provide preliminary information and background for the second dialogue. In the first dialogue, Frederick explains that he learned to write from Voltaire, but it was from Wolff that he learned to think. Voltaire is made to appear very proud and confident that his works will survive, until Frederick embarrasses him by asking if he always had a noble, benevolent purpose in mind when writing. Voltaire is humbled, and he and Frederick wander on to visit Lessing.

In the second dialogue Frederick and Lessing discuss problems that would naturally arise in a meeting between these two men, in particular their relationship to the French writers. Lessing explains to Frederick that he did not dislike the French writers, but rather learned from them. He admits that he adopted "Redewendungen" which lent themselves, he felt, to use in the German language. But he makes it clear that he did not imitate the French (1050). Frederick is amazed that Lessing preferred Diderot to Voltaire as an epic and tragic poet. The dialogue closes with speculation as to whether posterity will prefer Voltaire or Diderot. Lessing makes this comparison:

Voltaire machte mit einem leichten, netten Schiffe glückliche

Fahrten nach allen zu seiner Zeit bekanten Häfen, wo
gute Ladung zu bekommen war, er wußte jede Ladung
gut wieder abzusetzen. Diderot machte Entdeckungs-
reisen in unbekannten Gewässern. Er suchte, wie Diaz,
den neuen Weg nach Ostindien; er erreichte, wie Diaz,
das Kap, kam aber nicht nach Ostindien. (1051-1052)

Dialogues of the dead in miscellany magazines treated many kinds of
literary problems, not just questions of hierarchical order among the poets. The
Neues gemeinnütziges Magazin presents three expositions of literary problems in
the form of Totengespräche. All of them use figures from antiquity and show an
affinity to Lucian's style. One of the dialogues[24] centers on a topic that teased the
eighteenth-century critical mind: whether it was the material or the treatment that
made the classics great. This dialogue between Achilles and Homer opens with a
bit of humour – Homer has to remind Achilles that shades are not allowed to become angry. He issues this warning with a typical explanation of the nature of the
nether world: "Du hast nunmehr keine andere Waffen übrig, als vernünftige Schlüs-
se" (551). The argument developes from a personal conflict between the two conversants. Achilles demands gratitude from Homer for providing him with the material to write the Iliad. Homer's attitude, which is the prevailing one, is that Achilles should rather be grateful to him for having been given immortality through literature, for Homer could surely have found equal material elsewhere. Thus the
question is settled in favour of poetic inspiration rather than materials and events.
    This same dialogue developes further to a statement by Homer on the
role of a ruler in supporting the arts, in which the author gives expression to his
ideas concerning the relationship of the state to poetry. Great deeds alone cannot
perpetuate the fame of a ruler: only the Muses possess that power. The ruler who
desires honours must first make certain that he is virtuous enough to deserve them;
secondly he must know how to ingratiate himself with those favoured by the Muses.
If a ruler truly loves the "sciences", then talented men will gather under his aegis.
If a king has no Homer to celebrate his fame, then it is because he does not deserve
one. Correspondingly, a king's lack of good taste dishonours his nation.
    In the following year (1761) the Neues gemeinnütziges Magazin again
utilized the dialogue of the dead. The dialogue features Hieron and Pindar – a des-
potic ruler and the poet who praised him. This dialogue is one of the shortest of all
dialogues of the dead, consisting of only eighteen lines. Its principle device is the
Verkennungstopos: Pindar fails to recognize the tyrant in whose service he had
been on earth. In that this dialogue comments on the role of the Muses in political
affairs, it is related to the discussion between Achilles and Homer. Rather than
condemning Pindar for selling his talents, the author of the dialogue directs his
criticism at the prince, who was foolish for believing what the poet said about him.
The concern with the potentate's relationship to the arts was, of course, highly
topical in an age in which the arts depended in large measure for their sustenance
on patronage by the nobility. Both of the Totengespräche discussed above would
argue against the custom of paying a poet to sing the ruler's praise.
    The state of contemporary satire is the subject of the third dialogue of
the dead in the Neues gemeinnütziges Magazin.[25] Menippus and Lycambus review

the present situation, having as source of their information, naturally, a newly-arrived shade. The two figures are well chosen for discussing the subject, Menippus as an author of satire and Lycambas as its object. Menippus has little good to say of modern satire:

> Ich habe . . . gehört, daß die Macht der Dichtkunst jetzo
> so stark nicht mehr ist, als zu deiner [Lycambas'] Zeit.
> Die satyrischen Schriften sind meistens so frostig, daß
> die sich getroffen finden, gar nicht die Versuchung haben
> können, dich nachzuahmen: und wären auch die Satyren
> beissend, so würden sich die nicht henken, die sich abge-
> schildert finden. Nein, sie würden die Dichter henken las-
> sen. . . . [26]

Menippus argues like a modern man, who looks to the past nostalgically. However, he was probably correct in stating that contemporary satire led few to suicide, as it had Lycambas.

The miscellany magazines as well as the moral weeklies concerned themselves with linguistic reform. However, the miscellany magazines display less interest in the topic than do the moral weeklies. Yet a good example of the use of a dialogue of the dead to the end of linguistic reform is found in the Hanauisches Magazin.[27] The cause of linguistic purity is upheld in a "Gespräch im Reiche der Todten, zum Nutzen und Frommen der Lebendigen, zwischen Herrn Lithophus, Herrn Maron und Herrn Friedorf"; Friedorf represents linguistic purity, the simple and good; Lithophus and Maron, whose names suggest petrified usage and grumbling or growling, demonstrate poor usage: "Der eine spricht noch im Canzleistyl mit lateinischen, und der andere in der kauderwelschen Sprache mit französischen Wörtern gelapt" (306).

According to Friedorf, Pluto has issued a decree that all legal affairs in the underworld must henceforth be conducted in German. Pluto has further caused a "deutsche Akademie" to convene in order to pass judgement on the linguistic purity of every book printed. Maron and Lithophus protest that the German language is not yet capable of dispensing with certain French and Latin phrases. Friedorf contends that it is indeed, for Pluto has chosen the German language to be the "Hauptsprache Elysiums" (310) because it, of all the living languages of man, still possesses the most of the "Urstof" which is particular to it. Friedorf then defends the justness of this choice on the basis of the glorious past of the German language, calling to mind the "German" of Charlemagne and Otfried. The current usage in which French words are mixed with German arises from the "absurd prejudice" that it sounds more elevated, witty and scholarly to employ such terms.

Still arguing against purification, Lithophus presents his most cogent point: since people are accustomed to the present mixture, sudden change in usage to a more "German" vocabulary would create confusion. Friedorf counters with "Gewohnheit macht den Fehler schön!" and begins immediately with an extensive program of improvement. He suggests, for example, "wegen" with the genitive instead of the dative and more care in distinguishing "den" and "denen" and the avoidance of such legalistic forms as "obbelobter" and "beaugenscheinigen" (316-317).

At the end of each of the two sections of the dialogue he appends a list of translations from French and Latin phrases to German. Friedorf's purifications occasionally verge on the extreme, but not to the extent of the reforms advanced by zealots. His suggestion to substitute "Ansehen, Schutz" for "Autorität" is less than desirable and his assertion that the French have no word for Trinkgeld is highly questionable.

While the attempts at satire in this Totengespräch do not reach the same heights as those in other journals, it is nevertheless interesting for its creation of new fictions about the realm of the dead. In this dialogue Pluto seems more than mere judge in the nether world; here he is made a tyrant. Yet authority is necessary for statement of opinion in the realm of the dead. Although the dialogist does let Maron and Lithophus speak a mixed language in self-parody, the grace of the satire is impeded by the awkwardness of attempted German translations after each foreign phrase.

Again in 1782 the Hanauisches Magazin published a dialogue of the dead, this time a translation of Lyttleton's dialogue between Mercury, an English duellist, and a North American savage. [28] The translation is true to the linguistic purism advocated in the first Totengespräch presented in the magazine. The word "duellist" is translated as "Zweikämpfer" and "Tom Pushwell", the name given by Lyttleton to the English duellist, is transliterated as "Stoswol". [29]

Such social criticism as is found in Lyttleton's dialogues figures large in the subject matter of dialogues of the dead in the miscellany magazines. Aberrant social behaviour on earth receives condemnation in the nether world. Lyttleton includes in his Dialogues of the Dead a variation on the form of the Totengespräch. A translation of this dialogue between Mercury and "Frau Modisch" — the name betrays her character flaw immediately — is found in the Gesammelte Schriften zum Vergnügen und Unterricht. [30] Mercury advises the woman, who is not yet a shade, that she should wander forever on the nearer side of the Styx, lest Minos cast her into the Tartarus for her empty-headed cultivation of bon ton and consequent neglect of husband and family.

While in the above dialogue judgement is passed without the pronouncement of sentence, the Baierische Sammlungen und Auszüge presented a complete judgement scene in the same year (1767). [31] Here Rhadamanthus dispenses punishment for vice and reward for virtue. The judgement scene is a device employed by both moral weeklies and the miscellany magazines to illustrate proper behaviour and attitudes.

Social and ethical criticism of society, similar in form and content to Lucian's satires, is seen in a dialogue of the dead in the Westphälische Bemühungen. [32] Here the author of "Pluto, Merkur einige Schatten" parodies the language and lives of several social undesirables as they are brought before the judge; these include a monk, a self-centered lawyer (censured because he lived from the quarrelsome nature of mankind), a reprehensible bookkeeper (Plusmacher), a schoolman, and a young lady of questionable virtue, all of whom are condemned. Pluto admits only one shade to the Elysian fields — a poor shepherd-woman who has deceived no one throughout her life of penury.

The Totengespräch is rarely used in miscellany magazines to comment on religious affairs. One example concerning the controversy surrounding Lessing's publication of the Fragmente eines Unbekannten avoids dealing with the various points which that document raises. Rather the dialogue takes Lessing to task for endangering the faith of the common people. The dialogue is found in the Journal aller Journale,[33] and although most of the articles in this periodical are reprints, this particular dialogue, signed "H.", was probably the product of the editor, Jonas Ludwig Heß, himself. Heß had been acquainted with Reimarus and thus would have found Lessing's publication of the Fragmente a worthy subject for his comments. The dialogue is divided into two sections, the first a conversation between Lessing and Klotz. Here Lessing professes that he published the Fragmente with the idea that they could help people troubed by doubts and that he in no way regrets having done so. Klotz has only one question left unanswered; the country pastor arrives on the scene just in time to pose that question. The country pastor argues that even though Lessing was sincere in believing that all the doubts raised in the Fragmente could be refuted, he was nevertheless blind to the danger that they presented to certain people who look for doubt as a release from duties. The author of this Totengespräch lets the opinion stand that Lessing published the Fragmente more from confused thinking than from malicious intent. The country pastor maintains that such publications, when directed at a larger, non-scholarly audience, only cause unrest among the faithful. Finally, even Lessing has to admit the wisdom of the pastor's point of view.

This conservative criticism in the dialogue is typical of the tendency of writers of Totengespräche to protect the common man, "die einfältige Heerde" in the words of the country pastor. The use of the Totengespräch facilitates judgement and allows the author to state opinions with a degree of authority. Such a form was a boon to critics who liked to add dramatic weight to their aesthetic and moral pronouncements.

Dialogues of the dead appeared in the miscellany magazines with frequency and some regularity from the 1740's to the end of the century. (As late as 1798 W. G. Becker's journal Erholungen presented a Totengespräch by Bodmer.[34]) Concomitant with this phenomenon is the intense concern of the journals with Lucian, exemplified by the numerous translations of his works and the number of original pieces inspired by his style. Whether the inspiration for the dialogues of the dead in the miscellany magazines comes from Lucian or from other sources, the form is frequently used by them in a way in which Lucian did not use it: as a vehicle for literary criticism. None of Lucian's dialogues of the dead are primarily concerned with literary criticism. Yet the motifs of moral and ethical criticism — part of the earliest heritage of the dialogue of the dead — are not lacking in the dialogues of the dead that appeared in the miscellany magazines.

In the two subsequent chapters this study deals with dialogues of the dead used as "independent literary satires" and with dialogues which owe rather much to classical tradition. There is admittedly a certain degree of difficulty in distinguishing between dialogues found in the "miscellany magazines" or as "independent literary satires" or among the "classical" group; inevitably, some aspects of the dialogues could be as easily treated in one chapter as in another. In addition, a few of those Totengespräche treated in the last two chapters were first published in periodical sources. Nevertheless, the present order, while it results in part from convenience, lends clarity to the presentation.

70

NOTES

1   "Vorrede", Stück 1 (Lemgo, 1753).

2   Wolfgang Martens, Die Botschaft der Tugend (Stuttgart, 1968), p. 147.

3   "Vorrede", Vermischte, mehrenteils historische gelehrten Abhandlungen, von verschiedenen Verfassern (Rostock, 1767).

4   Because a great number of Totengespräche are found in these journals, it was not possible to discuss them all. Additional dialogues are listed in Appendix I.

5   Neue Beyträge zum Vergnügen des Verstandes und Witzes, I Stück 5 (Bremen, 1745), 471-495. Karl Goedeke ascribes the translation to Hagedorn (Grundriß zur Geschichte der deutschen Dichtung, IV^1 [Dresden, ^{3}1910], 55).

6   I, Stück 6 (Bremen and Leipzig, 1745), 527-536.

7   I, Stück 2 and Stück 3 (Bremen, 1744), 120-149; 221-253.

8   Vermischte, mehrenteils historische gelehrte Abhandlungen, von verschiedenen Verfassern, Stücke 22-25 (Rostock, 1767), pp. 169-200.

9   I (Leipzig, 1741), 101-126. Schwabe's colleagues included Gellert, J. E. Schlegel, J. A. Schlegel, Uz, Ewald von Kleist and Rabener. This dialogue is also found in Johann Elias Schlegel's Werke, ed. Johann Heinrich Schlegel, III (Copenhagen and Leipzig, 1764), 181-202. Subsequent references to this dialogue given in the text are based on this edition, which does not differ significantly from the earlier one.

10   The influence of Gottsched is still to be found here. In the preface to the third part of Die deutsche Schaubühne Gottsched comments on Regnard's "Democritus": "Denn wer in dem alten Athen zu Demokrits Zeiten Könige, Hofleute, Glockentürme, Fischbeinröcke und andere solche vortreffliche Dinge verdauen kann der muß ja von der Wahrscheinlichkeit kein Wort sagen."

11   Both Rentsch and Egilsrud point to Erich Schmidt's contention ("Zu 'Götter, Helden und Wieland'", Goethe Jb I (1880), 378-9) that Schlegel's Totengespräch influenced Goethe's farce. However, in light of more recent and specialized studies (discussed in Chapter VII) there seems to be neither need nor support for this hypothesis.

12   Rentsch, p. 28. Elizabeth M. Wilkinson in her study of Schlegel's aesthetics relates the satire to Schlegel's general theories (Johann Elias Schlegel A German Pioneer in Aesthetics [Oxford, 1945], pp. 83-86).

13   Neue Belustigungen des Gemüths (Hamburg and Leipzig, 1745), "Todtengespräche. Lucretia. Sappho. Cato", pp. 129-134; "Ein Todtengespräch. Diogenes und Alexander", pp. 338-343.

14   Neue Belustigungen des Gemüths (Hamburg and Leipzig, 1745), "Thais. Ein Todtengespräche", pp. 236-239; "Merkur und Momus. Ein Todtengespräch", pp. 508-513.

15   "Todtengespräche. Horaz. Orbil", Neue Beyträge zum Vergnügen des Ver-
      standes und Witzes, II, Stück 5 (Leipzig and Bremen, 1745).
16   "Todtengespräche. Horaz. Orbil", p. 373.
17   "Todtengespräch. Vasman. Schwift", Westphälische Bemühungen, Stück 17
      (Lemgo, 1754), pp. 332-338. Subsequent references to this dialogue are
      given parenthetically in the text.
18   Stück 3 (Hamburg, 1766), pp. 246-257. A footnote indicates that the dialogue
      entitled "Todtengespräch zwischen Horaz und einem neuern Gelehrten" was
      originally written in Danish and was taken from the Patriotischer Zuschauer.
      Subsequent references to this dialogue are given parenthetically in the text.
19   Chronologen, Wilhelm Ludwig Wekhrlin, ed., I (Frankfurt and Leipzig, 1779),
      38-48.
20   Friedrich Wilhelm Ebeling. Geschichte der komischen Literatur in Deutsch-
      land, II (Leipzig, 1869), 403-407.
21   "Dialog, wie K. Ludewig XIV. und Fenelon ihn gehalten haben könten",
      Deutsches Museum, VI (Leipzig, 1784), 417-420.
22   Meißner's literary satire in the form of a Totengespräch is discussed in
      Chapter VII.
23   Neues deutsches Museum, Heinrich Christian Boie, ed., III (Leipzig, 1790),
      749-757; 1048-1052.
24   "Todtengespräch. Achilles und Homerus", Neues gemeinnütziges Magazin.
      (April, 1760), 551-554.
25   "Todtengespräch. Menippus, Lycambas", Neues gemeinnütziges Magazin.
      (Feb., 1761), pp. 255-256.
26   Neues gemeinnütziges Magazin, (Feb., 1761), p. 256.
27   Stücke 38 and 40 (Hanau, 1779), 303-321; 329-336. Subsequent references to
      this text are given parenthetically.
28   Stück 26 (Hanau, 1782), 225-232.
29   The translation of the Hanauisches Magazin captures the sense and tone of
      Lyttleton's original better than the translation by Oelrichs does. However,
      a more thoroughgoing comparison of the two versions is complicated, since
      different editions of Lyttleton, the second changed significantly, were used
      by the translators.
30   "Gespräch der Todten. Merkur – Und ein heutiges feines Frauenzimmer",
      II, Stück 1 (Vienna, 1767), 70-75.
31   "Gespräch von dem Schaden, den ungeschickte Lehrer einem Lande bringen.
      Rhadamanthus und zween Schatten", Baierische Sammlungen und Auszüge
      zum Unterricht und Vergnügen, IV (Munich, 1767), 47-55. Reprinted from
      Der Bienenstock.
32   Stück 16 (Lemgo, 1754), 251-258.
33   "Gespräch im Reich der Schatten, zwischen Klotz, Lessing, und einem Land-
      priester", I (Hamburg, 1786), 362-372.
34   Erholungen, III (Leipzig, 1798), 191-204.

CHAPTER VI

THE SERIOUS DIALOGUE OF THE DEAD:
EIGHTEENTH-CENTURY CLASSICISM

In view of the high regard which both Lucian and Fontenelle enjoyed in
Germany in the eighteenth century, it would be surprising not to find serious attempts at creating new dialogues upon the inspiration or in imitation of the style
of these two masters of the form; and indeed, a great number of such dialogues in
the nether world were produced. These often appeared in the moral weeklies and
in the literary journals. But were there no writers who created series of Totengespräche as independent works of literature such as those of Lucian and Fontenelle?
In the preface to his translation of Lyttleton's Dialogues of the Dead (1761) Johann
George Henrich Oelrichs states the situation very succinctly:

> Bei der Fruchtbarkeit der teutschen Schriftsteller, können
> wir uns doch nicht rümen, dem Lucian, Fenelon, Fontenelle
> und Littleton eine teutsche Schrift in dieser Art an die Seite
> sezzen zu können: Wenigstens ist mir keiner bekannt gewor-
> den, der in dieser Art des Vortrags mit ihnen verglichen zu
> werden verdiene. [1]

With the exception of the dialogues of the dead in the periodicals, this was largely
the case. It remained for the second half of the eighteenth century to produce dialogues of the dead of high literary quality.
    The earlier lack is perhaps explained by the low regard for the genre
on the part of German writers, resulting from the quality and quantity of dialogues
in the style of the Entrevuen in dem Reiche derer Todten by David Faßmann and the
followers of that fashion. Such "trivial" Totengespräche still flourished in 1761 and
Oelrichs goes on to comment on them:

> Vielleicht werden einigen meiner Leser unsere bekannte
> Gespräche im Reiche der Todten eingefallen sein, woran
> wir so wenigen Mangel haben, daß wir noch täglich damit
> überhäufet werden: Würde ich aber meinen Landesleuten,
> nicht zu wenig Geschmak zutrauen, wann ich besorgen
> wolte, daß man mir diese Art Schrift entgegen sezzen
> könne? [2]

Diatribes against Faßmann and against the "trivial" Totengespräche are frequently
found in literary and critical sources. An example of this are Johann Salomo Semler's remarks on Faßmann and his Totengespräche from "Gedanken von Ueberein-

kommung der Romane mit den Legenden":

> Ich kenne einige, welche eine vollständige Sammlung
> teutscher Entrevues, oder Gespräche im Reiche der
> Todten haben. Wenn sie ihren schlechten Verfasser
> genauer kenten, so würden sie sich nicht halb so viel
> auf diesen Schatz einbilden. [3]

The quotations above serve as an apt summary of the situation before 1760. After that date there were a number of attempts at "serious" Totengespräche, perhaps the best of which are those by Christoph Martin Wieland. Significantly, the authors of classically-oriented dialogues of the dead avoid titles which would suggest any close connection with the style of Faßmann. Different terms are used in place of the popular formula Entrevue in dem Reiche derer Todten, which Faßmann had helped to make so universally familiar.

This chapter treats of such "serious" dialogues of the dead. The word "serious" is used because the writers to be dealt with here frequently show an awareness of the traditions of the genre and strive to add something to it; their purposes are often philosophic or moralistic. Some of the writers included literary criticism in their dialogues, although satire itself is a method infrequently employed. Format is also a factor in the designation of this category: many were published as single works in book form; some, however, were first seen in the more discriminating journals — Wieland's "Dialogen im Elysium" first appeared in the Teutscher Merkur, for example. That the authors to be considered under this heading wrote (with one exception) more than one dialogue of the dead, indicates, too, a more than passing interest in the form. Thus one may see here (as is rarely the case in the literary journals) whether an author is able to sustain the rather delicate balance of wit, drama and pedagogy for which the genre is so perfectly suited. However, dialogues of literary value are found both in the periodicals and among those works here labelled "serious".

Often the writer of the serious dialogue of the dead attempts a classicism in style which distinguishes his use of the form from that of other writers whose chief interest is satire or biography. Frequently the authors in this category were classical scholars, such as David Christoph Seybold, Christoph Martin Wieland and Johann Heinrich Merck. Consequently their dialogues display an awareness of the traditional forms of the dialogue to a much greater degree than do those of the Faßmann "school" or those of the writers of independent literary satires. The dialogues of the writers of "serious" Totengespräche reflect more clearly the strong informing tradition of Lucian and Fontenelle than do Totengespräche of journalistic intent.

This classicism of style manifests itself above all in choice of speakers. Greater emphasis is placed on characters from antiquity. Bodmer's Gespräche im Elysium und am Acheron, for example, are peopled entirely with characters from ancient, mostly Roman history. Although Jacob Wegelin and Johann Konrad Fäsi are exceptions to this generalization, partially because of their subject matter, their dialogues, too, avoid figures from the contemporary political scene.

Ribaldry is an element which is absent from the "serious" Totenge-

spräche; the authors occasionally allow themselves a wry turn of phrase, however.
Writers in this group choose to use the dialogue of the dead not as a vehicle for
verbal buffoonery, but rather to convey philosophical and moral truths. [4]

One of the first German writers to publish a series of dialogues of the
dead was Wilhelm Ehrenfried Neugebauer (1735?-1767), the author of the comic
novel Der teutsche Don Quichotte. [5] Neugebauer wrote five dialogues of the dead,
published together as a Versuch in Todtengesprächen in 1761. In these short dialogues (average length is about seven small octavo pages) Neugebauer displays a
skillful control of the medium to a degree which had rarely seen before his time.
The dialogues unfold their arguments through the personalities of the speakers.
The issues are well-expounded and the author presents the views of both sides
with a fairness which is rare. The dialogues evince some interest in satire, but
little of the humour and playfulness that is Lucian's; in their smooth intellectuali-
ty they more nearly approach Fontenelle's dialogues.

The first of the five dialogues is the most germane to the interest of
this study since it illustrates Neugebauer's dramatic technique of dialogue writing
and offers criticism of the world of letters. The dialogue takes place between "Sebastian Gryph" and "Thyrsis", the former a Buchführer (derogatory term for a
book dealer), the latter an unpublished poet.

Evidently Neugebauer intended this dialogue to be read from the page
silently and not spoken dramatically, for there is no positive evidence that the setting is in the nether world until the third speech in which Thyrsis mentions his
"frühzeitigen Tode". [6] The silent reader, of course, had the title "Todtengespräch"
to inform him of the circumstances. The merchant Gryph confirms the location in
the following speech with a sentiment frequently had in the realm of the dead:
"Aber, ihr wisset nicht, daß der Haß und alle Leidenschaften nach dem Tode auf-
hören sollen?" (72). This topos recurs in Neugebauer's dialogue between Justinian
and Juvenal. In general Neugebauer is fond of calling attention to the idealistic
qualities of the realm of the dead. He uses the device for humour also, occasionally inventing juxtapositions such as "ein aufrichtiger Todter".

The first person to speak is the pseudonymous poet Thyrsis, newly
arrived in the nether world. With characteristic conciseness Neugebauer introduces the conflict in the first two speeches: Thyrsis mentions his hatred of Buchführer and Gryph confesses that he was himself one. Thus characters are chosen
who are able to comment on the relationship between book-dealers and authors.
In the sixth speech Gryph assures Thyrsis that he too disdains the Buchführer and
excludes himself from their number by the fact that he lived much earlier. The
removal in time from the present serves two functions. First, the bitterness of
the enmity between Thyrsis and Gryph is abated, allowing them to discuss the issue reasonably as befits the realm of the dead; secondly, since Gryph belongs to
an older generation of booksellers, he is able to criticize present practices with
the authority of age and tradition.

When Gryph asks why Thyrsis hates the Buchführer, Thyrsis informs
him that he was "ein Poete, ein Philosoph und ein witziger Autor" (73), who was
robbed of his fame by the poor taste of dealers who refused to print his works.
Thyrsis argues that he might have been another Homer, a Klopstock or a Milton,
yet the publishers printed "Stoppens Gedichte, die sächsische Herkuliska, den

Philosoph Robine u. d. g. Skarteken" (73), but left Thyrsis' works to perish. Gryph presents the mercantile considerations: the businessman must live from his sales, and "Werke des Witzes" are especially dangerous items, subject to the vagaries of fashion. Thyrsis argues that esprit may appear in all the forms; the most important rule is that one follow nature in one's work. Gryph finds this dictum inadequate, for both Schönaich and Klopstock could claim that they follow nature. For Thyrsis this only reinforces his arguments that the taste of the Buchführer determines what gets printed. Gryph suggests other possible reasons for Thyrsis' misfortune.

A work may gain favour because of the reputation of the author, or because of the publisher's personal preferences or because the taste of a particular region acclaims it. He contends that no book is so bad that it does not make its way to its readers. "Selintes Gesundheiten" sells as well as "Noah". Indeed, many works − such as Christian Nikolaus Naumann's "Nimrod" − are sold by the poor taste of the public, and people often buy Amadis just to have something "thörichtes und ungeheures" (76) to read. Gryph comments again on "Nimrod", saying that since Germany had Klopstock, there was no need for a "Nimrod".[7]

Gryph's logic cannot convince the poet, who accuses him of siding with his colleagues in trade. Thyrsis declares that he will have to wait until he feels death's influence more strongly before he can continue the discourse serenely. Thus the dialogue breaks off when reasoned discourse is no longer possible.

In a short space Neugebauer has presented several ideas succinctly and dramatically. Two sides of the issue − embodied by the two shades − have been delivered in such a way that the reader's sympathies can lie neither with the merchant nor with the would-be poet. This is typical of Neugebauer's method. Arguments are put forth which enable the reader to see, or at least look for, a via media, an intermediate position between two extremes.

In the matter of literary criticism the author has been apodictic in presenting his likes and dislikes. Interesting for the understanding of Neugebauer's literary standards are his depreciatory remarks on the Amadis novels and Selintes' Gesundheiten (a collection of toasts), his dislike of Naumann's "Nimrod" and his preference for Bodmer and Klopstock. The views expressed on satire in the dialogue between Justinian and Juvenal further illumine Neugebauer's ideas about the writing of satire. In this dialogue he proceeds much as he did in the first. Justinian and Juvenal discuss the comparative value of laws and satire in effecting improvements in man. The two characters' lives make them qualified to comment on the issue of discussion.

The dialogue opens with the loss-of-anger topos: "Nun habe ich allen Zorn verlohren . . ." (93), spoken by Justinian, a law-giver and also the libelled object of Procopius' Secret History. The dialogue then developes out of a personal dispute between a satirist and an avowed satire-hater. In the course of the dialogue both characters modify their positions so that by the end of the piece Justinian can no longer maintain that satire is never effective and the work of slanderers; nor can Juvenal continue to believe that the making of laws is a vain process, although the idea of the futility of the law is never fully refuted. A compromise is struck which allows that the satirist may indeed have the improvement of man as his goal.

Neugebauer's collection of original German dialogues of the dead was indeed a step forward. Totengespräche of comparable quality are seen previously

only in a few of the moral weeklies and literary journals. Neugebauer's Totengespräche are carefully and compactly written: there is little in the text that does
not inform the reader or advance one or the other side of an argument.

The year 1763 saw the publication of a collection of twenty dialogues
of the dead by Jacob Wegelin (1721-1791). Wegelin was the preacher at the French
Church in Berlin, then professor of philosophy in St. Gall and later professor of
history in Berlin. It is not surprising that his Religiose Gespräche der Todten
should feature historical personages discussing religious issues. Wegelin was not
unfamiliar with the dialogue form, for in 1760 he had published Die letzten Gespräche Socrates und seiner Freunde (Zürich, 1760), dialogues only a brief step
removed from being Totengespräche.

The dialogues in this collection are consciously didactic. In his preface the author states that his dialogues are "instructive" and states further that
one must not expect the same qualities from them that one requires of those written for entertainment. Most of the dialogues attempt to impart practical teachings
as the author explains in the "Vorbericht" and were thus in accord with contemporary principles of literature:

> Die meiste von diesen Gesprächen betreffen praktische
> Gegenstände welchen Schaden es bringe, wenn in freyen
> Staaten Religionstreitigkeiten zu Staatsparteien erhoben
> werden . . . .[8]

The Religiose Gespräche der Todten was reviewed by the Ausführliche
und kritische Nachrichten the same year it was published.[9] So enthusiastic is the
editor that he reproduces both Wegelin's preface (in part) and the dialogue between
Erasmus and Luther. The editor praises the dialogues for their careful representa-
tion of the ideas of the speakers, yet he cannot refrain from commenting on the
lack of authenticity in imitation of language. Indeed, it is disturbing to hear an
eighteenth-century rationalist Luther speaking of "die erhabenste Religion des
Verstandes" (33). The editor apologizes for Wegelin's fault in the introduction
and states that "eine gedankenvolle Schreibart" (19) was necessary for the topic.
Unfortunately, the dialogues are less interesting literarily for all their alleged
fidelity to the thoughts of the speakers. Wegelin evidently did not find humour to
be an educational device, nor did he choose to make full use of the devices inherent in the form. Even the principle of selecting speakers from different centuries is employed only a few times. Yet if Wegelin made no other contributions
to the genre, he did lend greater respectability to the form by trying to teach
religion and morality with it. His success was such that the Ausführliche und
kritische Nachrichten could praise his dialogues at a time when scholarly magazines devoted little attention to Totengespräche.

While the name Johann Jakob Bodmer is frequently heard in other contexts, it is rarely mentioned in connection with Totengespräche, despite the fact
that "the Swiss Homer" wrote at least twelve dialogues of the dead in addition to
those which appeared in Die Discourse der Mahler and Der Mahler der Sitten.
Some of the dialogues which comprise Bodmer's Gespräche im Elysium und am
Acheron had appeared in periodical sources: nine dialogues were published together

with the Neue Critische Briefe (1763). [10] These dialogues of the dead, most of which
feature speakers from Roman history, reveal a broad knowledge of ancient history
and literature.

As early as Der Mahler der Sitten Bodmer expressed an awareness of
the structure of dialogues of the dead by way of an apology for his Totengespräch
between Romulus and Cartouche. In the preface to this dialogue Bodmer avows his
admiration for Fontenelle and explains Fontenelle's technique of dialogue writing:

> Man hat den Herrn von Fontenelle wegen seiner Gespräche
> der Todten mit allem Rechte gelobet, daß ein jedes von den-
> selben eine, und nicht mehr, als eine sonderbare Idee in
> sich schleust, welche, nachdem man sie eine kurtze Zeit
> lang erwartet hat, zulezt eröffnet wird. Es scheint, daß
> die Haupt Betrachtung, mit welcher er ein Gespräche en-
> diget, aus etlichen andern Betrachtungen, die ihr vorher-
> gehen, hervorfalle, und daß er nicht habe umhin gehen
> können, selbige zu machen, ungeachtet in der That das
> gantze Gespräche um dieser Hauptbetrachtung willen ge-
> schrieben ist. [11]

Bodmer states in conclusion that his own dialogues cannot boast of the same unity
of ideas found in Fontenelle's dialogues des morts, yet he hopes that his own dialogues will satisfy his audience, since the dialogues do possess unity of a kind,
admittedly to a lesser degree. This unity he sees in the close relationship between
the various ideas.

The dialogue between Cato and Homer from Gespräche im Elysium und
am Acheron[12] may serve as an illustration of Bodmer's method. Here Bodmer
brings together two figures whose basis for fellowship lies in posterity's treatment of them, rather than in shared history or similarity of activity. The dialogue divides easily into two sections, in the first of which Bodmer treats of
Homer's fate at the hands of contemporary eighteenth-century society and in the
second half, of Cato's.

The text requires a visual reading rather than a hearing. This distinction between hearing and reading a dialogue reflects one substantial difference between Lucian's dialogues and eighteenth-century dialogues of the dead. Lucian's
dialogues were often read aloud; the eighteenth-century dialogue of the dead was
more often read silently. It was Lucian's practice to introduce the speakers immediately, either by direct address or meaningful epithet. [13] Bodmer's text carries the superscript "Cato und Homer" and Homer is referred to directly in the
first speech ("guter Homer"). However, no allusion is made to Cato until he becomes the center of attention in the second half of the dialogue (40).

The first speech serves several functions: it introduces the problem-
atic nature of the ensuing dialogue ("Welcher Trübsinn verdunkelt deine heitere
Gestalt, guter Homer?") and identifies the locus dramatis ("Kan die Traurigkeit
in diese Wohnungen der Seligen sich einschleichen?"). Homer names as the cause
of his unhappiness the disturbing reports from the world above, employing the
frequently-appearing fiction of informational intercourse between the two worlds.

Homer adds that he does not understand his concern with the world of the mortals.
By allowing the shades to retain a vivid interest in the Oberwelt, the author thus
links the real world with the world below.

In subsequent speeches Homer laments that the earth has now only a
few people whose respect for his works is based on reason and good taste ("Vernunft und Geschmak"). Upon inquiring about the morals and inclinations which now
govern men, Cato learns that the present is an age without heroes, without patri-
ots, without persons desirous of honours ("Ehrbegierige"). The consequence is a
lack of understanding for Homer's poetry: "Gerade das betrübt mich, daß die Menschen in diese sclavische Feigheit gefallen sind, die meinen [Homer's] Gedichten
so schädlich ist" (39).

After a few remarks from Cato about the prevailing spirit of conformi-
ty, Homer politely inquires about Cato's own fate at the hands of posterity. Cato
is much disturbed that the modern world misunderstands the motives for his suicide, interpreted as the result of hate for Caesar rather than of love for the republic (40). Homer attempts to re-instate Cato's greatness; Cato is for him exem-
plary, "das Beyspiel eines Mannes . . . der starb, weil er kein Knecht eines Böse-
wichts seyn konnte . . ." (41). In the last speech Cato reiterates the central theme
of the piece: "Das iztlebende Geschlecht der Menschen ist so hartköpfigt, daß es
sich Tugend und Rechtschaffenheit kaum noch im Geiste vorstellen kan" (42).

Attached to the dialogue is a quotation from Montaigne in much the
same spirit as the dialogue itself; both texts aim at a vindication of Cato. This
was perhaps Bodmer's way of indicating his indebtedness to Montaigne. Elsewhere
Bodmer does Montaigne the honour of letting him converse with Cicero in the nether
world.

That Bodmer wrote than a dozen original dialogues of the dead (in addition to those in his moral weeklies) points to the respect which the genre enjoyed
among the more sophisticated reading public. Yet Bodmer's Totengespräche have
received little critical notice, even in the particular studies of dialogues of the
dead. Since Bodmer's collection deals with figures from ancient history, one could
reasonably expect a treatment of them in Anthony Scenna's The Treatment of Ancient Legend and History in Bodmer. [14] However, Scenna dismisses the dialogues
summarily as imitations of George Lord Lyttleton, [15] whose Dialogues of the Dead
had first been published in London in 1760. The historian of Swiss literature Baechtold exercises more moderation when he says, "Nach dem Muster des Litelton
schrieb Bodmer eine ganze Reihe stofflich zumeist der römischen Geschichte ent-
lehnter kleiner [Gespräche]". [16]

In the introduction to the Gespräche im Elysium und am Acheron Bodmer himself commented on his debt to Lord Lyttleton. Speaking of his own dialogues Bodmer says:

> Ihre Form ist Liteltonisch, und einige sind von Liteltons
> Abhandlungen veranlasset worden. Aber Sie werden bald
> entdeken, daß die Gedanken von des Engländers abweichen.
> Es hat seine Verdienste anderst als Litelton, und doch
> nicht unrichtig gedacht zu haben.

Here, as in his comments on Fontenelle's technique, Bodmer seems more interested in the ideas contained in the dialogue than in the technique of dialogue writing itself. Consequently the philosophic burthen of Bodmer's dialogues often outweighs their literary charm.

A comparison of Lyttleton's and Bodmer's dialogues reveals a number of major differences, not only in the subject matter, but also in matters of style and technique. Both Bodmer and Lyttleton evidently found the contemporary Romans T. Pomponius Atticus and M. Brutus suitable partners for conversation, for both writers featured the two Romans in a dialogue of the dead. This is the only instance in which the two dialogists unite the same two conversants, although many figures from Roman history are common to both writers' dialogues.

The historical background presented is much the same in both conversations. (Lyttleton lists Plutarch's life of Julius Caesar and Cornelius Nepos' Vita Attici as his sources. Presumably Bodmer knew the same sources.) Lyttleton, however, chooses to insert more biographical information into his dialogue than does Bodmer. For this and other reasons Lyttleton's dialogue has nearly twice the length of Bodmer's. Bodmer concisely introduces the conflict in the first speech, while Lyttleton delays it until the third, cautiously and politely developing the difference of opinion between the two men. Only Bodmer delineates the location of the conversation within the text of the dialogue.

The dialogues are similar in that they go beyond the presentation of biography and serve as vehicles for the thoughts of the authors. It is in the nature of the ideas expressed in the works, as Bodmer correctly stated, that his version of a dialogue between Atticus and Brutus differs from Lyttleton's. Lyttleton's Atticus reasons long and well for the virtues of prudence and temperateness. These ideals Brutus contests, urging that one must obey "the noble Feelings of [the] Heart"[17] and implying that Atticus lacks proper public spirit. The philosophical burden of Bodmer's dialogue much resembles that of the dialogue between Cato and Homer discussed earlier. The prevailing theme of the conversation between the two Romans is that the times are corrupt, that modern men are weak and cowardly.

To the corpus of German dialogues of the dead Bodmer added some of the most learned. By limiting his speakers to figures from antiquity Bodmer gave his Totengespräche a unity of which few other German collections could boast. However, it is difficult to deny that the dialogues lack liveliness and colour.

In 1798 a dialogue of the dead by Bodmer between Claudius Tacitus and Tiberius appeared in the magazine Erholungen; the editor of the periodical, W. G. Becker, claims to have received the dialogue from the hands of Bodmer himself[18]:

> Dieses Gespräch empfieng ich nebst andern theils unge-
> druckten, theils verbesserten Aufsätzen noch aus den
> Händen des ehrwürdigen Greises, dessen Verdienste um
> die deutsche Litteratur, wenn er schon zuweilen etwas
> einseitig war, bereits vergessen zu seyn scheinen. [19]

The literary worth of this particular dialogue is not stressed; the introduction seems to value the piece because it was written by the "grand old man" rather than for its intrinsic merits.

Bodmer's Gespräche im Elysium und am Acheron come at a time when he was concerned with the writing of "political dramas" based upon classical materials. In 1760 two tragedies by Bodmer, "Electra" and "Ulysses", had been published. Bodmer's dialogues of the dead immediately precede the publication of a number of tragedies on political themes. His "Julius Cäsar" appeared in 1763, "Marcus Tullius Cicero" in 1764; a group of dramas, Politische Schauspiele (1769), contain some of the same historical figures as the Totengespräche. It is possible that Bodmer regarded the dialogues of the dead as preliminary studies to the dramas. Because refinement of dialogue writing is necessary to drama as well as to Totengespräche, an examination of the criticism of the dramas should add to an understanding of the dialogues themselves.

Bodmer's political dramas met with the strongest critical reproaches.[20] Reviewers in Klotz's Deutsche Bibliothek der schönen Wissenschaften gave Bodmer's dramas consistently unfavourable, if lengthy, reviews, thus keeping alive the old conflict between Leipzig and Zürich. One critic writes of "Der vierte Heinrich, Kaiser" and "Cato der Ältere, oder der Aufstand der Römischen Frauen":

> Daß der Verfasser überhaupt keine Kenntniß des Theaters
> habe, versteht sich von sich selbst. . . . Aber den Dialog
> des Drama, die Sprache der Leidenschaften und der Empfin-
> dung hätte doch der Kenner der Griechen[21] wenigstens et-
> was genauer kennen sollen. Seine Aufsätze [the two plays]
> sind auch nur als politische Gespräche betrachtet, unaus-
> stehlich. Die Kunst zu dialogisiren fehlt gänzlich: die Per-
> sonen reden, und reden, und wissen nie wieder aufzuhören:
> wenn sie einmahl einen locum communem anfangen, so
> schütteln sie alles aus, was sie davon wissen . . . .[22]

Another critic attacks Bodmer's new "Gattung", the political drama:

> [The genre] erhebet Kayser zu Schwätzern, und Prin-
> zeßinnen zu Häringsweibern. Sie travestirt trotz der
> komischen Epopee, und dialogirt trotz Faßmannen.[23]

In an ironic turn of events Bodmer, who forty years earlier had castigated David Faßmann, now finds his own writings compared to Faßmann's. However, the fact that Bodmer returned to the dialogue of the dead after an interval of forty years is a testimony of his esteem for the genre. However, the literary quality of the Gespräche im Elysium und am Acheron is such that Bodmer's greatest service to the dialogue of the dead in German literature remains his contributions in that form to the moral weeklies.

A member of the "bardic" movement, Karl Friedrich Kretschmann (1738-1809), wrote two Totengespräche. The first of Kretschmann's dialogues,

"Gellert und Rabener", was written in 1772. In the introduction to his Sämtliche Werke Kretschmann states that this dialogue was written in time of famine for the benefit of the poor. [24] This dialogue, as well as another between "Basannia und Ikaste" (which had appeared in the periodical Für Altere und Neuere Lectüre in 1785), were published in the collected works of 1789.

Both Totengespräche are highly moralistic in tone; both make no attempt at humour; in both the characters are awaiting the judgement of Minos. The dialogues are marked by simplicity of form and by their tendency to emotional excesses. Neither Totengespräch is pure dialogue; Kretschmann has added paragraphs of descriptive narration in non-dialogic form.

Neither Gellert nor Rabener is formally introduced in Kretschmann's dialogue, although a few biographical details are mentioned in the course of the work. Nor is any personal quarrel between the two speakers developed. Rather, Gellert begins innocently by asking Rabener about his beloved Saxons: ". . . erfreun Sie mich doch durch eine recht umständliche Erzählung ihres Wohlstandes . . ." (201). Unfortunately Rabener can only report of the general famine in the land. Following Gellert's request, Rabener delivers the "portrait of a poor farmer" (205). In this passage and in the even longer description of the plight of the city dweller which follows, Kretschmann forsakes the dialogue form for narrative prose. Rabener completes his description of the poor with a complaint that the rich live sumptuously as before in the face of great poverty. Gellert then expresses the hope — indirectly a plea — that at least his former students have shown Christian charity. Next he inquires about his readers (Leserinnen): have they done nothing? Gellert is, of course, disappointed to learn that neither the former nor the latter group has done much to relieve suffering. Gellert and Rabener end the dialogue with a warning about the coming day of judgement: those who have not shown mercy will not obtain mercy.

The dialogue between Basannia, Ikaste and Charon also utilizes a narrative prose section to set the scene and another to introduce Ikaste, the third speaker in the dialogue. This second dialogue is more discursive. Two kinds of love — the passionate, Wonnetaumel (224) of Ikaste and the resigning mother love of Basannia — are judged by Charon, who is called a "Kenner weiblicher Vollkommenheiten" (215). First Basannia, who refused to follow her lover and leave her aged father, is introduced by her conversation with Charon; next Ikaste, who killed herself when she lost her own lover, is similarly introduced. Once the two extremes of love have been presented, there is debate between the two women as to who has loved the best. Kretschmann finally passes judgement — the genre allows him this — through the figure of Charon. Yet he casts the verdict in the form of hopes of what Minos will do: Ikaste should not be punished, but Basannia should be rewarded.

Perhaps Kretschmann's previous experience with dialogue in his dramas taught him to make the Totengespräche more vivid, for he invents netherworldly interjections for his characters. Thus Charon swears, "Bey meinem Strom!" (217) and Ikaste calls out "Ihr Stygischen Nebel!" (221). These phrases are typical of the picturesque quality of the dialogue, yet it is a picturesqueness which ultimately cannot be contained by the dialogue form and thus breaks into descriptive prose.

A member of the Göttingen Hainbund, Leopold Friedrich Günther von Göckingk, also produced a dialogue of the dead. Indicative of the degree to which the Totengespräch was now accepted as belles lettres is the inclusion of Göckingk's dialogue in the Auswahl der besten zerstreuten prosaischen Aufsätze der Deutschen of 1780. The dialogue had been earlier published in 1773.[25] Considered from several standpoints, the dialogue is well constructed. Although the use of Democritus and Heraclites as contrasting figures was not new, Göckingk uses the two figures skillfully for the topics under discussion.

Normally the nether world must wait for newly-arrived shades to bring the latest news of the Oberwelt. Göckingk, however, employs an innovation on the usual source for news: the dialogue opens with the reunion of Democritus and Heraclites after a period of wandering exploration in the world above. This gives the author wide possibilities for criticizing contemporary society. Göckingk inveighs against nostalgic adoration of the past (Antiquitätensucht), against the cult of the galant, and against the Germans' inclination to imitation of their neighbors' customs. In the famous quarrel between the ancients and the moderns, Democritus presents a good case for the moderns.

The introduction to the first selection of the Auswahl states that the purpose of the collection was neither mere amusement nor the improvement of taste, but rather the furthering of genuine, natural and moral taste. Certainly this dialogue of the dead, with its direct questioning of prevalent ideals, with its simple classicism and social criticism, was a worthwhile addition to the collection.

Johann Konrad Fäsi (1727-1790), a Swiss pastor, historian and friend of Bodmer, published two volumes of dialogues of the dead. The first volume Todtengespräche über wichtige Begebenheiten der mittleren und neueren Geschichte[26] contains, among other topics, three dialogues which compare the history of the Jesuit order with that of the Templars. Egilsrud thinks that these dialogues suffer from Fäsi's lack of objectivity. The fifth and sixth dialogues deal with "les principes politiques corrompus du pape".[27] Yet in other of the dialogues Fäsi preaches religious tolerance in the same tone as that of his second volume of Totengespräche which was called Unterredungen verstorbener Personen.

The persons brought together in the second volume are drawn mainly from the fifteenth, sixteenth and seventeenth centuries. The dialogues average about nine pages in length; several of the participants appear more than once. There is always some point of connection between the two speakers, as between Cosimo de Medici and Jacob Fugger or Copernicus and Galileo. Occasionally the connection is less obvious, for example the dialogue between Juan Rodríguez de Fonseca and Bartholomé de las Casas. Fäsi points out on the title page that both men were bishops, but a pithy summation is missing from the dialogue. Most of the conversations begin with a highly compact exposition which summarizes the speakers' meaning in history or gives an in nuce explanation of their exploits. The opening lines of these Totengespräche are terse and use such devices as "Treffen hier nicht zween . . . ?" or "Ich erblicke . . ." to establish both the identity of the speakers and their common experience or point of connection. While such introductions are well within the Lucianic tradition, the lack of variety in the method gives these dialogues an overtly didactic tone.

After the speakers are introduced, they proceed to discuss history in moral terms. Occasionally the dialogues present lists of names or a brief chronology of the developement of the particular topic under consideration; in the conversation between Copernicus and Galileo, for example, the author sketches the evolution of the academies of science in Europe.

A portion of the pedagogical effect Fäsi achieves by the political raisonnements and avis of his characters; at one point Cosimo de Medici states: "Jeder Staat, der einem andern die Handlung zu erschweren bedacht ist, beschädiget sich selbst."[29] The same dialogue deals in part with the different ways that England, France and Spain dealt with colonialism and its financial results. At times the dialogues are so filled with statements of moral opinion that there is hardly room left for real discussion or divergence of opinion. As a result some of the dialogues tend to become monologues.

Although Fäsi's dialogues, like Faßmann's, deal with historical and political topics, Fäsi seems more inspired by Fontenelle than by Faßmann. There is little in Fäsi's dialogues to suggest Faßmann's style or structure. Even though neither the contents nor the techniques employed in Fäsi's dialogues places them among the first of the genre, they may still be read with some profit and enjoyment.[30] Fäsi's inspiration could have come from his compatriot Bodmer, who encouraged Fäsi's work on local Swiss history.

David Christoph Seybold (1747-1804), known for his novel Reizenstein oder die Geschichte eines deutschen Officiers (1778-1779), edited Das Magazin für Frauenzimmer from 1782 to 1787; later he held a professorship of ancient literature in Tübingen. As the editor of Luciani opuscula selecta (which Wieland praised highly[31]) he must have been well aware of the stylistic qualities of the great satirist. Reizenstein, the protagonist of Seybold's epistolary novel, learns Greek and developes a great appreciation of Lucian. Like the translator Oelrichs, Reizenstein, too, wonders about the lack of German followers of the Syrian:

Aber schon tausendmal hab' ich mich indessen gewundert,
daß niemand auf den Gedanken gekommen ist — so viel ich
weiß — Gespräche im Reiche der Todten in Lucianischer
Manier, statt der albernen Fratzen zu schreiben, die diesen Titel führen.[32]

Following these prefatory remarks are seven dialogues of the dead which feature both ancients and moderns in conversation. In 1780 Seybold re-edited these Totengespräche and published them together with two new ones as Neue Gespräche im Reich der Todten. Nach Lucianischem Geschmack.[33]

Seybold's Totengespräche must be granted the distinction of being some of the best eighteenth-century German works in the manner of Lucian. Seybold's first dialogue, between Augustus and Louis XIV, his third, between Mesdames Maintenon and Pompadour, and his seventh, between Montezuma and Columbus, have their basis in the kind of mutual antagonism expressed in Lucian's popular dialogue between Alexander, Hannibal, Minos and Scipio. Seybold's eighth and ninth dialogues both feature Mercury, Charon and a dead man, the eighth "ein medicinischer Schatten", the ninth a "stummer geistlicher Schatten". The motifs mix the style of Lucian's fourth dialogue, in which Mercury and Charon settle their mutual debts, with his tenth dialogue, in which various shades are placed on Charon's bark for the crossing.

Seybold's second dialogue between Gottsched and Klotz contains many of the traditional devices and topoi of the dialogue of the dead, and provides an excellent example of his technique.[34] The title of the work bears the term "Gespräche im Reiche der Todten"; Seybold, in the Lucianic manner, repeats this information in the first and third speeches. Thus the first line of the dialogue, spoken by Gottsched, "Bist mir bald nachgefolgt, Bruder Klotz" indicates the transition from one world to the next. The first line fulfills another function: the naming of one of the correspondents. Without this naming within the text, the dialogue depends on an explanatory superscript and a visual reading of the work. Were the dialogue to be read aloud, however, without the title and speech headings, the listener would have positive identification of Gottsched only in the fifth speech, although various hints had been given in the second and third speeches.

Responding to Gottsched's initial vocative "Bruder Klotz", Klotz addresses Gottsched as "Euer Hochedelgebohrne Magnificenz" (2). This establishes Gottsched as a revered figure and is thus a form of judgement. In response to this flattering sobriquet Gottsched enunciates the theme of democracy in death: "Sez' das bey Seite!" (5). In the next lines Gottsched explains what it is that the two speakers have in common: "Wir saßen beyde auf papiernen Thronen, und beyden sind sie von unsern Feinden zu Asche verbrannt worden . . ." (7-8).

Klotz agrees that little remains of Gottsched's and his own fame, basing his information on the testimonies of newly-arrived shades (14-15). Angered by this loss of reputation, Klotz issues a threat to Lessing, Herder and Nicolai. Gottsched maintains that he has forgiven "the Swiss" and urges Klotz to forgive also. Klotz responds: "Ich kanns nicht so gleich" (22). The process in which the dead often have to learn gradually to put aside their anger occurs frequently in Totengespräche; in this dialogue the process is never completed. The topos has several functions. While it reminds the reader that the realm of the dead must be an unimpassioned land, at the same time it allows for a certain dramatic emotiveness necessary for interesting dialogue.

In the nether world the shades may continue the verbal thrusts and parries of debate with their former opponents. Gottsched provides an opportunity for Klotz to do this when the former inquires, "Wie schmeckt dir das Wasser aus dem Styx?" (39). Klotz answers, "Wie Leßings antiquarische Briefe, oder Nicolais Vorrede zum achten Bande der Bibliothek" (40-42). These jabs refer to the well-known literary and scholarly feuds. In the "Briefe antiquarischen Inhalts" Lessing, it will be remembered, makes a number of charges against Klotz. Klotz suffered under Nicolai's pen also. In addition to the unkind criticism in the Allgemeine deutsche Bibliothek of Klotz's books on numismology, there is also an unfavourable review of his "Ueber das Studium des Alterthums" (Klotz's first publication in the German language) in the same volume of Nicolai's publication.[35]

Klotz inquires about the men whom he himself had criticized, adding that he is uneasy about meeting these people in the present location. The dialogue ends in a mutually protective pact between Klotz and Gottsched, whom Klotz calls a "baumstarker Riese" — a punning reference to Gottsched's remarkable height.

Because Seybold's dialogues of the dead have a Lucianic freshness about them which is found in few others, it is unfortunate that previous writers on the genre have so neglected them.[36] While Seybold has been overlooked by some, he has elsewhere been charged with imitation of French authors.[37] While it may be true that Seybold was inspired by his reading of Fontenelle's dialogue between Montezuma and Cortez to create a fictive conversation between Montezuma and Columbus, it is wrong to suggest that the ideas are the same in both dialogues, as the following examination of the two will show.[38]

Fontenelle's dialogue between Montezuma and Cortez touches upon a number of problems. In the first part Montezuma labours to prove that his people were no more foolish than the Athenians, whom the Spaniards held in great respect; following that, he castigates the Europeans who act from a concept of politeness,[39] rather than from the dictates of the heart. Cortez attempts to defend European manners by an appeal to the rational necessity of social lies and other conventions. The idea is rejected by Montezuma, who moralizes that Europeans have become used to recognizing, then rejecting reason. The "sonderbare Idee" (to use Bodmer's terms of analysis) which comes forth at the end of Fontenelle's dialogue is that the Aztecs had as much right to cross the ocean and conquer Spain as the Spanish had to conquer the Aztecs.

Seybold's Montezuma and Columbus discuss other problems entirely, often on a very personal level. Montezuma is at pains to show that Columbus' endeavours were based on glory seeking (34). Montezuma states ironically that he expected the newly-discovered lands to be "Kolomina" or "Kolumbina" (35); Columbus rejoins that Montezuma and his ancestors mined gold just for a Cortez to take it. Two other issues are mentioned briefly in the dialogue: the ill effects of Columbus' discovery on Europe (33) and the hypocrisy of the Christian religion, which, according to Montezuma, taught love but practiced brutality (35-36).

Seybold's own epithets for his Totengespräche might serve as concluding remarks to this examination of his work. On the title page (above the near-obligatory "Miscet utile dulci") stands the following assessment: "Lustig zu lesen, wohl zu studieren, und nicht wie andere Skelets von derley Fratzen zu betrachten!"

This study of dialogues of the dead in the classical tradition turns now to an author whose literary endeavours crown the eighteenth-century renascence of the form. Christoph Martin Wieland's original dialogues in Elysium and his translations of Lucian are lasting literary achievements. Although Wieland's five Totengespräche number among the most sophisticated and profound of any written in German lands, they have not yet been adequately treated by scholarship.[40] Even Hirzel's major study of the dialogue allots them only brief mention.

Like most of the other authors discussed in this chapter, Wieland knew the works of the Syrian satirist very well. Indeed, Wieland has been called a Lucianus redivivus, and Goethe once spoke of Wieland as "der deutsche Lucian".[41] Wieland acknowledged the satirist to be one of his favourite authors.[42]

Julius Steinberger places the date of Wieland's earliest reference to Lucian as 1751.[43] Evidently Wieland knew the original Greek dialogues of the dead as well as Gottsched's translation of 1745. In a letter of November, 1762, Wieland announced to Johann Georg Zimmermann his intention of publishing selections of the classical writers, among them, to be sure, Lucian. By 1767 Wieland was discussing with Salomon Gessner plans for publication of the translation of Lucian, which, however, was not yet begun. Wieland had explained to Gessner that the translations were to take second place to original creation. Therefore, the news that J. H. Waser was undertaking a translation of Lucian did not disturb Wieland; in a letter of May, 1767, Wieland expressed his pleasure at Waser's venture and in a review for the Erfurtischen gelehrten Zeitung he welcomed Waser's translation as a substitute for d'Ablancourt's; at the same time he criticized the new translation for lack of Lucianic grace. [44]

A number of quotations and letters show that Wieland's interest in Lucian continued during the 1770's. [45] However, the translation of Lucian's Eikones, which appeared in the Teutscher Merkur in 1780, [46] was his first translation of an entire work by Lucian. [47] Significant of Wieland's creative scholarship is the appearance of two "Dialogen im Elysium" in the same issue of the Teutscher Merkur [48]; the third of this series, "Phaon. Ein Dialog im Elysium", [49] was published in the journal two years later.

Work on the translation of Lucian, which was to be more inclusive and stylistically superior to Waser's, was actually begun in 1786. [50] By August, 1787, Wieland was translating Lucian's dialogues of the dead. In the preface to "Eine Lustreise in die Unterwelt" [51] Wieland attributes the work to Lucianic inspiration, stating that the dialogues of the dead caused him to want to see the nether world. [52]

In 1788 Wieland's third volume of Lucian's Sämtliche Werke was printed. [53] This volume contained "Das Lebensende des Peregrinus", sections of which Wieland published in the Teutscher Merkur in July, 1788. [54] The Peregrinus material was later to become the basis for Wieland's late novel Peregrinus Proteus (1797). [55]

The year 1789 was the period of Wieland's most intense work on Lucian. There are clear statements from Wieland that indicate his growing satiety with the task. In a letter to K. L. Reinhold, Wieland wrote characteristically: "Ich übersetze mich am Lucian — zum Invaliden, und sehe meiner Erlösung mit Ungeduld entgegen . . . Auch Lucians kriegt man in 2 Jahren endlich genug." [56]

After the completion of the translation, reference to Lucian and to passages from his works continue to occur in Wieland's writings. [57] The feelings of the mature Wieland for Lucian were recorded by Karl August Böttiger: "Gewisse Bücher habe ich als Tröster in der Noth. Wenn mir der Geschmack zu allen übrigen vergangen ist, so bleiben diese, als eine feine Hauslectüre. Hierher gehören einige Stücke Lucian's." [58]

Wieland returned to that particularly Lucianic form of dialogue when in 1800 he published "Agathon. Hippias. Ein Gespräch im Elysium" in the Attisches Museum. [59] This dialogue was to be his last exercise with the form.

That Wieland intended to write a long series of dialogues of the dead is indicated in his footnote to the conversation between Diocles and Lucian. [60] Only three dialogues, the "Dialogen im Elysium", were forthcoming at this time. In these conversations there is much of Lucian and yet much of Wieland, too. All the dialogues are set in Elysium and not in the larger Reich der Toten. The title itself is so formulated to indicate that Wieland's dialogues had little to do with "trivial" Totengespräche; at the same time it indicated that there was a kind of idealism to be found in them.

The dialogue between Diocles and Lucian begins with the arrival of Diocles the poet in Elysium. [61] A short, expository monologue by Diocles sets the scene with the aid of reference to poetic and philosophic views of Elysium. [62] The quotation of older literary material is, of course, frequently employed by Lucian himself. In his new condition Diocles notices that flakes and clumps keep dropping from him, causing him to feel lighter and more sentient; this process of Abschälung is an idea which features in all three of the "Dialogen im Elysium". Both Kurrelmeyer and Steinberger suggest that Wieland received the idea from Lucian's tenth dialogue of the dead. Yet it should be more strongly emphasized that in Lucian's dialogue the newly dead must part with all inessentials before crossing the Styx, while in Wieland's dialogues the process takes place in Elysium itself. Within the same opening monologue Diocles introduces himself and in the second speech Lucian, too, is identified. Such early introductions follow the Lucianic method.

The dialogue proceeds with a discussion of Diocles' condition. Lucian tells him that his senses (Sinne) have not yet been cleansed (282), that his state is similar to birth, and explains that only good will come of the Abschälungen (282). Diocles exclaims, ". . . was für ein Puppen- und Fratzenspiel von Täuschung und Blendwerk war das, was ich mein Leben nannte!" (282).

Of the truths that Diocles learns in Elysium one of the greatest is that he was only an ordinary human being (ein gemeiner Mensch). Lucian instructs him:

Das ist wohl die dickste und häßlichste von allen Schuppen,
kein gemeiner Mensch seyn zu wollen, wenn man im Grunde doch nur ein gemeiner Mensch ist. Siehst du, was für
ein Klumpen wieder von dir fällt? (283)

The quotation illustrates a technique which Wieland employs several times. As Diocles apprehends a new truth, a particle (Klumpen), which is directly proportionate to the magnitude of that truth, falls from him. The device is repeated at the end of the Socratic dialogue which follows this section of the dialogue.

Lucian next explains the nature of Elysium, which in the traditional description by negation, is a place without envy, a place where no one desires revenge. Lucian emphasizes the truthful nature of Elysium: "Kurz, bey uns ist alles wahr, und eben darum sind wir glücklich" (284). The explanation prepares the way for a short question and answer section which follows.

By the principle of reductio ad absurdum Lucian shows that Diocles' understanding of his own motives of behaviour had been illusory. (When Diocles comprehends this truth, a large bit of matter falls from him.) Lucian tells Diocles: "Du büßest hier für — deine Tugenden" (285). The cynical Lucian surmises that Diocles had been a poet in life. Diocles' claim that he loved truth above all Lucian questions mockingly. He ends the dialogue by advising Diocles to visit the baths which exist for the newly-arrived shades.

The second of the "Dialogen im Elysium" divides into three main sections: the first in which Diocles and Lucian continue their discussion from the first dialogue, the second, containing lighter, more frivolous repartee between Lucian and Panthea, and the third section, a return to more serious philosophical discussion.

The dialogue begins with the topic of Diocles' spiritual progress since the last meeting between the two speakers. Improvement consists of discarding one's (false) image of oneself; all one's merits and excellencies, for example, are seen to be delusion (286). In this dialogue Diocles has advanced from birth to a stage of childhood (286). A point difficult for Diocles to accept is that one's earthly merits gain one no respect in the nether world. Is not Lucian's Panthea, the ideal of perfect beauty, worth more than the "erste beste Bürgersfrau von Smyrna" (287)? Lucian then delivers a monologue in which he explains why and under which conditions of illusion he chose Panthea as his ideal.

With the arrival of Panthea the second section of the dialogue begins. Diocles now steps aside and allows Lucian and Panthea to converse; during this section Diocles restricts himself to ironic asides which create some of the humour of the dialogue. In the ensuing conversation both Lucian and Panthea confess their mutual folly concerning Lucian's writing the "Essay on Portraiture" (Eikones), which Wieland rendered as "Panthea, oder die vollkommne Schönheit." The section ends when Panthea announces all too conveniently, "Ich muß einen kleinen Flug nach der Oberwelt thun" (291).

Panthea disappears, leaving Diocles and Lucian to discuss the apparition. Diocles learns that the people of Elysium, free from the distorting effect of desires, see beauty as it really is; further, they are capable only of Platonic love. They are also free from enthusiasm (Schwärmerey), which is equated with drunkenness, and its ill effects. [63] Trying to refine his question, Diocles asks, ". . . giebt es nicht eine art Begeisterung, wo das Anschauen der Schönheit . . . die Seele ergreift . . . ? (293). This kind of enthusiasm (Begeisterung) Lucian accepts and even welcomes. Wieland evidently realized that this was uncharacteristic speech for Lucian for he allows him to say, "Aus meinem Munde sollte es dich wohl befremden Ja zu hören? Aber bilde dir ein, daß es Pythagoras oder Plato sey, der dir durch mich antwortet" (293). The condition of Begeisterung, "Lucian" continues, is better known to Elysium's inhabitants than to mortals; for that which on earth is sensory illusion is in Elysium Truth. Thus the second dialogue extends a theme begun in the first dialogue. All those in Elysium are initiated into certain mysteries; however, they do not speak of them. Those who have perceived the divine do not speak of it but rather enjoy it contemplatively.

To this Diocles raises an objection, "Aber woran erkennt Ihr, daß es nicht auch bey Euch Täuschung ist . . . ?" (293). "Lucian" replies that when the soul is in a state of health, nothing is less deceptive than the sign (Kennzeichen) by which truth and falsehood are distinguished. "Licht und Finsterniß sind einander nicht mehr entgegen" (293-4). Thus it would seem that while Schwärmerey remains unacceptable behaviour for mortals, it or a more moderate form, Begeisterung, is part of the nature of Elysium.

The third dialogue, "Faon, Nireus, hernach Saffo, zuletzt noch Anakreon", is likewise concerned with the concept of beauty. The dialogue was published in the Teutscher Merkur in 1782, and like the other two dialogues it relates to Wieland's interest in Lucian's Eikones, for two characters, Phaon and Nireus, mentioned at the beginning of Lucian's "Essays in Portraiture Defended" (Hyper tōn eikonōn) recur in this third dialogue. [64] Here the newly-arrived shade of Phaon, Sappho's former lover according to the tale of Ovid, approaches a handsome stranger, the shade of Nireus; Phaon has not yet been cleansed of earthly illusions and is unable to understand the concept that in Elysium outward beauty counts for naught.

The third dialogue is reminiscent of Lucian's dialogue in which Nireus, the most handsome man among the Greeks, and Thersites, the ugliest, appeal to Menippus to judge who is the more beautiful. Menippus replies: "Neither you nor anyone else is handsome here. In Hades all are equal, and all alike."[65]

Citing among other things Sappho's suicide, Phaon tries to convince Nireus that the world had held him (Phaon) for a great beauty. At length Nireus reveals his identity to Phaon, who thinks that the two men ought to be accounted equal in beauty. Nireus, however, finds Phaon repulsive, and in reply to Phaon's plea for a means to return to his former beautiful form, prescribes that Phaon learn to love and be loved by Aesop, the bald, misshapen dwarf. Phaon's re-education has already begun, for he states that in Aesop's presence he feels like an ape (297).

The second section of the dialogue is initiated by the arrival of Sappho. The reunion of Phaon and Sappho could be embarrassing to both, were it not for Sappho's having been through the process of enlightenment in the nether world. Now that she has been freed from the "childish condition" she finds the very sight of Phaon repulsive; this she all too histrionically illustrates by placing her hand on her stomach (299). She explains that her punishment has been to be surrounded by seven beautiful but stupid young men for six days of the week; the monotony is relieved once in seven days by a visit from Nestor, Simonides or Solon. Most of all she enjoys the company of Anakreon. Phaon fails to understand why Sappho considers these old men handsome.

The mention of the name Anakreon serves as the beginning of the third section of the dialogue. Sappho bids farewell to Phaon, informing him that by the process of Abstreifung he can become someone "der in guter Gesellschaft einen Platz behaupten kann" (300). Anakreon enters crowned with roses and carrying a goblet full of Lethe's water. He announces that Sappho's penitence is completed. Sappho then drinks the potion and exits with Anakreon singing. Phaon is left to ponder what will become of himself and remarks sarcastically "Ein feines Elysium!" (300).

The "Dialogen im Elysium" display a number of Lucianic characteristics. The method of introducing characters, the quotation of "the classics" within the text, wittiness of dialogue — these traits Wieland's dialogues share with Lucian's. Yet Wieland's dialogues are not mere imitation; rather, Wieland uses the older dialogues as a point of departure. It has been suggested that a crucial difference between the dialogues of the two writers is a lack of the grotesque in Wieland:

> . . . was [Wieland's dialogues] im Gegensatz zu den
> [Lucian's] fehlt, ist die eigentliche Satire, oder viel-
> mehr der groteske Zug, der durch den Kontrast der
> zusammen redenden Personen und die scharfe Charak-
> terisierung besonders derjenigen, denen der Spott gilt,
> hineinkommt.[66]

However, in fairness to Wieland it should be remembered that he did not propose

to write satirical Totengespräche, but to edify through "Dialogen im Elysium".
Indeed, it is true that the grotesque elements so frequent in Lucian's dialogues
are not so numerous in Wieland's dialogues (where the concept of gracefulness
could not be sacrificed). Yet certainly the falling particles (Klumpen) approach
the grotesque in their grave corporeality.

When in 1788 Wieland published a dialogue between Peregrinus Proteus and Lucian in the Teutscher Merkur, he once again brought together Lucian
and one of Lucian's own characters. Because Lucian had described Peregrinus so
unfavourably in "The Passing of Peregrinus" (that account of the last days in Peregrinus' life before his self-immolation), the meeting of the two in Elysium has
conflicts built into the situation.

The methods and themes which Wieland employs in "Peregrin und
Lucian" are much like those of the "Dialogen im Elysium". Both characters are
named at the beginning of the dialogue, and Wieland bases the introduction and
the setting of the scene on the mutual animosity of the speakers. Lucian is naturally surprised to find Peregrinus in Elysium and does not at first recognize him,
because in the realm of truth Peregrinus appears much different from Lucian's
perception of him on earth. Later it is intimated that both Lucian and Peregrinus
have gone through the process of Abschälung.

The exposition leads directly to a discussion of the relationship between human folly and satire. Lucian defends satire as one of the very few reme-
dies against folly; not even the smallest, most "innocent" folly will he allow. In-
veighing against mysteries, Lucian restates the theme of the worth of mankind
much as he had in the first of the "Dialogen im Elysium":

> Wer zum Menschen gebohren wurde, soll und kann nichts
> edleres, größeres und besseres seyn als ein Mensch —
> und wohl ihm wenn er weder mehr noch weniger seyn
> will![67]

From this point the discussion leads to the nature of man. Peregrinus postulates
a dichotomous man, caught between heaven and earth, who becomes an animal
unless he strives to become a god. Lucian argues that man has a talisman against
such nonsense, namely reason — "gesunder, gemeiner Menschenverstand" (182).

Peregrinus announces that he hopes to impart to Lucian a better opinion of his life than the one Lucian set to paper. The rest of the dialogue then is
concerned with the way Lucian had characterized Peregrinus. Peregrinus accuses
Lucian of having been a not impartial witness; Lucian refutes the charge in part.
Peregrinus asks about Lucian's sources and whether the "wakerer Unbekannte"
of Lucian's story was a real or a fictive person. Lucian confesses that he added
anecdotes to the report of the unknown man. [68] Near the end of the dialogues Peregrinus questions the veracity of Lucian's excuses for not reporting Peregrinus'
dying words:

> Denn daß die angeführte Entschuldigung "Du wärest, der
> Menge und des Gedränges wegen, zu weit entfernt gewe-
> sen, um etwas davon zu verstehen" nicht eine bloße Aus-

rede gewesen sey, wird sich schwerlich irgend ein unbe-
fangener Leser überreden lassen. (189)

Lucian defends his truthfulness as a narrator and strives at the same time to be
conciliatory. His statements are particularly interesting since they reflect in
some measure Wieland's own opinion of Lucian:

Wir waren beyde zu ganz das was wir waren, ich zu kalt,
du zu warm, du zu sehr Enthusiast, ich ein überzeugter
Anhänger Epikurs, um einander in dem vortheilhaftesten
Lichte zu sehen. (189)

Lucian, the lover of truth, next urges Peregrinus to rehearse his
story, for he wishes to have a more correct understanding of Peregrinus' character. At Lucian's suggestion they seat themselves under a shade tree which
bears a striking resemblance to that Socratic tree on the bank of the Ilyssus.
Thus the scene is set for Peregrinus' narration of his life's story which constitutes the bulk of the novel Peregrinus Proteus.
Wieland's last use of the dialogue of the dead was "Agathon und Hippias ein Gespräch im Elysium", which appeared in the Attisches Museum of 1800.[69]
If Agathon may be considered a "philosophical" novel, the "Agathon und Hippias"
is a "philosophical" dialogue of the dead. It will be possible here only to sketch
the larger ideas of the piece; unfortunately it is difficult to reproduce in short
space the subtlety of the argumentation. Similarity of method and themes betrays
the relationship of this dialogue to the "Dialogen im Elysium". As Wieland's
Lucian had been surprised to encounter Peregrinus in Elysium, so Agathon expresses surprise upon discovering his former mentor Hippias in Elysium. Hippias is in Elysium only for a short sojourn, however; both the speakers plan to
leave for the "Unterwelt" at the end of the conversation. In this dialogue alone
Wieland seems to have placed Elysium above the earth!
A variation on the theme of Abschälung is the initial topic of discussion. Hippias shrugs aside the necessity of Abschälungen: "Ich bin nun einmal
Hippias, und ihr könntet mich bis auf die letzte Haut abschälen, ich würde doch
nie Agathon werden" (270). From this point the dialogue developes into a discussion of human perfection; Hippias argues for perfection in many forms (vielgestal-
tige Vollkommenheit), Agathon for an ideal of perfection against which every individual may be matched: "Es muß also ein Ideal der Vollkommenheit geben, das
für alle gilt . . ." (273).
The conversation progresses to the question, What is man? Agathon
cannot accept men because they fall short of what they should be. This Hippias
counters by questioning the standard and by accusing Agathon of establishing himself as the measure of perfection. The question of what man ought to be leads, of
course, to a peroration on free will. As concrete example Agathon chooses the
life of Dionysius of Syracuse: was he that which he was because of entelechy, or
was it within his volition to choose what he wished to be? Neither nor, answers
Hippias, for no one is forced by irresistible necessity to be that which he is. It
certainly was possible for Dionysius to change to some degree, despite the enor-

mous influence of nature, fate and chance (Zufall) (280-282). Hippias argues then for limited freedom of will, Agathon for complete freedom, which one perceives by an inner feeling that one has it. Did Agathon have this feeling when kneeling before Danae, Hippias asks. Nevertheless Agathon cannot be dissuaded of his belief in the independence of the will.

Ranging even further, the topic turns to the cause of evil in man. Agathon suggests social corruption (sittliche Verderbniß) (286). No, argues Hippias, the source lies yet deeper; it is in the make-up of man himself (187). Then Wieland allows Hippias to deliver a five-page disquisition on the nature of man. Interestingly, Hippias postulates wide-ranging gradations of human existence based mainly on degree of intelligence. The great differences which do, in fact, exist are not the result of training, says Hippias, but of the inner form of the creature (289-90).

The dialogue ends in accord, however, for the speakers recognize that they strive for the same goals (294): "Warum sollten Vorstellungsarten und Hypothesen uns trennen, wenn Wahrheit das Ziel unsers Forschens, und Menschenwohl der Gegenstand unsrer Thätigkeit ist?" (294). Having satisfied himself that they both agree on the possibility of human perfectibility, Agathon announces their plans to return to the world of men (Unterwelt), and after explaining how they hope to better man's lot, they depart. Hippias, however, has the last word: Wieland allows him to mutter a cynical aside against idealism.

Wieland's own sympathies would seem to lie with Hippias since he allows Hippias not only disproportionate space but also the final word of the dialogue, aimed directly at the reader. However, it is Agathon who mentions truth, a theme in all the other Totengespräche by Wieland, as the goal of their investigations. In this dialogue Wieland does not emphasize that Elysium is a place of truth; in fact, Hippias makes the suggestion that Agathon is still in a state of delusion even while in Elysium. In general Wieland makes less use in "Agathon und Hippias" of the possibilities which the fictive setting in the nether world offers than he does in the earlier dialogues, and there is less gaiety, less lightness than in his previous dialogic compositions.

Wieland did not omit to write down theoretical comments on the dialogue, albeit he wrote none on the dialogue of the dead per se. Some of his ideas on the origin and nature of the dialogue may be found in the Attisches Museum. Here he contends that the dialogue could only have developed among the Greeks. For Wieland the dialogue was a high form of art which incorporated a diversity and profundity of material within itself: the dialogue is based on "unsrer Gedanken, und Gesinnungen, zwanglose Darstellung unsrer eigenthümlichen Art zu seyn . . . ."70

Remarks of a more technical nature are imbedded in the late epistolary novel Aristipp und einige seiner Zeitgenossen (1800-1802). In the fourth book of this lengthy work Wieland's "Aristipp", writing to Eurybates on the subject of Plato's "Republic", tries to determine what constitutes the "most essential beauty" (wesentlichste Schönheit) of the dialogue:

> Vorausgesetzt, daß die Rede nicht von Unterweisung eines
> Knäbleins durch Frage und Antwort, sondern von einem Ge-

spräch unter Männern über irgend einen wichtigen, noch
nicht hinlänglich aufgeklärten, oder verschiedene Ansich-
ten und Auflösungen zulassenden Gegenstand ist, so läßt
sich doch wol als etwas Ausgemachtes annehmen: ein er-
dichteter Dialog sei desto vollkommener, je mehr er
einem unter geistreichen und gebildeten Personen wirk-
lich vorgefallenen Gespräch ähnlich sieht. In einer solchen
gesellschaftlichen Unterhaltung stellt jeder seinen Mann;
Jeder hat seinen eigenen Kopf mitgebracht, hat seine Mei-
nung, und weiß sie, wenn sie angefochten wird, mit star-
ken oder schwachen, aber doch wenigstens mit schein-
baren, Gründen zu unterstützen. Wird gestritten, so
wehrt sich jeder seiner Haut so gut er kann. [71]

"Aristipp" here demands the presentation of several points of view. [72] A prerequisite of proper dialogue is that the topic be on a subject which is open to differ-
ing opinions. The militant terms of Aristipp's description imply that he places a
premium on vigorous debate. In a later section Aristipp seems to value versimili-
tude in the dialogue: the dialogue is more nearly perfect the more it resembles a
conversation which actually took place among educated persons. Related to the demand for "realism" in the dialogue is the call for lack of artifice:

Was . . . nicht wenig zum Vergnügen der Leser beizu-
tragen scheint, ist die anscheinende Unordnung oder,
richtiger zu reden, die unter diesem Schein sich ver-
bergende Kunst, wie der Dialog, gleich einem dem
bloßen Zufall überlassenen Spaziergang, indem er sich
mit vieler Freiheit hin und her bewegt, unter lauter
Digressionen dennoch immer vorwärts schreitet und
dem eigentlichen Ziel des Verfassers (wie oft es uns
auch den Augen gerückt wird) immer näher kommt.
. . . [D]ie größte Kunst des Dialogendichters ist,
seinen Plan unter einer anscheinenden Planlosigkeit
zu verstecken, und nur dann verdient er Tadel, wenn
er sich von seinem Hauptzweck so weit verirrt, daß
er sich selbst nicht wieder ohne Sprünge und mühselige
Krümmungen in seinen Weg zurückfinden kann. [73]

Here Aristipp requires that the dialogue have a seeming disorder, that the craft
of the writing never be too obvious. The dialogue should resemble a walk which
is governed by chance. The author's plans must be concealed behind a seeming
absence of purpose.

These are strong demands of any writer of dialogues, and that Wieland did not struggle to meet their strict requirements in every instance might
indicate a difference of opinion between "Aristipp" and his creator. Vigorous
debate is found in Wieland's Totengespräche, especially in the last-discussed
"Agathon und Hippias". In this work he clearly succeeds in presenting different

points of view. Both partners speak well, and to use "Aristipp's" phrase, each one "hat seinen eigenen Kopf mitgebracht", although Hippias is the more forceful of the two speakers. That Wieland's dialogue between Agathon and Hippias resembles a casual walk, is shown by the language of the opening lines:

> Agathon:
> Seh ich recht? auch Hippias — im Elysium?
> Hippias:
> Sey ohne Sorge, Agathon! ein bloßer Zufall hat mich
> durch eure Grenze geführt. (269)

From the announcement that the meeting is a chance one, the audience may deduce that the ensuing dialogue or conversation will likewise be unrehearsed. "Agathon und Hippias" illustrates the manner in which progress is made through digressions. Although one topic seems to lead to the next quite naturally, the reader never feels that the author is directing the process with a heavy hand.

On occasion, however, one feels that Wieland is making a "leap" to get back to the path. Such an example is the exit of Panthea from the second dialogue of the "Dialogen im Elysium". Once Panthea has stated the circumstantial facts of the Eikones, she must be disposed of quickly. Wieland allows her the excuse of a flight to the Oberwelt (291). Even if Wieland does on occasion have to make a "leap", he never relies on "mühselige Krümmungen" to return to the subject. In the instance given above Diocles follows her remark by saying that she will make a lovely ghost. This leads Lucian back to the subject of beauty.

On the whole Wieland's dialogues convey a sense of unpredictability: one can never guess just which direction the path of discourse will next lead. Such seeming spontaneity is Wieland's art of concealing his plan behind a seeming lack of order.

Johann Heinrich Merck, the journalist, friend of Goethe, and natural scientist, produced a dialogue of the dead during his association with Wieland's Teutscher Merkur. The dialogue "Die schöne und die häßliche Seele. Scenen im Elysium" was published in 1783, signed simply by "M.***".[74] It was not Merck's first attempt at dialogic art, for as early as 1776 he had published in the Teutscher Merkur a conversation between Hogarth and Burke entitled "Über die Schönheit." The work is an attempt to contrast Hogarth's "Analysis of Beauty" with Burke's "Philosophical Inquiry of the Sublime and Beautiful".[75]

Merck's dialogue is more drama than strict dialogue: it is divided into two acts, the first act having four scenes (Auftritte), the second act, one scene. The first act even calls for a shade to address the parterre. It might easily be staged; in fact, some stage directions are supplied, e.g., "[Die Schatten] schleichen, in weissen Leichentücher gehüllet, langsam über die Bühne . . ." (33).

Despite some rather serious flaws this short two-act play makes interesting reading and poses a ticklish question for students of the eighteenth century. The "schöne Seele" of the title is "Glycerion"; "Aspasia", strangely enough, is the ugly one. Other speakers in the scenes are the people who frequented Aspasia's salon in Athens — Perikles, Phidias, Xenophon, Socrates — and in the second act, the judgement scene, Minos. Although the characters are classical there are a number of noteworthy divergences from the traditions of the nether world. The shades dressed in white winding sheets contrast starkly with the naked dead of Lucian's dialogues. Elsewhere Socrates has a name called in the groves in order to find a particular shade. Flaws in the work result from Merck's inability to blot lines; consequently the piece is burdened with unnecessary repetitions. Even Wieland, who edited the piece before publication and who certainly had an appreciation for fullness of detail, found it necessary to omit a non-functional segment from the version printed in the Merkur.[76] The love scene between Socrates and Glycerion might be distasteful to some. There Socrates is made to say: "Sanftes, liebes Mädchen, ich liebe dich, meine Seele schmiegt sich an die deinige, und ihre Vereinigung wird himmlische Wollust uns schmecken lassen" (42).

Whatever its faults may be, the work still holds its reader because of its peculiar subject matter. The piece has at least two main themes, the representative plots of which interact with each other. The first is the problem of Aspasia; graceful, beautiful, respected, accounted a "schöne Seele" on earth, she arrives in Elysium only to find that no one there considers her a "beautiful soul". Although she was lauded by Socrates and Perikles in Athens, in Merck's Elysium she is called a "Buhlerin" and a "Kupplerin" (253). These men then viewed her through the distorting air of the earthly city and not with the true vision of Elysium. Only Phidias, who in carving her statue concealed her flaws with the sculptor's chisel, realizes that Aspasia cannot be the "schöne Seele" whom all the nether world awaits. Quite interesting is that portion of the dialogue in which Phidias envisions a "schöne Seele" from the viewpoint of a sculptor. This, of course, reflects Merck's own interest in sculpture. Merck's Elysium emphasizes the plastic arts in yet another way. There the outer form truly does reveal the inner nature: "Beym Eintritt in die Unterwelt bildet sich die Gestalt nach der Seele, ist ihr wahres Gemälde" (40). Thus the idea of Elysium as a land of truth appears in Merck's Totengespräch as it did in Wieland's: "[I]n der Gegend der Unterwelt hilft nichts als — Wahrheit" (36).

The second figure is Glycerion, the "beautiful soul" acclaimed by Socrates. Glycerion was a simple, hardworking girl, who with her kind stepmother read every evening of the lives of good people: "[W]ir lasen die Leben guter Menschen die von guten Menschen aufgezeichnet waren . . ." (44). Thereupon they went to sleep and dreamed of these noble characters. Glycerion's imagination arranged the characteristics of the various figures and created more and more nearly perfect ideals. She falls in love with the highest ideal of her imagination, or as Socrates says, "das wesentliche Schöne, die Urform des Guten" (46). Glycerion then describes in a very effusive manner her reaction to the discovery. The perception of such was as intense as fire and her enthusiasm resulted in her early death, which she can only partially explain: "Das Leben nahm nach und nach ab, mein Blut floß langsamer, meine Kräfte schwanden, und ich war nicht mehr" (42). Clearly the girl was an enthusiast. Could she be both "schöne Seele" and enthusiast?

Aspasia and Glycerion are brought before the netherworldly court. The matter of Aspasia's claim to be a "schöne Seele" — already made ludicrous by the testimonies against her in the first act — is there solved by having her (and other shades) peer into the "mirror of truth".[77] Minos then awards the title of "schöne Seele" to Glycerion. In jealousy Aspasia tries to discredit her rival by revealing that Glycerion is an enthusiast. Minos supports the challenge: "[I]ch finde Schwierigkeiten, Schönheit der Seele mit einem Exceß von Liebe, Liebe zu Undingen, mit Schwärmerey, vereinigen zu können" (256). If she was an enthusiast, she cannot be a "schöne Seele". It will be remembered that a similar figure is encountered in the person of the Stiftsdame of Goethe's "Bekenntnisse einer schönen Seele"; she likewise suffers from too lively an imagination.[78]

The court next hears opinions on this subject from Perikles and Anaxagoras, both of whom argue against Glycerion's being the beautiful soul. Anaxagoras' reply mocks the philosopher's actual teachings in a manner reminiscent of Lucian's "Philosophies for Sale" (Bion prasis). Only Socrates comes to Glycerion's defense, enumerating the positive qualities which make her a beautiful soul. Concerning her enthusiasm he says: "Schwärmereyen sind oft besser als — Würklichkeiten" (260). Yet Socrates can suggest a more empirical method of proof. Since he believes that the creature of Glycerion's imagination either existed or will exist, he urges Minos to let all "great souls" of the past appear before Glycerion. If she recognizes one of them, that will prove that her own ideals are not "Hirngeburten" and "Undinge", as Aspasia claims. Minos orders that Socrates' proposal be realized and there the dialogue ends.

Unfortunately Merck does not supply the details of the examination. Wieland added in a footnote to the work[79] some hints of the outcome. He reports that Minos was compelled to resign from the case when Proserpine asked for a review of the trial. Wieland assures his readers that he is not the author of these "Scenen im Elysium". No one, he reasons, could think the author of Agathon to be the author of a work in which Aspasia was called a "Buhlerin" and a "Kupplerin" (262). Wieland also implies that he sees no great difficulty in reconciling beauty of the soul with enthusiasm.

The dialogues of the dead of Wieland and Merck certainly represent a high point in the more classical use of the form. These authors, as had so many others, employed the genre to present in a dramatic fashion ideas about central controversies of eighteenth-century intellectual life.

NOTES

1 Gespräche der Verstorbenen eine Englische Schrift, trans. Johann George Henrich Oelrichs (Berlin, 1761), "Vorrede", p. xxi.

2 Oelrichs, p. xxii.

3 Johann Salomo Semler, "Gedanken von Uebereinkommung der Romane mit den Legenden" (Halle, [1749]), p. 22.

4 There are, of course, eighteenth-century Totengespräche in which the role of humour is of great importance. These will be dealt with in a subsequent chapter.

5 A new edition of this novel, now under preparation by Harold Jantz and Lieselotte E. Kurth, will contain more extensive biographical information.

6 Wilhelm Ehrenfried Neugebauer, Die Fabeln des Fuchses nebst einem Versuch in Todtengesprächen (Glogau, 1761), p. 71. Subsequent references to this work are given in parentheses.

7 "Nimrod" is a lengthy verse epic.

8 Jacob Wegelin, Religiose Gespräche der Todten (Frankfurt and Leipzig, 1763), p. i.

9 Ausführliche und kritische Nachrichten von den besten und merkwürdigsten Schriften unsrer Zeit nebst andern zur Gelehrtheit gehörigen Sachen, Issue 1 (Lindau, Frankfurt and Leipzig, 1763) 17-51. Subsequent references to Wegelin's dialogues are cited from this reprinting and parenthetically in the text.

10 Jakob Baechtold, Geschichte der deutschen Literatur in der Schweiz (Frauenfeld, 1892), "Anmerkungen", 192. Here the places of publication of the various dialogues are listed in detail.

11 Der Mahler der Sitten, Stück 69 (Zürich, 1746), 196-197.

12 s. l. & a. [1763], pp. 37-42. Subsequent references to this text are given in parentheses.

13 Alfred R. Bellinger, "Lucian's Dramatic Technique", Yale Classical Studies, I (1928), 14.

14 New York, 1937.

15 Scenna, p. 7.

16 Baechtold, p. 644.

17 George Lord Lyttleton, Dialogues of the Dead (London, 1760), p. 166.

18 III (Leipzig, 1798), 191-204. To judge from style and subject matter this dialogue appears to have been written near the time of Bodmer's Gespräche im Elysium und am Acheron.

19 Erholungen, III (1798), footnote on p. 191.

20 A review in Christian Heinrich Schmid's Almanach der deutschen Musen begins: "Ohnerachtet mir, außer Hrn. Bodmers Studierstube, kein Winkel der Erde bekannt ist, wo man an diesen politischen Schauspielen Gefallen fände . . ." (1770, p. 73). There is little in Schmid's career to suggest

strong partisanship either for Leipzig or Zürich, and his intense work on matters of drama and theater would imply competence in this area.

21 Bodmer so refers to himself in the Neue theatralische Werke.

22 Deutsche Bibliothek der schönen Wissenschaften, ed. Christian Adolf Klotz, II (Halle, 1768), 92.

23 Deutsche Bibliothek der schönen Wissenschaften, III, 1769, 397.

24 Karl Friedrich Kretschmann, Sämtliche Werke, V (Carlsruhe, 1790), "Introduction". Subsequent references are taken from this edition and are given parenthetically in the text. K. H. Jördens adds that the proceeds from the sale of this dialogue were given to the "bedürftigsten Nothleidenden" (Lexikon deutscher Dichter und Prosaisten, III [Leipzig, 1808], 110).

25 Hannover, 1773. Holzmann-Bohatta attributes the dialogue to Göckingk (Deutsches Anonymen-Lexikon I [1902], 391).

26 Leipzig, 1775.

27 Egilsrud, 134.

28 Halle, 1777.

29 Unterredungen verstorbener Personen (Halle, 1777), p. 43.

30 Egilsrud notes that Fäsi's style is "clair et simple" (p. 134).

31 Wieland wrote in the Teutscher Merkur: ". . . Seybold . . . , der sich seit kurzem durch eine anpreißenswürdige Ausgabe einiger auserlesener Stücke Lucians und durch eine mit feinen kritischen Anmerkungen begleitete Uebersetzung der Alcestis . . . als einen Mann gezeigt hat, der die Griechen nicht blos als ein Wortklauber studiert, sondern in ihren Geist eindringt, und durch ihren vertrauten Umgang seinen eignen vollkommner macht. Dieser Gelehrte macht uns Hoffnung, daß er uns, auf die nehmliche Art, wie er die opuscula selecta behandelt hat, eine neue . . . brauchbarere und ungleich wohlfeilere Ausgabe der sämtlichen Werke Lucians liefern werde . . ." (1774, VI, 358-359).

32 David Christoph Seybold, Reizenstein I (Leipzig, 1778), 298.

33 Hanau, Frankfurt and Leipzig, 1780. Subsequent references to Seybold's dialogues in this study are cited from this revised edition, in which Seybold made a few changes for heightened clarity and added the eighth and ninth dialogues.

34 The complete text may be found in Appendix II.

35 Allgemeine deutsche Bibliothek, VIII (Berlin and Stettin, 1768), 118-125.

36 Rentsch does not even mention Seybold at all. He does, however, list "Plaudereyen aus der Unterwelt" (p. 31). Three dialogues named from this collection (1791) would seem to be the same as three in Seybold's Neue Gespräche. Unfortunately the "Plaudereyen" are no longer available in German public libraries. Egilsrud's appendix includes "Plauderreyen Auss der Unterwelt" (sic), yet he may simply have copied the entry from another source.

37 It is in the treatment of Seybold that Egilsrud's francophilism may be seen in its most negative form. Egilsrud attempts persistently to make Seybold dependent on the French — not only on Fontenelle but also on French culture and ton. A serious discrepancy comes to light in Egilsrud's reporting of the preface to Seybold's Neue Gespräche im Reich der Todten. Although both the version of 1778 and that of 1780 carry basically the same prefatory remarks

(quoted in this study on page 84), Egilsrud's translation into French carries a phrase which is found in neither version. Seybold questions why no one has written dialogues of the dead in Lucian's style "statt der albernen Fratzen zu schreiben, die diesen Tittel führen" ("Kleine Vorerinnerung", p. [ii]). Egilsrud translates thus: "pourquoi personne n'a, autant que je sache, écrit des dialogues des morts dans la manière de Lucian, au lieu d'adopter la manière française" (p. 135, italics added). To be absolutely fair one could imagine that Egilsrud's quotation was taken from another version. Yet his own reference — Leipzig, 1780 — agrees with the version of the dialogues used in the present study.

Egilsrud then suggests that Seybold insisted that Lucian was his model in order to draw attention away from the French influence on the dialogues: "C'est, en réalité, en passant par l'intermédiare de la France qu'il approchait Lucien, malgré sa connaissance de l'original grec" (p. 135). However, Egilsrud can marshal little by way of proof for this allegation even though much would be needed to detract attention from Seybold's superior knowledge of Greek.

38 Concerning Seybold's dialogue number seven between Montezuma and Columbus, Egilsrud states: "C'est Fontenelle aussi qui fournit à Seybold la frappant figure de Montézuma discutant avec Christophe Colomb les même idées que dans le modèle français" (p. 136). Such a statement implies at best that its author has misread one of the two dialogues involved.

39 Fontenelle writes "civilté"; Gottsched's translation gives "Höflichkeit".

40 A study by Marga Barthel, Das "Gespräch" bei Wieland (Frankfurt, 1939) contains pertinent remarks about the relationship of eighteenth-century aesthetics to Wieland's aesthetics and to the dialogue of the dead in general. The dialogic style is seen to arise from the hegemony of wit (Witz) and grace and Bildungsstreben (p. 14). The brief treatment of the "Dialogen im Elysium" contends that a basic quality of Wieland's Totengespräche is the unqualified honesty of the conversants, and relates the theme of Abschälung to other of Wieland's works.

41 Johann Wolfgang Goethe, Werke (Sophienausgabe) I, 36, 327.

42 The matter of Wieland's indebtedness to Lucian has been well documented by Julius Steinberger's Lucians Einfluß auf Wieland (Dissertation Göttingen, 1902), to which the present study makes grateful reference.

43 Steinberger, p. 1.

44 Steinberger, pp. 2-7.

45 Steinberger, pp. 6-7.

46 IV (Nov.), 97-121; (Dec.), 201-216.

47 Steinberger, p. 7.

48 IV (Oct. 1780), 67-75; (Nov. 1780), 122-138.

49 I (Jan. 1782), 55-66.

50 Steinberger, p. 10.

51 Teutscher Merkur, III (Aug. 1787), 119.

52 Steinberger, p. 15.

53 Steinberger, p. 14.

54 "Peregrin. Ein Auszug aus Lucians Nachrichten von dem Leben und Ende

dieses Schwärmers", III (July), 61-96.

55   Wieland's Peregrinus Proteus has been excluded from this study for several
      reasons. First, Wieland makes little use in this work of the devices peculiar
      to the dialogue of the dead. Indeed, the setting of the dialogue in the nether
      world does make it possible for the two speakers to meet, but since the two
      were roughly contemporary, the exotic setting is hardly indispensible.
      Secondly, Peregrinus Proteus is clearly much more a novel than it is a
      Totengespräch. although it is admittedly a combination of the dialogue and
      the novel. However, the dialogue within a novel is a characteristic Wieland-
      ian trait as Marga Barthel points out in Das "Gespräch" bei Wieland. Fried-
      rich Sengle has commented succinctly on the form: "Im Peregrinus Proteus
      und Agathodämon ist die Auflösung des Epischen nicht so weit fortgeschrit-
      ten, daß man nicht noch von wirklichen Romanen sprechen könnte. . . ."
      (Wieland, p. 480).
56   Steinberger, p. 16.
57   Steinberger, p. 20.
58   Literarische Zustände und Zeitgenossen, I (Leipzig. 1838), 166. Cited in
      Steinberger, p. 20.
59   III (Lucerne and Leipzig, 1800), No. 2, 269-295.
60   Teutscher Merkur, IV (Oct. 1780), 67.
61   Wilhelm Kurrelmeyer suggests that Wieland had in mind the Athenian writer
      of comedies. See Wieland's Schriften, I, Vol. 14, 142 A.
62   Christoph Martin Wieland, Schriften, ed. Wilhelm Kurrelmeyer, I, Vol. 14
      (Berlin, 1928), 281. Subsequent references to this source given in paren-
      theses in the text. Kurrelmeyer traces Wieland's borrowings to Pindar and
      Aeschines.
63   Wieland's general advocacy of moderation is already evident in the title of
      his first novel: Der Sieg der Natur über die Schwärmerey, / oder / die
      Abenteuer / des / Don Sylvio von Rosalva, / Eine Geschichte / worinn alles
      wunderbare natürlich zugeht.
64   Steinberger, p. 95.
65   Lucian, VII, 175.
66   Steinberger, p. 96.
67   Teutscher Merkur, III, (Aug. 1788), 181. Subsequent references to this text
      are given in parentheses.
68   Steinberger treats "Peregrin und Lucian" as a disputation concerning Lucian's
      "The Passing of Peregrin". See especially pp. 18-19.
69   (Lucerne and Leipzig), III, 269-295.
70   Attisches Museum IV (Lucerne and Leipzig, 1802), No. 2, 106.
71   Wieland's Werke XXVIII (Berlin, 1879), 23-24.
72   The extent to which the character Aristipp speaks for Wieland himself is a
      matter too intricate for the present study to treat justly. The traditional idea
      that Aristipp is the spout from which the wisdom of Wieland's old age pours
      forth should be called into question; however, it will be remembered that some
      of the material in Aristipp was published elsewhere (notably in the Attisches
      Museum) under Wieland's name.
73   Wieland's Werke XXVIII (Berlin, 1879), 67.

74   Teutscher Merkur, I (Jan. 1783), 29-49; (Mar. 1783), 252-262. Subsequent references to this text provided in parentheses in the text. A number of factors point to Merck's authorship. The initial "M." could of course stand for Merck. Secondly, the date of the dialogue coincides with the period of Merck's contributions to the journal. The dialogue contains references to and an interest in sculpture which corresponds to Merck's own inclinations. Merck's reputation for a sharp tongue is borne out by the snide remarks to the audience in the fourth scene.

75   Hans Wahl, Geschichte des Teutschen Merkurs. Ein Beitrag zur Geschichte des Journalismus im 18. Jahrhundert. (Berlin, 1914), p. 119.

76   See his footnote, p. 255.

77   Merck's importation of the "mirror of truth" into the realm of the dead is evidently his own invention. It appears in no other dialogue of the dead known to this author.

78   For a discussion of this problem see Lieselotte E. Kurth, Die zweite Wirklichkeit (Chapel Hill, 1969), pp. 225-228.

79   "Wiewohl der Herausgeber schon öfters erfahren hat, daß er, um sich unkenntlich zu machen, nur sein W. hinter einem Aufsaz, (und wenn es auch Clelia und Sinibald wäre) wegzulassen braucht: so darf er doch hoffen, daß niemand auf den Argwohn kommen werden, eine Scene im Elysium, worin Aspasia für eine Buhlerin und Kupplerin erklärt und in ein Ungeheuer verwandelt wird, auf Rechnung des Verfassers des Agathon zu setzen, oder für eine Fortsetzung derjenigen zu halten, die er in zwey vorgehenden Jahrgängen des Merkurs geliefert hat. Die gegenwärtige Scene kann indessen zum Beweise dienen, daß sogar die Richter in Elysium nicht immer unfehlbar sind; auch soll der Lord Oberichter Minos — dem es etwas so simples scheint, Schönheit der Seele eher bey Mantel und Bart als bey einer Glycerion zu vermuthen, und dem es so schwehr ist Schönheit der Seele mit Schwärmerey zusammenzudenken — soll (wenn wir unsern Nachrichten aus der Unterwelt trauen dürfen) bey einer von Proserpinen veranstalteten Revision dieses Processes, sich genöthiget gesehen haben, um seine Entlassung anzuhalten. Sollten wir so glüklich seyn, durch irgend einen unsrer Geister die Acta dieser Revision zu handen zu bekommen: so werden wir uns ein Vergnügen daraus machen, unsern Lesern einen Auszug derselben mitzutheilen" (262-263).

CHAPTER VII

THE DIALOGUE OF THE DEAD AS INDEPENDENT LITERARY SATIRE

Throughout the eighteenth century the dialogue of the dead and the fictional setting in the "realm of the dead" were used to satirize literary trends as well as particular literary figures. Such works included anonymous contributions to journals as well as signed works.[1] Most of these satires of literary subjects were published independently of any journal or magazine and are thus related to "serious" attempts at Totengespräche.[2] Also included in this grouping are academic and literary "Streitschriften" which have the form of a dialogue of the dead.

The writers of independent literary satires show less desire to imitate classical predecessors; these satirists tend rather to experiment with ideas and motifs borrowed from antique sources in a casual fashion. The unusual titles of their works reflect this freedom of imagination. Characteristic of these literary satires is their tendency to enlarge both the setting of discourse and the number of speakers. The scene may include perambulation to various parts of the netherworldly empire. The speakers tend to be specific individuals rather than archetypal characters.

In the first half of the century these writers often voiced opposition to Faßmann and his "school", as did the authors of some of the moral weeklies. An early example of a Totengespräch satirizing Faßmann appeared in 1724;[3] in 1751 Faßmann was severely criticized in the "Freundschafftliche Unterredungen der Seelen David Fassmanns und Thomas Hobbes, durch welche beyder Charakter moralisch zergliedert werden . . .". Such satires of literary figures persist throughout the eighteenth century in Germany.

An important and early (1739) Totengespräch among the literary satires is Johann Wilhelm Steinauer's "Gespräch zwischen Johann Christian Günthern aus Schlesien In dem Reiche der Todten / und einem Ungenannten In dem Reiche der Lebendigen."[4] This is a literary "Streitschrift" of some 156 pages in length, written in part to criticize the biography of Günther by Christoph Ernst Steinbach (1698-1741) which appeared in Dresden in 1738. Steinbach used as nom de plume Carl Ehrenfried Siebrand. In the opening lines of the "Vorbericht" to this dialogue Steinauer points to his former opposition to Faßmann:

> Bis hierher bin ich ein Feind von dem ehrlichen Herrn
> Faßmanne gewesen / und zwar dieserwegen / weil er
> der Verfasser einiger Gespräche im Reiche der Todten
> ist. Ich liebe das Natürliche / und ich hasse alles dieses /
> was diesem zuwieder läuft. Nichts aber ist mir unnatür-
> licher vorgekommen / als eben die Gespräche des Herrn
> Faßmanns. (12)

This the author offers more as apology for his use of the form than as real reconciliation with Faßmann. The fact that Steinauer is so careful to enumerate Faßmann's faults indicates that he still holds some of his former views. Further evidence of this may be found in the text itself: the dialogue bears but faint semblance to Faßmann's Entrevuen in any point from vocabulary to artistic intention, and Steinauer's views on using "pure" German set him at odds with David Faßmann. This contrast to the Entrevuen echoes the opposition expressed by Steinauer's mentor Gottsched in the Vernünftigen Tadlerinnen and elsewhere.

The dialogue is surrounded by a frame in which the narrator describes the events which led to his knowledge of the nether world. He writes that "he" left his body at four in the morning; through the fireplace in his room his spirit finds its way to fresh air, thence to the Elysian fields. At the end of the dialogue his spirit is picked up by a strong wind and is carried away from the realm of the dead. This fanciful frame helps to lighten what is otherwise rather leaden criticism.

The dialogue itself may be divided into three sections according to content. The first consists of criticism of Steinbach's biography of Günther. In the dialogue Günther supports the position, then and since generally held, [5] that the author of the biography is Christoph Ernst Steinbach (21). The unnamed visitor argues that it could not be by Steinbach, who is a true gentleman and scholar, but is rather the work of Carl Ehrenfried Siebrand, who "speaks like the rudest Silesian peasant whose village borders on Poland" (21, translation mine).

The second section of the dialogue continues to defame Steinbach-Siebrand, listing the various wrong opinions which he espouses. In section two Steinbach-Siebrand's deviations from the path of Gottschedian orthodoxy are severely criticized. Unfortunately, the level of criticism of the poor biographer's personality rarely rises above the level of common libel.

Günther opens the third segment of the dialogue by requesting "Neuigkeiten" from the realm of the living. The report, which centers around the literary world of Germany, contains some information and quite a bit of pontification in matters of taste. To Steinauer's credit one could say that he is more positive than negative and that he does attempt to give reasons for some of his judgements. There are chiefly three villains in his eyes: Henrici-Picander, Johann Ulrich von König and Daniel Stoppe. The Erste und Andere Sammlung of Stoppe's poems (1728-1729) are reviewed specifically. Steinauer goes so far as to quote twelve verses of "Gratulation auf den Namenstag eines guten Freundes", to which Günther replies:

> Man sollte in Wahrheit nicht glauben / daß ein Mensch
> seine gesunde Vernunft recht mit Fleiß zu verleugnen
> gesinnet wäre. Ich habe jederzeit auch das Lustige ge-
> liebt. Allein das Lustige und Scherzhafte von dieser
> Art habe ich als der kleinste Knabe gehaßt. So spasen
> die Bauernbuben auf den Erndtenschmäußen. (106)

Even the meanest gossip about von König's marital affairs is thought worthy of inclusion in the report! König could not be forgiven his association in the translation of Marino into German.

The report is full of praise for Gottsched, who is called "the German

Horace" (100), while his wife is lauded for her translations (92). The attitude of
the author to the Gottscheds is adulatory, if not slavish. Schwabe and Haller receive their due of praise, as does Brockes, who in Steinauer's opinion, is unfortunately not beyond the corrupting influence of Marino (122). Interesting also
is Steinauer's concern with contemporary poetesses, which does not end with "die
Gottschedin". Of the female writers then active Steinauer prefers "Jungfer Zäune-
männin" of Erfurt. Here too he mixes criticism of the person with criticism of the
work: "Sie reimt dann und wann ganz hübsch. Sie verdienet vieles Lob; aber doch
etwas weniger / als sie sich selbst giebt" (126). When Günther learns that Miss
Zäunemann has been crowned by the University of Göttingen, he remarks that the
crowning of women is becoming quite customary. Der Ungenannte also mentions
favourably "Frau P. Lincken und ihre Tochter / die Fr. P. Wittern" of Straßburg (123), recognizing the contributions of women to the scholarly world (Mrs
Linck translated from the French). "Die Neuberin" and her whole troupe receive
Steinauer's benediction.

    While it is true that the kinds of criticism found in this dialogue of the
dead are not of the first water, the dialogue is nevertheless important because it
presents an expansive view of the literary scene of its day. In this dialogue is contained a commentary on the literary world from the pen of a disciple of Gottsched.
It is also one of the first incidences in which a Totengespräch in a non-periodical
source is used extensively for literary criticism.

    The author of "Das verwirrete und wieder beruhigte Reich der Todten.
Eine Lucianische Satyre, ohne Vorrede" likewise makes a comment on writers of
Totengespräche:

> Zwar war das Reich der Todten eine Zeit her nicht gar
> wohl zufrieden mit einigen Sterblichen, welche sich mit
> denen Unterredungen im Reich der Todten beschäftiget
> hatten; doch ließ man sich daran gnügen, daß man diesen
> elenden Gesprächs=Schreibern bey ihrer Ankunft aus der
> Ober=Welt einen derben Verweis gab. Es waren sehr we-
> nige darunter, welche noch ziemlich gelinde davon kamen.[6]

    As the title intimates, the influence of Lucian is strong. In some as-
pects the satire continues the tradition of Lucian's "Philosophies for Sale" (Bion
prasis), but the principal device is not an auction, but rather a war in the realm
of the dead. (The author adds humourously that he hopes that his revelation of
these events will not gain him the same rejection which the writers of Totengespräche find.) The author's source for the events is a chance meeting with Lucian
himself, who has returned from the nether world to report on the war as "Warnung
und Erbauung"; Lucian, says the author, enjoys such high esteem in the scholarly
world that surely no one would question his honesty.

    The incident that sparked the feud in the nether world was a review by
a theologian of the latest developements in the field of philosophy. Here the author
employs one of the most frequent of the literary topoi used in connection with the
fictional setting in the realm of the dead, that is the narration of news from the
Oberwelt. Yet it only serves as a device to lead to the rest of the satire and is not

the principal reason for the writing of the dialogue. The theologian's manner of presentation offends the philosophers; insults are exchanged and their personal feud soon widens to include most of the inhabitants of the nether world, who divide into theological, philosophical and neutral factions.

A civil war in the realm of the dead presents some problems. According to the unbreakable rules of the realm, such feuds are forbidden. Further, the quarreling factions forgot their present condition and re-adopted the opinions and passions that they had followed on earth. War is soon found to be the best means of revenging the insults traded by the theologian and the philosopher. Here, as in other places, the author of the satire suggests that this agitated and unreasonable, but temporary state of the <u>Reich</u> <u>der</u> <u>Todten</u> is the real state of the <u>Oberwelt</u>.

The rest of the satire concerns itself with the problems of setting up counsels of war, electing leaders and winning shades over to the two principal sides. The selection of a leader is a difficult task for theologian and philosopher alike. Although several popes voice strong contention for the honour, it falls to three bishops. The philosophers select Aristotle, much to Plato's chagrin. It is in the making of these plans that the satire most resembles Lucian's "Philosophies for Sale", for in the course of discussion, various theologians and philosophers are satirized. The philosophers begin their war counsel with the question, Is the proposed war just or not? The first speaker, Machiavelli, finds the question superfluous. Aristotle speaks next:

> Er fieng zuerst an, von der Materie und Form des Kriegs
> ein langes und breites herzuschwatzen, wovon er das wenig-
> ste selbst recht verstehen mogte. Die Versammlung ward
> seines Vortrags bald überdrüßig. Die meisten davon fiengen
> an sehr zu jähnen, als wann sie alle Augenblick hätten ein-
> schlafen wollen . . . . (19)

Other philosophers are satirized as well; Leibniz's monads are also found in the realm of the dead, but cannot participate in the war because they cannot move about. Such satire is more topical than that of other eighteenth-century imitations of Lucian which hark back to Pythagoras and his beans.

Nor are poets exempt from satirical treatment. In this satire, as in many dialogues of the dead, the poets have their own separate quarters. But the poets were so splintered that a second war threatened to break out within the "Lust=Wäldlein" where they resided:

> Sie zanckten sich wegen der Rechte und Grentzen der Schau-
> bühne: Einige verwarfen die Opern, und trieben ihr Gespötte
> damit; andere wolten sie beybehalten wissen. Daraus ent-
> stand eine andere Zwistigkeit, nemlich ob ein Epischer und
> Tragischer Dichter auch könne und dürfe Opern machen. Sie
> konten sich nicht ein mahl darüber vergleichen, was ihr
> Handwerck, nemlich die Dichtkunst für ein Ding sey. Der
> ärgste Lermen war darüber entstanden, wer unter ihnen
> der beste und gröste Dichter sey, dem man sich im Dichten

zu einem Muster vorstellen könte. Die Frage ob man in
der Poesie die Reime beybehalten solte, oder nicht, ward
nebst andern nichtswürdigen Grillen unter ihnen so eyferig
getrieben, als ob die gantze Wohlfahrt des Reichs der Todten daran hienge. Das artigste war, daß sich die Harlekins
in einen besondern Haufen versammlet hatten, und sich über
die andern beschwereten, daß man sie aus den Lust=Spielen
gäntzlich verbannen wolte. (33)

The author finds that the poets are more concerned with <u>Witz</u> than with <u>Vernunft</u>.
The poets let their passions guide them more than reason. One poet quickly com-
poses a battle song.

It is unfortunate that the author does not name individual writers as
he does philosophers and religious. But in refusing to specify particulars he displays a closer affinity to Lucian, who rarely involved himself with specific literary problems. This satire in the realm of the dead is particularly interesting for
its extensive picture of Elysium's areas and processes.

When the recruitment is over and the sides are chosen, there remain
the more practical aspects of the war, and the satire necessarily comes to its end,
for there can be little action in the realm of the dead. The philosophers discuss
which weapons are to be used. With a witty parry, the author lets the philosophers
decide to use a bellows ("Blasebalg . . . das bequemste Instrument zum Windma-
chen . . ." [35]) to upset the enemy. None of the shades have funds for financing
the war, nor have they means for crossing the Styx to encounter an opposing army.
Someone thereupon suggests Kaysersberger's <u>Narren=Schif</u>, [7] "welches so gerau-
mig ist, daß darin alle Sterbliche gnugsamen Platz finden können" (36). This comment is in keeping with the satirist's view of man.

The episode is ended by divine intervention in the form of a thunderbolt
which jars everyone back to his senses. The author draws the conclusion (mentioned also in the Afterword) that human reason is weak and imperfect, allowing
the passions to exert an unwholesome influence on human behaviour.

One of the most famous of all literary satires has the form of a dialogue of the dead. This piece is known to many who are unfamiliar with the tradition of the <u>Totengespräch</u>, for Goethe's "Götter, Helden und Wieland" has received
frequent scholarly attention. In this <u>Totengespräch</u> of some 3500 words Goethe ridi-
cules Wieland and his <u>Singspiel</u> "Alceste". Perhaps even more offensive to Goethe's
mind were Wieland's letters in the <u>Teutscher Merkur</u> on Euripides and "Alceste".
If Goethe's <u>Dichtung und Wahrheit</u> is to be believed, he wrote the farce in one sit-
ting on a Sunday afternoon over a bottle of good burgundy. [8] After writing the satire
in 1773, Goethe mailed it to Johann Michael Reinhold Lenz, who insisted that it
be published. "Götter, Helden und Wieland" was first printed at Kehl in 1774.

In the same section of <u>Dichtung und Wahrheit</u> Goethe includes his reasons for writing the piece. There Goethe grants Wieland the right to re-shape poetic
tradition according to his purposes, yet he finds that the letters in the <u>Teutscher
Merkur</u> justify the procedure in too partisan a manner:

Allein in den Briefen, die er über gedachte Oper in den

"Merkur" einrückte, schien er uns diese Behandlungsart
allzu parteiisch hervorzuheben und sich an den trefflichen
Alten und ihrem hohen Stil unverantwortlich zu versündi-
gen, indem er die derbe gesunde Natur, die jenen Produk-
tionen zum Grunde liegt, keineswegs anerkennen wollte. [9]

Other clues to Goethe's reasons for writing the farce are to be found
in two letters from near the time of its appearance. Writing to Sophie von La Roche
during the latter part of May, 1774, Goethe states simply: "Ich dachte Wieland sollte sich so albern nicht gebärden."[10] In a letter of early June, 1774, Goethe writes
to G. F. E. Schönborn of the farce which he calls "ein schändlich Ding": "Ich tur-
lupinire ihn [Wieland] auf eine garstige Weise über seine moderne Mattherzigkeit
in der Darstellung iener Riesengestalten der marckigen Fabelwelt."[11]

Although Goethe maintained in the letter to Sophie von La Roche that
he had burned down "ein Gartenhäusgen seines [Wieland's]Papiernen Ruhms",[12]
Wieland's review of the farce in the Teutscher Merkur reveals no fear of fire.
Here Wieland calls the piece an "heroisch-komisch-farcicalischen Pasquinade"
and a "kritisches Wrexekekek Koax Koax".[13] Wieland is highly complimentary
of Goethe and even compares him to Shakespeare and Aristophanes. In self-de-
fense Wieland argues that Goethe's treatment of Wieland resembles Aristophanes'
satire of Euripides.

The main points of criticism in the farce are well summarized in the
quoted section of Goethe's works. Other studies have presented resumés of the
action and the subject matter.[14] Critical attention in this study will focus on placing Goethe's farce in the tradition of the dialogue of the dead.

There have been several scholarly attempts to link Goethe's "Götter,
Helden und Wieland" to earlier dialogues of the dead. A supposition that Goethe
received the form from Elias Schlegel's "Demokritus. Ein Todtengespräche" re-
mains unproved.[15] Imaginative work on the sources of Goethe's Totengespräch
has been done by Hanna Fischer-Lamberg,[16] who points out that Goethe's teacher,
J. G. Albrecht, held Lucian in very high esteem. Goethe records in Dichtung und
Wahrheit that Albrecht kept a volume of Lucian as a constant companion.[17] Yet
Fischer-Lamberg finds — after arguing that Lucian's dialogues of the dead and
Goethe's satire have little in common structurally — another source for one section of the satire: the early folk plays about the Faust legend. The oldest treat-
ments of this material often included a "prelude in hell"; this occurs in at least
three of the Faust plays. Goethe could have known these plays from the English
comedians who toured Germany.[18]

Another element of "Götter, Helden und Wieland" suggests that influence from Lucian is less direct: the inclusion of Pluto in the role of "Höllen-
fürst". Pluto's voice is heard in the piece only at the very end; however, these
last lines bear certain resemblances to the appearance of Pluto in the Straßbur-
ger Faustspiel.[19] Yet to suggest strong influence of the early Faust plays on this
section of "Götter, Helden und Wieland" risks overlooking their vast differences
in tone and purpose. Seen in this light such a source of inspiration for Goethe's
farce becomes unlikely.

Influence from Lucian is thus a highly complex matter. It is improbable that the question of sources for "Götter, Helden und Wieland" can ever be answered with certitude, for Goethe did not comment on Lucian at any time before he used the dialogue of the dead as a form for his satire. The fictive device of the realm of the dead was employed for many kinds of literature in eighteenth-century Germany and was used by writers for situations other than "pure" dialogues of the dead. In consideration of the facts that in 1773 new dialogues of the Entrevue type were still being published, that the German moral weeklies and literary journals had earlier adopted the form, and that Totengespräche had been successfully employed by historical and religious writers, then it seems both impossible and unnecessary to establish a single source for Goethe's knowledge of the form.

A "Gespräch zwischen Voltaire und Hr. D. Bahrdten im Reiche der Todten . . .",[20] published anonymously in 1780, concerns itself chiefly with presenting a critical biography of the controversial Carl Friedrich Bahrdt. The subtitle of the work, "in welchem dieselben einander ihre Begebenheiten erzählen", recalls the tone of the Entrevuen and the emphasis in the dialogue on biography and controversies suggests even more strongly the possibility of influence from the Faßmann "school". Although much of the text deals with Dr. Bahrdt's philosophical and religious Streitigkeiten, there are a few references to literature. In particular there are disparaging references to Werther and the "Wandsbecker Bote".

Voltaire acts as authority figure in the dialogue. After the relation of a particular episode in Bahrdt's life, Voltaire draws the conclusions and points out Bahrdt's faults. The exposition itself is lively and well done, even suspenseful. Voltaire is the first to speak: "Was hat Sie denn die Oberwelt gethan, daß Sie sich nicht länger auf derselben verweilet haben? -- Ich sollte es fast errathen. Sie werden den Orthodoxen so scharf in die Flanquen gefallen seyn, und die können gar nichts leiden" (3). Here the anonymous author is letting Voltaire speak as much to the reader as to Bahrdt. For complete appreciation of these lines the reader must already know who the speakers in the dialogue are.

Bahrdt does not recognize Voltaire immediately, but guesses that he might be Duns Scotus, Petrus Lombardus or Thomas Aquinas. The author presents his character "Bahrdt" by the character's own speech: " − wenigstens sind Sie kein Kezzer, denn sonst müßte ich eine Sympathie fühlen" (4).

Uttering the topos that vision in the nether world has not the clouding veil before it as on earth, Voltaire tells Bahrdt (and the reader) who the newly-arrived shade is: "Sie sind Hr. Doctor Carl Friedrich Bahrdt, − von der Welt gehaßt, − von den Orthodoxen verfolgt . . ." (4). At the revelation of Voltaire's identity Bahrdt utters words of praise. Later in the dialogue Bahrdt too articulates the theme of improved understanding after the crossing of the Styx: "Ja freilich, ich glaube es selbst, die Augen sind mir schon etwas aufgegangen. − Ich sehe itzt alles ohne Hülle, aus einem ganz andern Gesichtspunkte und ohne alle Partheilichkeit an . . ." (5).

In this Totengespräch there is a short episode of perambulation, in which Voltaire and Bahrdt journey (at Voltaire's suggestion) to meet a man who was once the scourge of the majority of poets (161). The man − identified only as "G.R.K." − was once Bahrdt's critic and enemy,[21] but since they were reconciled before death, the reunion in the nether world is a pleasant one.

A dispute between the physician Dr. Ernst Platner and the writer Johann Karl Wezel in 1781-82 prompted three dialogues of the dead which appeared as Streitschriften. The dispute centered on certain derogatory remarks made by Wezel on Leibniz's Theodicée to which Platner took exception, leading him to criticize Wezel's talents as a writer. Wezel then challenged Platner to defend the critique publicly.[22] The two principals in the dispute, Platner and Wezel, are the featured speakers in one of these dialogues concerning the "Miniaturfehde".[23] With the two disputants facing each other, the dialogue is very direct and leads to criticism of Wezel's novel Tobias Knaut by "Platner":

> Ich glaube in Ihren Schriften auch manche Wiederholungen, leere Worte und ermüdende Langweiligkeiten bemerkt zu haben, vorzüglich im Tobias Knaut, welches vermuthlich die erste Frucht Ihrer Lenden oder vielmehr Ihres Kopfs ist, und ich wundre mich sehr, daß dieser Roman, den wir füglich entbehren konnten, einen so guten Abgang gefunden hat, ob gleich dieser gute Abgang, der oft den elendesten Schmierereyen zu gute kommt, nicht den Werth und die innere Güte eines Buchs beweiset, welche vielmehr aliunde aus Horazens lectione decies repetita konstiren muß. Und schwerlich dürfte dies der Fall bey unsern gangbaren Romanen seyn.[24]

In reply to this the author of the dialogue lets Wezel distinguish between belles lettres and philosophy and take a mild slap at Platner's writings:

> Der Beyfall des Publikums, sonderlich des schönen Geschlechts und aller der Leute, die Kopf und Geschmack haben, hat für mein Buch entschieden; was dürfen wir weiter Zeugniß? Freylich schrieb ich keine trockene Aphorismen, wozu ich den Stoff aus andern Büchern entlehnte, denn es war mein Beruf nicht, Weltweisheit zu lehren, und hätte ich welche geschrieben, oder wär ich zu dem Fall gewesen, nach Professorart und dem lieben Herkommen gemäß ein eigenes Lehrbuch herauszugeben zu müssen, ich denke, die Kunstrichter sollten mehr damit zufrieden gewesen seyn, als mit dem Ihrigen.

Platner replies with some basic criticism of the novel and the writing of novels:

> Sie beliebten vorher des Berufs zu gedenken. Sagen Sie mir doch, was hatten Sie für einen Beruf? Zum Romanschreiben? Warlich, ein elendes Verdienst um die Menschen, sie einige Stunden vertändeln zu helfen, und sie von reelen Dingen abzuhalten. (10)

Platner further suggests that Wezel should have kept his position as "Hofmeister" in Berlin so that he would have had "Protektion" to look for a position:

> So wären Sie doch für den Staat ein brauchbarerer Mann
> geworden, als Sie es mit Ihrer Schriftstellerey je werden
> konnten. Aber das ist jetzt, die herrschende Mode unsrer
> schönen Geister, zu privatisiren, weil sie nicht gern ar-
> beiten und fein gemächlich nach ihrem Gutdünken leben
> wollen. (10)

"Wezel" is able to defend himself against these charges; he attempts to negate the suggested alternatives and defends his own writings on the basis of utility:

> Ich liebe die Unabhängigkeit . . . ein sklavisches Leben
> ist mir von je her verhaßt gewesen, und Sie müssen es
> aus meinen Schriften abgenommen haben, daß ich kein
> Empfindler war, der die Leute zu weinen, und die Nar-
> ren noch närrischer machte. . . . Ich glaubte vielmehr,
> mich in einem stillen Privatleben durch gut ausgearbei-
> tete Schriften um meine Zeitgenossen eben so Verdienst
> machen zu können, als wenn ich Hofrath und Professor
> geworden wäre. Ueberhaupt hat jeder Mensch seinen be-
> stimmten Wirkungskreis, den er erweitern, oder ver-
> engern kann, je nachdem die Lage der Umstände es mit
> sich bringt. (11)

The conflict between the practical man and the "schöner Geist" is presented very clearly in this dialogue. This social problem is also recorded in other literary forms of the period as well.

Two other Totengespräche resulted from this feud, one between the publishers of each author[25] and another between two book sellers in Leipzig.[26] Neither is directly concerned with literary criticism, nor do they make a signi- ficantly interesting contribution to the developement of the Totengespräch to war- rant further discussion.

A Totengespräch by August Gottlieb Meißner, published in 1782, is no longer a simple dialogue, but rather a scene from the nether world, or as Meißner subtitled his work, "Eine Anekdote aus der Unterwelt".[27] Meißner also wrote a love poem "Zwey Schatten aus Elysium", and a "Dialog wie K. Ludewig XIV. und Fenelon ihn gehalten haben könten"; the dialogue appeared in the Deut- sches Museum.[28] Both the poem and the dialogue between Fénelon and Louis XIV display gracefulness and an interest in the well-executed turn of phrase.

The "Anekdote" has as its speakers Lope de Vega, Lessing and "Pas- tor Richter" and presents literary criticism of a gentle nature. Meißner places Lessing in the role of hero in this dialogue, which opens with Lessing's being greeted by the shades of the great in Elysium. As Meißner puts it: "Selbst Vol- taire vergaß der Dramaturgie, (die er iezt verstand) gab seine Merope und Semi- ramis Preis; und freute sich des wetteifernden Witzes" (3). While Lessing plays the hero, the buffoons of the dialogue are Lope de Vega and Spanish chauvinism.

After the introduction there follows a section in which Lessing and Lope recapitulate their lives. Lope arrogantly prides himself on his unique fecundity. Lessing, too, relates his achievements in the theater, during the course of which he enumerates a critical principle: "Was häufig ist, ist selten vortreflich" (11). When Lope cannot be convinced that mere quantity counts for little in the theater, Meißner brings out "Pastor Richter", an object of scorn for his having composed 6,000 sermons. The situation further allows Lessing to propound the idea that the theater should both teach and improve morally. The topicality of the idea is more easily seen when one remembers that Schiller's essay, Die Schaubühne als moralische Anstalt betrachtet, was published two years later than Meißner's satire.

Since Lessing's role is that of worthy authority, he wins his arguments against Lope. Yet Lope is not totally rejected: Lessing decrees that Lope nevertheless deserves acclaim. Rather than try to rank the poets in Elysium as in suggested by one shade, Meißner ends his dialogue with remarks about the absence of class or hierarchical stratification in Elysium.

A dialogue of the dead by the playwright and editor Georg Karl Claudius (1757-1815) bears some relation to Meißner's "Anekdote aus der Unterwelt". Claudius' "Die Schatten. Erster und zweyter Transport"[29] is a dramatic scene in the nether world; like Meißner's, it too is chiefly concerned with literary criticism. In this piece Claudius gives Meißner a dose of his own medicine by casting him in an inglorious role, just as Meißner had done to Lope. As the objects of his criticism, Claudius chooses the luminaries of eighteenth-century German literature, including Ramler, Klopstock, Jacobi, Wieland, Schiller and others. Claudius inverts the names so that Ramler must be deciphered from "Relmar", Klopstock from "Kostpolk" and so forth.

As the title indicates, the work is divided into two parts. The first is a mixture of badinage and burlesque connected with Charon's ferrying the dead across the Styx. In this section the interaction between Charon and the various poets anticipates the formal judgement which awaits the shades in the second half of the work. Claudius did not hesitate to break with the traditions about the nether world. Normally shades are allowed to bring nothing with them across the Styx, yet Klopstock is allowed to bring some of his poems into the bark:

> Der Schatte Kostpolk.
> Mach Charon, daß ich überkomme.
> Charon.
> Gleich, gleich. Sie haben gar, wie ich sehe, Equipage mit?
> Kostpolk.
> Ja --- Einige Dutzend meiner neuesten Sinngedichte.
> Charon.
> Gebens her, gebens her − (er legt sie in den Kahn) Hat
> nichts zu sagen, sie sind ziemlich leicht −
> Kostpolk.
> Und hier meine Aufsätze über die teutsche Orthographie −
> Charon.

Damit verschonen Sie mich; lassens zurück, lassens zurück . . . .
(72)

Thus Claudius has intimated through Charon which of Klopstock's contributions he considers most worthy. In the second half of the work Klopstock comes before Minos to receive his reward; here the actual sentence is passed:

> Der Schatte Kostpolk.
>> Ich habe meinem Volke eine Epopee gegeben.
> Minos.
>> Sie ist die Freude der Musen.
> Der Schatte.
>> Ich warf die Rechtschreibung meiner Nation um.
> Minos.
>> Und das bricht deinem Ruhm den Stab . . . Am Morgen
>> soll dein Lorbeer grünen; und am Abend verwelken. (81-82)

The passing of sentences by various means in Totengespräche is not unusual. More unusual is Claudius' originality in devising fitting sentences in which poetic justice may be carried out. These contribute much to the humour of the dialogue.

Claudius treats Schiller in a similar manner. Schiller climbs into the boat carrying a copy of Kabale und Liebe. As they cross the river, Schiller begins declaiming from one of the stormiest passages, "Aber soll mir der Dintenklecker einmal in den Schuß laufen!" (75). When Charon discerns the title of the work from which Schiller is reading, he begins to row as fast as possible. Schiller questions:

> Rellisch:
>> Tod und Teufel, was hast du vor, Charon, das geht zu
>> schnell —
> Charon:
>> Nichts vor ungut. Lassen Sie uns machen, daß wir davon
>> kommen, denn man ist bey Ihnen das Leben nicht sicher.
>> Sie morden in Ihren Stücken, was nur Hofnung zum Leben
>> hat, und Ihre Geschöpfe sind so bestialisch schön — aber
>> für mich nicht verdaulich — (76)

Here Claudius employs one of the most venerable humourous devices of the Totengespräch: fear of death within the very sanctum of death. The scene also foreshadows the severe judgement of Schiller by Minos:

> Rellisch.
>> Ich bin der Verfasser — der Rebuär, Gnuröwschrev, Elabak
>> und Ebeil, und habe weiter nichts zu sagen.
> Minos.
>> Eben so lakonisch soll mein Urtheil seyn. Weil du denn an
>> dem unnatürlich grausenden dein Behagen findest, so geh
>> und leiste dem Tityos Gesellschaft. (85)

By associating Schiller with the violent giant Tityus, Claudius states his opposition to the "Geniebewegung". Here, too, there is criticism of the "unnatural" in literature, as there had been in the dialogue between Günther and the unnamed man. It should not be forgotten that the criticism of "Kabale und Liebe" was highly topical, for the drama was first performed in 1784. Claudius was presenting serious, relevant criticism in humourous form.

The charge of unnaturalness is also levied against Meißner and Wieland. As evidence against them, Minos calls forth a tragic couple, Naide and Alexis. Naide relates how she came to love Alexis more and more until her natural emotions were spoiled by a work of literature:

> Von ohngefähr kriegt ich Dnaleiw-s Sirdi und Edinez in
> die Hände; ich las; ich legt das Buch weg; floh, kam wie-
> der und las weiter. Mein Busen schwoll; meine Wangen
> glühten; Alexis kam, benutzte den Augenblick; die Götter
> der Unschuld verliesen mich und ich sank. Gesättigt floh
> Alexis. (83-84)

Alexis in his turn tells that he really loved Naide and wanted to be faithful to her; however, he had learned from reading Meißner's "Alcibiades" "daß Treue gegen ein Mädchen Schwachheit sey" (84). Minos' judgement on Meißner and Wieland is stern:

> Weh euch, daß ihr die Eumeniden zu Grazien machtet.
> Euer Loos sey: Ewig dafür den Eumeniden die verder-
> benleuchtende Fackel vorzutragen. (84-85)

Of the twelve poets that Claudius presents, only Christian Felix Weiße gains entrance into Elysium. The basis of criticism is in large part moral: Weiße merits Elysium because he is virtuous, his writings have never spread dangerous principles, nor has his wit made mockery of worthy accomplishments (86). Weiße is presented as an eighteenth-century praeceptor germaniae. The healthy naturalness of the Volk finds expression in Claudius' dialogue. Claudius seems to combat foreign, especially French, influence on German literature by his severe and almost scatological sentence on Magister Dyk, playwright, translator and editor of the Komisches Theater der Franzosen für die Deutschen:

> Minos:
> . . . Ich verweise dich [Dyk] zu dem Parnaß, wo du
> den Auswurf des Pegasus aufsammeln und nach deinem
> Gutdünken verarbeiten kannst. Magst ein französisches
> Lustspiel verdeutschen, oder eignes Trauerspiel schrei-
> ben. 'S gilt mir alles gleich. (88)

All things considered, Claudius' scenes in Elysium are some of the most readable and most humourous of all German dialogues of the dead. While it seems slightly repetitious to have the shades pre-judged by Charon before the actual judgement by Minos, Claudius alleviates the problem somewhat by introducing shades into the second scene whose traversal of the Styx with the ferryman is not shown the reader.

Claudius is one of the few writers of Totengespräche to include the still-living among the dead. He comments on this as a concluding remark and final thrust at the poets, saying that if he had to wait until they died to use their shades in a dialogue, then he would not have been able to write one at all, because the writers all think themselves immortal.

One of the other authors of Totengespräche who placed in Elysium the shades of those who were not yet dead was Frederick the Great. Monarchs, of course, enjoy special privileges. However, after his own death Frederick would have found — had there been messengers to the nether world (and who can doubt it?) — that he figured into many dialogues of the dead himself.

One such dialogue which honours Frederick is Samuel Jacob Schröckh's "Friedrich in Elysium";[30] the first edition of this dramatic scene in the nether world was published in 1786 and it enjoyed a second publication in an improved version in 1790. The piece consists of eighteen separate scenes, each of which features Frederick the Great and one or several famous persons. After a personal reception in the Elysian fields by Minos, Frederick is greeted by a host of historical celebrities, who welcome him to their company with words of praise. The principal device for indicating Frederick's greatness is accumulatio; for in the course of 127 pages, Frederick is visited by Maria Theresia, Pope Clement XIV, Luther, Solomon, Homer and Hercules, just to name the more notable! Unfortunately the level of criticism never goes beyond implication, and Schröckh takes little interest in lauding or enumerating items in Frederick's literary oeuvre. However, Schröckh's Homer and Voltaire (the two poets he places in Elysium) praise Frederick, an indication that Schröckh included Frederick's literary production as an aspect of his greatness.

While Jacob Schröckh lauded Frederick, Carl Ignaz Geiger (1756-1791) criticized him severely in a generic variation on the Totengespräch entitled "Friedrich II. als Schriftsteller im Elisium. Ein drammatisches Gemälde."[31] This work is one of the most elaborate uses of the dialogue of the dead in eighteenth-century German satirical literature. As the subtitle indicates, the piece tends to break out of the limitations of the dialogue form into the dramatic. The work is divided into four "scenes" and leads climactically to the condemnation of Frederick by the judges of Hades. The "cast" includes Maria Theresia, Pope Clement XIII, the Grand Inquisitor and various classical and contemporary writers, among them Virgil, Homer, Horace and Lessing.

The first scene depicts the customary arrival in the nether world, but to Frederick's disappointment he finds that his works are known and disliked by the great men of the past. Epicurus promises to introduce him at the weekly meeting of the "Gelehrtenklubb". The second scene presents a conference of the opposition forces. Here the major political and ideological charges are laid against Frederick as Emperor Franz reads from the Collected Works of Frederick and the Pope interrupts to pronounce anathemas. Frederick is labelled atheist and blasphemer and a danger to public morality (Verderber der Sitten). All his opponents agree that he deserves no place in the Elysian fields.

The third scene shows the meeting of the "Gelehrtenklubb", during which some rather thorough criticism of Frederick is offered. Frederick is ridiculed for having presumed to judge the Greek and Latin poets without having been able to read the texts in the original languages. Virgil asks for the critical reasons behind Frederick's statement that Voltaire and Racine were better than the ancient writers; and Frederick is, of course, unable to answer the question. Lessing then accuses Frederick of condemning the German writers of his day (Geiger provides the reader with the texts in footnotes) without a sound familiarity with them. To document Frederick's incompetence further Lessing quotes two of Frederick's poems from memory. The poems are so bad that the entire company is embarrassed by them. One of the poems is "An eine Hündin",[32] which leads Geiger to make some very uncomplimentary remarks in the footnotes on the subject of Frederick and dogs, relying for his information on Büsching's biography of Frederick. Frederick's letters are characterized by "abgenützter Epikurismus, Deismus und Skeptizismus unter allerlei Nonsens und Fadetäten" (37).

Yet Frederick was considered great by many of his contemporaries. One poet in particular wrote a revealing poem on his death. Schubart is named explicitly here by "Lessing" and receives some rather severe criticism, in which the linguistic usage of the Storm and Stress is ridiculed and rejected:

> . . . Schubart's Sprache ist nachläßig, voll Fehler,
> schmutzig aber voll Metaphoren und Grobheiten — er
> bemüht sich die alltäglichsten Redensarten in lauter
> Bildern zu sprechen — er sagt Dir z. B. nicht: der
> Kaiser erschüttert das Gleichgewicht von Europa, son-
> dern: Habsburgs Adler faßt mit mächtiger Kralle Frau
> Europa am Schopfe und schüttelt sie, daß ihr die Zähne
> klappern — seine Bilder haben alle was ungeheures, was
> Monströses, und was Pöbelhaftes. Dieß heißt in unsern
> Tagen Dichtkunst und Geniesprache.
> Homer.
> Den Kerl hätte man bey uns vor einen Wahnsinnigen, oder
> doch vor einen ungezogenen und niederträchtigen Men-
> schen gehalten.
> Lessing.
> Kluge die ihn kennen, halten noch izt auf der Oberwelt
> das Nämliche von ihm: aber doch hört man so gar in
> einer gewißen Litteraturzeitung von ihm die tollsten
> Lobsprüche verkündigen. (40)

Horace surmises that the situation of poetry must be as bad as that of politics. To this Lessing replies:

> Du irrst dich, wenn Du unsre Dichter alle nach dem
> Maaße dieses Pygmäen, der auf Stelzen geht, um
> groß zu seyn, oder nach dem verderbten Geschmake
> unsrer Zeit beurtheilst. Es gibt viele, die die Ehre

der Nation bei alldem noch in ihrer ganzen Größe
aufrecht halten . . . . (41-42)

Criticism of the popular taste is quite usual for Totengespräche: unusual in this
dialogue, however, is the degree of affirmation of the contemporary literary situation.

The fourth scene presents the three judges of the underworld in a splen-
did reception hall, here intended as the court room. The opposition voices its
charges, again quoting from Frederick's works. Geiger's faint effort to show Frederick's point of view is less kind than might be expected: In his own defense Frederick proudly calls upon "reason and truth" and expresses his contempt for the
charges. The sentence next read by Minos is a parody of legal terminology, including lengthy phrases and Latin abbreviations. The court finds Frederick guilty
of blasphemiae, claumniae, heterodoxiae & similium and sentences him to be
taken to Tartarus.

If Geiger's attack is one-sided and unfair, it still comes as a welcome
change from the usual laudations of Frederick which are found in other Totengespräche. The questioning of his competence in matters literary is certainly needed
as an antidote to the deference usually granted his pronouncements in such pieces
as Schröckh's "Friedrich in Elysium" (published three years prior to Geiger's
dialogue). A few such eulogies may even be found in belletristic magazines. David
Christoph Seybold, for example, wrote two Totengespräche laudatory of Frederick
for the Deutsches Museum (1787).[33]

From the colourful world of the Austrian comic theater came several
dialogues of the dead or dialogic scenes in Elysium. Two of these, "Der weyland
Casperl aus der Leopoldstadt im Reiche der Todten" and "Laroches Todtenfeyer
oder Des sog. Kasperls Gespräch am jenseitigen Ufer des Styx . . .", were published in Vienna in 1806 by Johann Joachim Perinet (1763-1816), the wellknown
actor, dramatist and writer of travesties. Both of Perinet's Totengespräche and
a third dialogue which appeared the following year are in Knittelversen, a characteristic which makes them rather unusual within this genre.

The third Totengespräch from this milieu, the "Gespräch über . . .
Herrn Weidmann im Reiche der Todten und Bartholomäus Zitterbarths . . . Ankunft im Elisium",[34] contains a conversation and an arrival scene. Speaking persons in the dialogue are Johann La Roche, who popularized the figure Caspar,
theater director Gottfried Prehauser, the comedian Brenner and the wife of J. J.
Perinet. With the arrival of Bartholomäus Zitterbarth, a Viennese theater director and patron of Schikaneder, the dialogue is enlarged. The conversation contains
news and gossip concerning prominent theatrical personages. Untraditionally the
piece opens with La Roche reading the Theater Zeitung. The paper, however, does
not satisfy the hunger of the inhabitants of Elysium for news from the Oberwelt.
Zitterbarth arrives in Elysium by the usual ferry, but here commandeered by a
Charon jokingly dubbed a "Neuigkeitskrämmer", who enters the scene unclassical-
ly exclaiming "Bona Dies! meine Herrn und Damen nach dem Tod" (9). Another
striking break with the traditions of the genre is the planned light meal (d'Jausen)
in Elysium.

A number of factors suggest either that Perinet may also be the author of the "Gespräch über Herrn Weidmann . . . und . . . Zitterbarths Ankunft", or that the dialogue is in imitation of him. The figures Charon, Prehauser and Brenner appear in both the "Weidmann/Zitterbarth" and "Der weyland Caspar"; an anonymous shade plays a role in both dialogues. In the "Weidmann/Zitterbarth" Madame Perinet plays a part.[35]

Evidence within the text likewise suggests a relationship. Charon's "Bona Dies!" illustrates Perinet's knowledge of Latin, of which he was quite proud.[36] Furthermore, the word "Auschelm" occurs in both "Der weyland Casperl" and "Weidmann/Zitterbarth".

Noteworthy also in "Weidmann/Zitterbarth" is the presentation of Perinet himself. Madame Perinet complains that Perinet cannot stop writing travesties. To which Brenner replies: "Laß ihn gehen, er bringt dadurch manche Wahrheit an den rechten Mann" (7). La Roche adds his opinion: "Mit allen, was über ihn geschrieben wird, treibt er sein Jux; / Ich für mein Theil hab ihn gar viel gratias z' sagen" (8). Perinet's name occurs once more near the end of the dialogue. There, too, the reference is flattering in its implication that director Schikaneder's continuing success depends heavily on Perinet.

Whoever the author of "Weidmann/Zitterbarth" may be, he is naively Lucianic in that he plays with the received traditions about the seemingly serious topic of life after death. This lightness is exemplified in the epithet applied to Charon: at one point in the dialogue he is called a "Wiener Kreisboth" (9)!

Lucian was the most important classical source for eighteenth-century writers of dialogues of the dead, but he was not the only source. Johann Daniel Falk's netherworldly satire owes a greater debt to Aristophanes than to Lucian, although Lucian was one of Falk's first reading materials and Falk felt a strong kinship between himself and the Syrian.[37] Lucian had also been recommended to Falk by Wieland.[38]

Early in 1806 Falk began his curious journal Elysium und Tartarus. Zeitung für Poesie, Kunst und Neuere Zeitgeschichte, which he issued twice weekly through September of the same year when it was suppressed by the authorities. Falk used the two classical locations, one installment of the journal being devoted to "Elysium", the next to "Tartarus", as a device for praising and blaming, respectively, various aspects of German culture. Falk, like so many other literati of the eighteenth century, perceived the relevance of the netherworld to this world, for he says in the introduction to Elysium und Tartarus: "Und dennoch steht diese schöne Schattenwelt mit der wirklichen in einem äußerst nahen und innigen Zusammenhang."[39] In the journal Falk expressly solicited "Gespräche im Reiche der Todten" to be submitted by his readers. The magazine contains only a few dialogues of the dead, but a great many letters from the dead.[40] One of the dialogues of the dead is a literary satire entitled "Die Dichterwaage",[41] written by Falk himself.

This short judgement scene was not inspired by Lucian so much as by the famous segment of Aristophanes' "The Frogs" in which Euripides' and Aeschylus' verse is weighed on a scales. In fact, Falk styled his work "Die Dichterwaage. Nach Aristophanes." While in Aristophanes' play the actual judging of the poets is left to the character Dionysius, the patron of theatrical performances, Falk returns the duty to Minos, Aeacus and Rhadamanthus. For Aristophanes' two poets

Falk substitutes Uz and Schiller, and for contrast he adds a third, Friedrich Wilhelm August Schmidt of Werneuchen.

The scales used by Falk corresponds fairly closely to the Aristophanean model: Uz and Schiller are to lay on their end of the balance that which of their works seems heaviest to them. Uz, since he is the senior poet, declaims first. Uz's first lines contain the words "I fly": "Mit sonnenrothem Angesicht / – Flieg' ich." Here Rhadamanthus interrupts and warns him to avoid the fate of Phaeton who flew too close to the sun. When Schiller later "flies" also, he is ridiculed just as Uz had been. Falk, it would seem, prefers a poetry more firmly attached to the ground.[42]

With the lines "Blumen lockt sie aus den Keimen, / Sonnen aus dem Firmament" Schiller is declared the victor, for little could outweigh the sun itself (47). Then Schmidt walks upon the scene dragging with him junk (Plunder), second-hand goods (Trödeleyen) and household wares which he throws into the scales. Minos remonstrates that such things belong more properly to a cheese scales (Käsewaage) than to this netherworldly one. This quip is reminiscent of Dionysius' complaint in the "Frogs" that he "needs must weigh / the art poetic like a pound of cheese."[43] In the battle of giants Schmidt has the audacity to declaim his own poetry, of which the following is a representative sampling:

> Nimm, mein Liebchen, diesen Löffel,
> Hier aus Spillbaum schön geschnitzt,
> Weil ein solches Hausgeräthe
> In der Wirtschaft immer nützt.

The spoon in the verse indicates the generally culinary nature of all the verses attributed to Schmidt.

At the end of the scene Minos accords Schiller the first prize for lyric poetry; Uz is granted a place next to him. Schmidt, however, is sent away, and the document is sealed with an appropriate Latin inscription and signed by the three judges from "Tartarus i[n] d[er] gr[oßen] Gerichtsstube" (48).

In an "Erklärung" at the bottom of the page, Falk takes responsibility for the satire. There he praises Wieland[44] thus:

> Hoffentlich wird es Niemand einfallen einen so liebens-
> würdigen Dichter, wie unsern Wieland, jemals im Tar-
> tarus, am wenigsten unter den 3 Höllenrichtern Minos,
> Aeakus und Rhadamanthus, zu suchen. Er gehört auf
> immerfort ins Elysium.

A work which despite its late date clearly belongs in a discussion of eighteenth-century satirical Totengespräche is the "Dramatisches Gespräch im Reiche der Todten, zwischen Schiller, Wieland, Iffland, Kotzebue und Göthe", which appeared in 1833.[45] The title of the work itself is old-fashioned, and the sympathies of the anonymous author[46] lie with the previous century rather than with his own. The work is divided into four sections, all written in blank verse. In style it tends toward epic description rather than dialogic discussion. The author has even made suggestions for appropriate musical selections to accompany parts of the piece. He introduces the third segment of the piece with the death march from Paer's <u>Achilles</u>, for example.

In the first section only Schiller and Wieland are present. Together they discuss personal and national problems before wandering on to visit the great artists of past times, amongst whom is, of course, Lucian.

The second section contains an enumeration of the virtues of Elysium, which in this politically conscious dialogue is free from human vices and from tyranny. Iffland next arrives on the scene and praises Schiller and Wieland at some length; they reciprocate the eulogy. Iffland adds to their knowledge of Germany's more recent history by relating the emancipation from the French.

Section three has to do in part with literary criticism; evidently the dramaturgic quarrel between Shakespeare, the Greeks and the French continues even in Elysium. Wieland and Schiller begin the third section with a discussion of Schiller's indebtedness to Shakespeare. Like the bard, Schiller, too, broke those rules "which Aristotle found necessary for his times" (29, translation mine). Wieland confirms. Genius, says the Wieland of this <u>Totengespräch</u>, tolerates little regulation:

> . . . Das Genie,
> Das wahre, duldet keine engen Grenzen,
> Worin die Dürftigkeit des Geistes oft
> Sich selbstgefällig zu verstecken pflegt. (30)

Schiller relates that even in Elysium Crébillon, Corneille and Racine still defend the old rules against Lope, Calderón, Shakespeare, Thomas Otway, Ben Jonson, "Beaumont=Fletcher" and himself. The Greek masters Sophocles, Euripides and Aeschylus, however, remain proudly aloof from the argument. Wieland finds a compromise: "Verschieden ist der Genius der Völker" (31).

Schiller and Wieland are next met by Kotzebue and Iffland. Kotzebue does not receive the encomion which the other poets heard on their arrival. In the familiar tradition of the dialogue of the dead Kotzebue tells the story of his murder to a sympathetic audience.

The last segment of the work is opened by none other than Goethe, who delivers first a monologue about his life, then a <u>précis</u> of the history of the French Revolution. The four other authors in this <u>Totengespräch</u> enter the scene and pay homage to Goethe. They are of course curious about the course of events in Germany since Kotzebue's arrival (an interval of thirteen years). Goethe obliges with a "Kriegs= und Staatsgeschichte" which brings them to the year of his death.

Having apprised them of the political scene, Goethe next speaks of the state of the arts in Germany in very pessimistic terms. For Goethe, Europe herself has long since passed the period of flowering. The great age is no more: "Wir dürfen . . . wohl sagen, daß der deutschen Dichtkunst Aera / Mit uns geschlossen ist" (59). Hardly any poems are written and even if they were, they would find few readers. Goethe comments on the rise of the novella: "Ja, nicht einmal Romane liebt man mehr. / Sie sind zu lang. Novellen machen noch / Ihr Glück." (59). The dramatists wish to know how they have fared with posterity. Iffland, reports Goethe, has lost popularity, while Schiller's and Kotzebue's plays are still seen on the stage (61). Ballets, operas and melodramas have replaced comedy and tragedy.

Wieland summarizes Goethe's report: "Es hat mich der allmählige Verfall / Der Dichtkunst und der Bühne tief betrübt" (63). The situation is so bad that the poets thank the gods, no longer to be in the <u>Oberwelt</u>. The poets turn their attention away from the world ("wir [wollen] aus dem Gedächtniß / Die Schwächen menschlicher Natur verbannen" [67]), and the scene ends with a banquet (<u>Gast-mahl</u>) in the poets' quarters of Elysium.

Franz Grillparzer wrote two dialogues of the dead, both of which feature Frederick the Great as principal speaker. The first, a political dialogue written soon after the 14th of October, 1806,[47] remains a fragment. In the dialogue Voltaire informs Frederick of the current political situation. The dialogue breaks off with the arrival of many shades from the battle of Jena.

The second dialogue is of a much later date (1841) and is a literary satire of genuine quality In style both dialogues are well within the eighteenth century. The later piece has as its speakers two major figures from the eighteenth century, Frederick the Great and Lessing, and is a survey and evaluation of eighteenth-century German literature.

The dialogue between Frederick and Lessing opens with a strong satirical thrust:

> Friedrich.
> Ich ennuyiere mich und habe Lust, zu plaudern.
> Lessing.
> Und wenn ich meinesteils nun keine Lust dazu hätte?
> Friedrich.
> Du mußt dich eben fügen. Denk, ich war ein König.
> Lessing.
> Und ich ein deutscher Gelehrter. Ich füge mich.[48]

After this oblique attack on scholarly obsequiousness, the dialogue developes at once into a disputation on nature and art which contains at the same time a critique of the German literary world of the eighteenth century. The piece conveys a sense of true conversation; the speakers react to one another's remarks, yet Frederick is clearly the figure of authority. (Voltaire had been the authority in Grillparzer's earlier dialogue.) The dramatic quality of the conversation seems to result from a series of reversals of the ordinary; what is expected is not delivered, rather its reverse! One of the traditional <u>topoi</u> of the realm of the dead is overturned by Frederick in this dialogue. Speaking of the occupations of the dead Lessing states, "Man setzt eben diesseits fort, was man jenseits geübt" (134). This Frederick denies, for he is here pursuing German literature. Thus Grillparzer has cleverly turned the topic towards criticism of literature.

Frederick finds the Germans simply boring. Gellert was the best of them all. Lessing himself was an exceptional (<u>ausgezeichneter</u>) writer, but not a great poet. To this Lessing replies: "Ich weiß es, Sire" (135). Another reversal of the expected is Frederick's diagnosis of the German's problem: they have "Sitzfleisch" and "Fleiß beim Sammeln", but none for "Reifwerdenlassen" and "Ausarbeiten" (135). They do not have the kind of energy to produce literature (Frederick contrasts "books", which the Germans can produce, with "literature") such as Gibbon's opus or Montesquieu's autobiography.

Frederick denies that there is a German literature in the same sense that there is a French, Spanish or Italian literature. German literature is rather a resumé of all other literatures, consisting of imitation and drawn from secondhand experiences. Some of the Germans have been able to establish an individual style, such as Goethe, whom Frederick, however dislikes (136).

Next Frederick theorizes about art:

> Die Kunst beruht auf einer Steigerung des Wirklichen und
> unterscheidet sich eben dadurch von Natur. Nun haben
> aber gerade jene kleinen, hausbackenen Empfindungen,
> deren Wert in der Wirklichkeit ich nicht leugnen will, das
> Besondere, daß sie zu nichts werden, wenn man ihnen nur
> das Geringste nimmt oder zusetzt. Es muß daher auch die
> Darstellung, wenn sie sich an solche Zustände macht, aus
> einer künstlerischen zu einer bloß natürlichen werden,
> was das größte Unglück ist, das der Kunst irgend passieren kann. Solange das nun nur die ausgezeichneten Geister
> treiben, geht es noch an, denn Leute dieser Art fassen
> die Natur mit scharfen Sinnen auf, und das Wirkliche ist
> immer interessant, wenn auch nicht immer schön . . . .
> (170-171)

Thus only the truly great writers are able to describe the emotions tastefully. The Germans cannot appreciate good literature because they have no taste; they have feelings (Gefühle), but not Empfindungen (137). Lessing counters that German literature is presently admired by all of Europe. Frederick replies that foreigners praise what they do not know (137), and turns again to Goethe.

Goethe's earlier works are too natural, his later works too artificial. The best of them is Wilhelm Meister, which Frederick compares in stature and quality to Don Quixote. Schiller is for Frederick the German Racine, despite the deleterious influence of Shakespeare. Frederick suggests that Wallenstein, if compressed into five acts, would be incomparable (138). Shakespeare is "ein großer Wilder" (138), who gives a précis of nature, but not nature herself. The theme of lack of fealty to nature brings Frederick back to Goethe, who for Grillparzer's "Frederick" is an immoral poet: "Die gefallenen Mädchen sind seine Lieblingsfiguren, und die Wahlverwandtschaften sind abscheulicher als die französischen Schmutzromane" (139). Goethe not only brought German poetry to its height, he also was the cause of its decline (139). Lessing gives partial assent, and the dialogue comes to a close.

To what extent is this rather harsh indictment of German letters representative of Grillparzer's own views? Is Grillparzer here using his former hero Frederick as a mouthpiece for his own ideas? Could Grillparzer have agreed

with Frederick's denunciation of German literature? The critic Josef Nadler,
stating that Frederick voices the same opinions on German literature which Grillparzer had expressed a few years earlier in two essays on dramatic art in Germany, implies the affirmative.[49] In point of fact, however, "Frederick's" opinions are much more extreme than those in the essays on the dramatic arts, where
Grillparzer at one point contrasts German dramatic production before the eighteenth century unfavourably with that of the French and the English.

Further, it is difficult to accept that Grillparzer could earnestly have
believed Goethe's Wahlverwandtschaften to be as profligate as "Frederick" described it, even taken hyperbolically, yet if Grillparzer is equated with "Frederick"
then those words must also be Grillparzer's. Fortunately more direct expression
of Grillparzer's criticism of the novel is found in non-dialogic form. In his mem-
oirs Grillparzer says of Goethe's novel:

> Was in diesen Wahlverwandtschaften am meisten stört,
> ist gleich von vornherein die widerliche Wichtigkeit die
> den Parkanlagen, kleinlichen Baulichkeiten und derglei-
> chen Zeug, fast parallel mit der Haupthandlung, gegeben
> wird. Es ist als ob man ein Stück aus Göthes Leben läse,
> der auch seine unvergleichlichen Gaben dadurch zum Teil
> paralysirt hat, daß er fast gleichen Antheil an derlei Zeit-
> verderb wie an den wichtigsten Angelegenheiten seines
> eigentlichsten Berufes nahm.[50]

Grillparzer does not seem unduly disturbed by the moral issues of the novel; rather,
his criticism is aesthetic:

> Angedeutet ist Manches: Z. B. daß Charlotte früher
> selbst ein Verhältniß zwischen Eduard und Ottilien
> habe einleiten wollen, aber die abgeschmackten Park-
> geschichten nahmen allen Raum zur genaueren Entwick-
> lung fort. Abscheulich ist, wie sie jetzt dasteht, die
> Geschichte jener ehelichen Nacht, gleich in Verbindung
> mit der Gelegenheitsmacherei zwischen dem Grafen und
> der Baronesse.[51]

A form of the word "abscheulich" occurs both in Grillparzer's mem-
oirs and in Frederick's speech, yet the contexts are different. The comparison
shows that Frederick's comments must be taken as exaggerations and not as Grillparzer's opinions. It is more likely that Grillparzer, true to the tradition of the
eighteenth-century form, was presenting two points of view, both exaggerated to
achieve the dramatic effect. In the next to the last speech of the dialogue Frederick
admits that he is exaggerating: "Es hört uns niemand, da können wir schon ein wenig übertreiben" (139). Ending the dialogue with a shocking idea was Grillparzer's
way of heightening the sense of drama.

Nadler in his study of Grillparzer calls the poet's Totengespräch a
"sehr gescheite und gründliche Betrachtung der deutschen Literatur des achtzehn-

ten Jahrhunderts."[52] While its ideas may be "clever", they are hardly thorough. So many writers are omitted that it is impossible to suggest that it is thorough; nor is its scope limited to the eighteenth century. A dramatic dialogue of the dead is not really a suitable place for meticulous and detailed criticism of literature. It is rather more effective at presenting ideas impressively and vividly. Grillparzer realized the nature of the genre and utilized it to his best advantage.

Although the dialogue of the dead continued in the nineteenth century with Grillparzer as its central representative, the genre was as lonely during that period as Grillparzer himself. Relatively few Totengespräche were written in the nineteenth century, although a series of Moderne Totengespräche by "Lucian der Jüngere" did appear in Berlin in 1894. A translation of Walther Savage Landor's Imaginary Conversations of Literary Men and Statesmen was done in 1878. However, the relationship of Lucian and the nether world to nineteenth-century literature is a matter which needs further investigation.

NOTES

1 Satirical Totengespräche found in magazines have been treated in Chapters IV and V; this chapter will consider literary satires which for the most part are in non-periodic sources.

2 These are discussed in Chapter VI.

3 This piece is treated in Chapter III.

4 s. l., 1739. Subsequent references to this text will appear in parentheses in the present study.

5 G. Waniek, Gottsched und die deutsche Litteratur seiner Zeit (Vienna, 1897), p. 352.

6 Cologne, 1746, p. 3. The author does provide an Afterword for the satire which he signs "Der Wohlbekannte Verfasser". The work is not known to Holzmann-Bohatta.

7 Johann Geiler von Kaisersberg (1445-1510) was the author of Nauicula sive speculū fatuorū or Des hoch / wirdigen doctor Keiserspergs na- / rrenschiff . . ." (Straßburg, 1498), a collection of sermons based on Sebastian Brant's Narrenschiff.

8 Johann Wolfgang Goethe, Sämtliche Werke (Jubiläums-Ausgabe), XXIV (Stuttgart and Berlin, 1902), 244. Cited in Julius Zeitler's Goethe-Handbuch, II (Stuttgart, 1919), 49.

9 Goethe, p. 244.

10 Goethes Briefe, I (Hamburg, 1962), 160.

11 Goethes Briefe, p. 162.

12 Goethes Briefe, p. 160.

13 Wielands Werke, ed. Wilhelm Kurrelmeyer, XXI (Berlin, 1939), 123.

14 Synopses of the "plot" as well as division into "acts" may be obtained by consulting the studies by Bernhard Seuffert, J. E. Gemeinhardt and Roger Aryault.

15 Erich Schmidt, "Zu 'Götter, Helden und Wieland' ", Goethe Jb, I (1880), 378-379.

16 "Eine Quellenstudie zu Götter, Helden und Wieland", Beiträge zur Goethe Forschung, XVI (1959), 139-142.

17 Sämtliche Werke (Jubiläums-Ausgabe), XXII, 146.

18 Fischer-Lamberg, p. 140-141.

19 Fischer-Lamberg, pp. 141-142.

20 "Gespräch zwischen Voltaire und Hr. D. Bahrdten im Reiche der Todten, in welchem dieselben einander ihre Begebenheiten erzählen". [Mühlhausen], 1780. Subsequent references to this text are given parenthetically.

21 These initials probably stand for "Geheimer Rat Klotz". Biographical information given in the satire concurs with the facts of Klotz's life. In the thirty-second chapter of his autobiography Bahrdt speaks of "Geißelungen" by Klotz's journals and in the thirty-fifth chapter he refers to "Geh. Rat Klotz".

22 Hermann Schletter, Platner und Wezel. Kriegsscenen aus der Leipziger Literaturgeschichte 1781-82 (Leipzig, 1846), p. 4.

23 Rentsch, p. 36.

24 "Gespräch im Reiche der Todten zwischen D. Ernst Platner und Johann Karl Wezel über die in ihrem Leben mit einander geführten Streitigkeiten" (Halle, 1782). Subsequent references to this text are given in parentheses.

25 "Gespräch im Reiche der Todten zwischen den Leipziger Buchhändlern Adam Friedrich Böhme und Karl Friedrich Schneider, die Platner- und Wezelschen Streitschriften betreffend" (Halle, 1782).

26 "Gespräch im Reiche der Todten zwischen dem Antiquar und Sprachmeister, Adolph Friedrich Kritzinger, und dem Antiquar Petschke in der Ritterstrasse" (Halle, 1782).

27 August Gottlieb Meißner, "Lope di Vega, Leßing und Pastor Richter. Eine Anekdote aus der Unterwelt" (Leipzig, 1782). Subsequent references to this work are given in parentheses in the present study.

28 VI (Leipzig, 1784), 417-420.

29 Taschenbuch für die Verdauungsgesellschaft (Spashausen, 1784), pp. 69-89. Subsequent references to this work are given in parentheses in this study.

30 Leipzig, 1786. Schröckh is also credited with "Joseph II. in Elysium" (1790).

31 Constantinopel [Augsburg], 1789.

32 In order that the reader may judge for himself, the poem is reprinted here in the French original (see Oeuvres posthumes de Fréderic II, Roi de Prusse, VII (Berlin, 1788), 56).

> Je t'envie, ô bichon! ta fortune prochaine,
> > Mon coeur voudroit te la ravir;
> Le fort te fait passer dans les mains de la Reine,
> > Et te dévoue à la servir.
> > Ah! si le ciel vouloit par grâce
> Me métamorphoser sous ton extérieur,
> > D'abord j'occuperois ta place:
> La servir, l'admirer, ce seroit mon bonheur.

33 "Pluto, Hannibal, Alexander, Scipio, Epaminondas, Condé, Turenne, Marschal von Sachsen" and "Pluto, Asträa, Viele stumme Personen", II (1787), 7-14. For a discussion of Seybold's "Neue Gespräche" see Chapter VI. A few Totengespräche dealing with Frederick the Great are mentioned in Chapter III also.

34 Vienna, 1806. Reprinted by Hugo Thimig for the "Deutscher Bibliophilen-Tag in Wien 1928" (Vienna, 1928). Subsequent references to this text are given parenthetically.

35 Gustav Gugitz points out ("Joachim Perinet. Ein Beitrag zur Wiener Theatergeschichte", Jahrbuch der Grillparzer-Gesellschaft, XIV [Vienna, 1904], 179) that after her death Perinet had written a part for "Madame Perinet" in "Der Jahrmarkt in der Unterwelt".

36 Gugitz, p. 176.

37 Richard J. Allen, Johann Daniel Falk and the Traditions of German Satire. (Johns Hopkins University Dissertation, 1969), p. 178.

38 Allen, p. 202.

126

39 Elysium und Tartarus (January, 1806), p. [iv].
40 Elysium und Tartarus has been examined only through July. However, in its
    year of existence the magazine became progressively more and more politi-
    cally oriented.
41 Elysium und Tartarus (January, 1806), pp. 47-48.
42 For a detailed study of Falk's aesthetics see Richard J. Allen, "Johann
    Daniel Falk and the Theory of Characteristic Art", MLN, LXXXVI (1971),
    345-377.
43 Aristophanes, trans. Benjamin Bickley Rogers (Loeb Classical Library
    Edition), II (London, 1924), 423.
44 Notices at the beginning of each issue often explained which poets were in
    Elysium and which in Tartarus. Wieland is consistantly places in Elysium,
    Falk himself sometimes in Tartarus.
45 Quedlinburg and Leipzig, 1833. Subsequent references to this work are
    given parenthetically in the present study.
46 The work is not to be found in the usual reference works.
47 "Todtengespräch. Friedrich der Große, Voltaire, Prinz Louis von Preußen,
    Prinz von Braunschweig", Sämtliche Werke, ed. August Sauer, II, 6,
    (Vienna, 1923), 3-5.
48 Sämtliche Werke, I, 13 (Vienna, 1930), 168. Subsequent references to this
    piece are provided in parentheses.
49 Franz Grillparzer (Vienna, 1952), p. 216.
50 Grillparzers Werke. Erinnerungsblätter 1822-1841. VI (Vienna, 1924), 430.
51 Grillparzers Werke, p. 430.
52 Nadler, p. 216.

CONCLUSION

The many aspects of the dialogue of the dead, as they have been presented in this study, indicate the vitality which the form enjoyed in eighteenth-
century Germany, in the time of its renascence. The richness and quantity of these
dialogues testifies against the suppositions of previous scholars, whose evalua-
tions can be sorely misleading, especially where they attempt to assess the worth
of German Totengespräche.

The chronological appendix of dialogues at the end of this study provides a repository of materials for scholars of the social and intellectual life of
the period; the wide range of subjects within this list, moreover, attests the popularity of the form. This appendix, the most comprehensive bibliography presently available, is an essential contribution of this study, since it helps to make clear
that the dialogue of the dead is not so limited either to the satiric or the political
traditions as other writers have supposed. However, in the text of the study the
genre has been presented in all its important uses, emphasizing those which relate more directly to literary matters than to fields such as theology or political
history for which the form was also frequently employed.

The dialogue of the dead must be seen as an important literary genre
of the eighteenth century, for a surprising number were produced in Germany. Although it is difficult to estimate the exact figure since multiple and pirated editions proliferated, the number 500 would still be a conservative one. A great many
writers, including some of Germany's best known men of letters, realized the op-
portunities which the form offers and used them to good advantage. In some future
conversation in Elysium Goethe, Wieland, Bodmer Schubart, Meißner, Gottsched, Seybold and Grillparzer may recall with pleasure their contributions to the
form while on earth.

Several particular characteristics of the dialogue of the dead made it
attractive to a broad spectrum of writers. Often the dialogist's purposes were
moral, and to this end the dialogue in the form of a judgement scene provided an
excellent forum for the condemnation of vices and the rewarding of virtues. The
dialogue of the dead is also able to present an issue from multiple points of view,
since in the nether world the dead of all eras may engage in informative conversation. For the force of its judgement scenes and its presentation from several
points of view the Totengespräch owes much to its setting in the world below.

Many eighteenth-century dialogues of the dead tended to discursive-
ness since the form so perfectly complemented contemporary theories of didacticism in literature. While the dialogue of the dead usually stresses wit and intellectual discussion, it is not by nature static; rather it tends toward the dramatic.
And it is this dramatic quality which lends itself to a plurality of purposes and
imbues the form with a commendable flexibility.

Lucian's dialogues of the dead are satiric in purpose. Not surprisingly, satiric Totengespräche appear in Germany from an early date and remain

a constant throughout that period which so favoured Lucian. While Lucian's dialogues derive in part from literary situations, they rarely touch upon matters of literary criticism; that, however, is a principal raison d'être of many German dialogues of the dead. Often such satires offer insights into the critical controversies of the times and lampoon specific poets in revealing ways. Goethe's dramatic farce in the nether world best illustrates the use of the dialogue of the dead for the criticism of literature.

David Faßmann, a secretary and teacher of English in Leipzig, is usually credited with being the instigator of the dialogue of the dead in Germany. Although Faßmann was not without antecedents in the political field, it seems that he did start an important fashion which continued for many years. His monthly Entrevuen im Reiche derer Todten aroused vigorous emotions in many corners; most of the Entrevuen enjoyed several editions despite opposition from both Bodmer and Gottsched. Typically these lenghty dialogues relate matters of politics, history and biography. Yet David Faßmann was not the sole creator of dialogues in this style; Johann Zacharias Gleichmann and Christoph Gottlieb Richter must also be acknowledged for their contributions and innovations. While earlier studies held that these men were for the most part mere imitators of Faßmann, this study enumerates some of the significant differences between them in matters of style and intention.

Among the most vociferous of Faßmann's literary opponents were the editors of the German moral weeklies. Yet despite their opposition, these periodicals also availed themselves of the dialogue of the dead; by adopting the simpler styles of Lucian, Fénelon and Fontenelle they were able to maintain another tradition of the genre. The present study points out that the inclusion of dialogues of the dead in moral weeklies is a feature which the German editors did not take over from the English moral weeklies, but is a feature peculiar to the German publications. The moral weeklies employ the form for the castigation of vices such as galant behaviour, preoccupation with improper literature and pedantry. An esteem for the dialogue of the dead is also to be found in the miscellany magazines of the middle and last half of the century. These magazines display a particular fondness for Lucian and employ his method often to present particular poets in a different light.

Beginning in the 1760's German writers wrote collections of dialogues of the dead as had Lucian and his French disciples. Such writers of multiple dialogues of the dead tend toward classicism in style and form. One of the first of these was Wilhelm Ehrenfried Neugebauer, in whose dialogues, appropriately entitled "Versuch in Todtengesprächen", most characteristics of the classical orientation can be seen. Here, too, discussion of literary matters plays and important part. Other writers in this group are Bodmer and David Christoph Seybold. It is, however, in Wieland's dialogues, which contain such a charming mixture of wit, scholarship and grace, that the German Totengespräch reaches its zenith. While the tradition is continued in the nineteenth century by Franz Grillparzer, it remains neither a vital nor a widespread form after the first decade of that century. The genre is represented in the twentieth century by Fritz Mauthner's Totengespräche and Paul Ernst's Erdachte Gespräche.

This study hopes to raise the genre from the waters of Lethe which have covered it, and to restore a proper understanding of the illustrious talking shades. It also raises a number of problems which are not within the bounds of its investigations. That the dialogue of the dead needed a thorough study has been shown; a re-evaluation of the larger genre, the dialogue itself, and its place in eighteenth-century German literature is now necessary. Certainly more work on Wieland's dialogues is mandatory, for no existing study adequately outlines his many achievements with the dialogue.

Other possibilities for future research have been intimated by this study, among them the relationship between the dialogue of the dead and the drama. May not an author's dialogues be regarded as preliminary studies or preludes to his dramas? In the case of Bodmer the question is especially intriguing. Other questions concerning the dialogue of the dead, a form which brings together two (or more) figures from the past, and the historical drama stand in need of investigation since Leipzig, the place of publication of the Entrevuen, also saw the developement of theories of the historical drama by several of her literary sons.

Once the eye has become accustomed to recognize references to Totengespräche in the printed word of the eighteenth century, the frequency of such allusions to the Greek nether world is surprising. The implications of the claims of Sterne's Yorick to know the Elysian fields better than heaven itself must be investigated. Henceforth, studies of eighteenth-century critical controversies, social criticism and Motifgeschichte will have to take into consideration the activities in the fictive nether world since the shades so perfectly mirror the concerns of those more corporeally endowed.

This chronological listing of dialogues of the dead in the German language is intended to display the multifaceted nature of the genre. It will serve as a reference source, it is hoped, for other scholars.

Although complete title listings were, despite their length, regarded as the ideal, several exigencies of the research made this goal unrealizable. Many of the titles listed by Heinsius and Kayser are greatly abbreviated and often the works themselves are unavailable. Often the sources disagree. In instances where it was not possible to examine the dialogue firsthand, that information which seems the most reasonable and pertinent is given. Unless otherwise noted the works are anonymous.

After most titles a reference source is given. In some cases these show where the work is actually available; in others, however, it shows only the contributing bibliography from which the reference was taken.

The following abbreviations are used for frequently cited sources:

BasUB	=	Universitätsbibliothek Basel
BM	=	British Museum Catalogue
D	=	d'Ester
E	=	Egilsrud
Fdf	=	Faber du Faur
G	=	Georgi
GöUB	=	Niedersächsische Staats- und Universitätsbibliothek Göttingen
H	=	Heinsius
HbgUB	=	Staats- und Universitätsbibliothek Hamburg
HG	=	Hayn–Gotendorf
HJ	=	Harold Jantz Collection, Baltimore
JHU	=	Milton S. Eisenhower Library of the Johns Hopkins University
K	=	Kaschmieder
LpzUB	=	Universitätsbibliothek Leipzig
M	=	Meusel
MbgUB	=	Universitätsbibliothek Marburg
NsZk	=	Niedersächsischer Zentralkatalog
PrStB	=	Preussische Staats-Bibliothek
R	=	Rentsch
Ros	=	Rosenbaum
WidL	=	Widener Library, Cambridge

1542

Drei neue und lustige Gespreche wie der Wolf so etwan doch nicht lang ein Mensch
Heinz Wolfenbüttel genant in Abgrunt der Hellen vordamt sei. Reinweis
ausz dem Latein ins Deutsch geben. 1542. In: <u>Satiren</u> und <u>Pasquille aus</u>
<u>der Reformationszeit</u>, Oskar Schade, ed., I (Hannover, 1856), 99-144.
Ein lustig Gespräch der Teufel und etlicher Kriegsleute von der Flucht des großen
Scherrhansen Herzogen Heinrichs von Braunschweig. 1542. In: <u>Satiren</u>
<u>und Pasquille</u>, I, 54-67.

1683

Historische / Politische und Philosophische Krieg= und Friedens=Gespräch / Auf
das jetzt neu=eingehende 1683. Jahr. Worinnen auch allerley leß= und
merckwürdige <u>Discursen</u>, unter dem so genannten frantzösischen
Kriegs=<u>Simplicissimo</u>, in den Elisäischen Feldern / Aller Monatlich
deß gantzen Jahrs / abgehandelt werden.
s.l., 1683.
Kirchner   E   HG

1718

[Faßmann, David]. Gespräche in dem Reiche derer Todten. Leipzig, 1718-1738.
(Issued monthly; titles of the 240 <u>Entrevuen</u> vary.)
E   R   HJ   GöUB   WidL   FdF   LpzUB

1719

[Faßmann, David]. Die Gantz unvermuthete und plötzliche Ankunfft Caroli XII.
Letztern Königs von Schweden, In dem Reiche derer Todten, . . .
Nebst einer curieusen Entrevue und Gespräche, zwischen ihm und
seinem Schwager, dem in der Bataille bey Cliscow oder Bynschoff
in Polen, 1702. gebliebenen Herzog von Holstein-Gottorp . . . .
Zweyte Edition, Verbessert und . . . vermehret . . . .
Frankfurt and Leipzig, [2]1719. [4]1720. [5]1723.
K   HbgUB

1720

Ges räche im Reiche der Todten zwischen Gottlieb Wernsdorffen und . . . Gott-
fried Arnolden . . . .
Freystadt, 1720.
LpzUB
Unterredung in dem Reiche der Todten zwischen Pabst Innocentio XI . . . . und
dem Cardinal . . . . Julio Mazarini . . . .
Leipzig, 1720.
LpzUB

Abgenöthigte Critique der sogenannten Gespräche in dem Reiche derer Todten.
Halle, 1721.
E   R   PrStB   Stiftsbibliothek Zeitz, DDR
"Gespräch des Pluto, und des Diogenes, mit zween deutschen Romanhelden", Die
Discourse der Mahler, Stücke 13 and 14 (Zürich, 1721).
GöUB
Besonders curieuse Entrevue in dem Reiche der Todten zwischen den Gold=Machern,
dem Grafen Cajetani und dem Baron von Klettenberg . . . .
Hamburg, Halle, Leipzig und Nürnberg, 1721.
D   PrStB

1722

[Edzardus, Sebastian]. Des Welt=bekandten Neulich zu Paris durchs Rad executir-
ten Cartouche, Gespräch im Reiche der Todten mit Calvino und Jan-
senio. Den itzigen Vereinigungs=Schreibern zum sonderbahren Nach-
sinnen mitgetheilet.
s.l. & a. [Hamburg ?, 1722]
GöUB
[Edzardus, Sebastian]. Unterredung im Reiche der Todten / zwischen Cartouche,
Zvinglio, und Tossano. In die Feder gefasset / von Jacques de Villétes.
Aus dem Frantzösischen übersetzet / A. 1722.
s.l.
GöUB
Gespräche in dem Reiche derer Todten zwischen dem Güldenen Tafel-Dieb Nickel
Leisten und dem Kirchenräuber Lips Tullian. Erste Entrevue.
Frankfurt, Hamburg, and Leipzig, 1722.
[Zweite Entrevue] zwischen dem französischen Spitzbuben und Räuber
Cartouche und der im Hamburger Spinnhause gestorbenen Erzbetrügerin
Falsette.
Leipzig, [1722].
Landesbibliothek Hannover   D

1723

"Übereinstimmung der Mahler und der Scribenten" (= Diogenes and ten shades),
Die Mahler, oder: Discourse von den Sitten der Menschen, IV (Zürich,
1723), Stück 1
GöUB
"Pirrhus, Apicius", Die Mahler, oder: Discourse von den Sitten der Menschen, IV
(Zürich, 1723), Stück 7.
GöUB
Gespräche in dem Reiche der Todten unter den Spitzbuben, 4. Entrevue zwischen
dem englischen Strassen-Räuber Thomas Wilmst und dem moquanten
Nicol-Listischen Cammeraden Christian Müllern, worinnen beyde ihr

übelgeführtes Leben . . . auch die neuesten Begebenheiten . . . der
   Cartouchianer in Frankreich . . . .
   Frankfurt, Leipzig and Hamburg, 1723.
   HG
Vertraute Conferentz derer Einwohner im Reiche derer Todten über ihre im Rei-
   che derer Lebendigen gehabten Fata und Zufälle. Sechs Zusammen-
   künfte.
   Altona, 1723.
   D   R   HG

1724

Gespräch im Reiche derer Todten zwischen den abgeschiedenen Geistern eines
   Ochsen und eines Schweines.
   Leipzig, 1724.
   R

1725

"Lucretia, Cleopatra und Proserpina" and "Proserpina, Mercurius, etliche
   Geister verstorbener Weibesbilder", Die vernünftigen Tadlerinnen, I
   (Leipzig, 1725), Stück 26.
   Hamburg, [3]1748.
   GöUB
Faßmann, David. Extraordinaires Gespräche in dem Reiche derer Todten, Be-
   stehende In einer Entrevue zwischen dem Tornischen Ober-Präsiden-
   ten Roessner, welcher, im December des letztverwichenen 1724ten
   Jahres, decolliret worden, Und dem Stamm-Vater, auch Stiffter des
   Jesuiten Ordens Ignatio von Loyola . . . .
   s.l., 1725.
   LpzUB   K
Dramatisches Gespräch der enthaupteten Thornischen Bürger in Elysium.
   s.l., 1725.
   R
Besonderes Gespräch im Reich der Todten zwischen dem . . . Praesidenten . . .
   der Stadt Thorn, Johann Gottfried Rößner, . . . und M. Jos. Weiland.
   Frankfurt and Leipzig, 1725.
   LpzUB
Unpartheiisches Gespräch im Reiche der Todten zwischen Johann Diazio und Jo-
   hann Gottfried Rössnern . . . .
   Berlin, Frankfurt and Hamburg, 1725.
   LpzUB
Gebundenes Gespräch im Reiche der seeligen Todten zwischen dem Bürgermeister
   Rößern und denen . . . enthaupteten Thornischen Bürgern.
   s.l., 1725.
   LpzUB
Neu=eingelauffene und nöthige Continuation zu der, in dem Reiche der Todten, ge-

136

haltenen Entrevue zwischen Rösner und . . . Luther.
Leipzig, 1725.
PrStB
Die Assemblée Unglücklicher Verliebten im Reiche der Todten . . . worinnen
Aminandors und Rosimena . . . Leben und Liebes-Händel . . . .
Assemblée 1-3.
Frankfurt and Leipzig, 1725.
Kirchner   E
Die Andere Assemblee Unglücklicher=Verliebten im Reiche derer Todten, Worin-
nen Melidors, Einer von Geburt schlechten an Schönheit aber vollkom-
menen Person, Und Amaliere, Einer schönen Coquette Leben und
Liebes=Händel, auch die daraus erfolgten unglücklichen Fälle dieser
beyden Personen mit beygefügter Moral beschrieben sind.
Frankfurt and Leipzig, 1725.
HbgUB
[Gleichmann, Johann Zacharias]. Gespräch im Reiche der Todten zwischen Luther
und dem Jurist Stryck über die Abschaffung der weitläufigen Prozesse
und des iuris canonici aus protestantischen Ländern.
Frankfurt and Leipzig, 1725.
M   R   MbgUB
[Gleichmann, Johann Zacharias].(Meusel credits dialogues of the dead to Gleichmann between the following persons:) zwischen der Päpstin Johanne
und einem Lutherischen Magister
zwischen einem Pilgrim nach Rom und Heinrich von Zütphen
zwischen Pallavicino und Trajano Boccalini
zwischen Paulo Odontio und Roberto Barns
zwischen Kaiser Günther und Johann Tetzel
zwischen Churfürst Johann Friedrich von Sachsen und dem Cardinal
von Sachsen-Zeitz
zwischen Herrmann, Churfürst und Erzbischoffen zu Cölln und D.
Johann Pfeffinger
zwischen Bartholom. Bernh. von Feldkirch und Bonifacio, der Thürin-
ger Apostel.
Frankfurt and Leipzig, 1725-1730.
M

1726

"Eudoxia, Ashasverus", Die vernünftigen Tadlerinnen, II, (Leipzig, 1726),
Stück 44.
GöUB
Besonders Curieuse Gespräche im Reiche derer Todten . . . [zwischen dem]
schwedischen Obristlieutenant Koch von Güllenstein und [Franz]
Laubler, Mörder des Dresdner Pastors Hahn.
Halle and Zerbst, 1726.
Frankfurt and Leipzig, 1730.
LpzUB   E

Curieuses und extraordinaires Gespräch in dem Reiche der Todten zweyer Königl.
    Phln. Geheimbder Cabinets-Ministers . . . August Ferdinand . . .
    Grafens von Pflug und . . . Friderici . . . Grafens von Vitzthumb.
    Halle and Magdeburg, 1726.
    R   LpzUB
Vertraute Unterredung zwischen dem . . . ermordeten Lutherischen Prediger
    . . . Hahn und . . . Johann Huß . . . .
    Frankfurt and Leipzig (also Dresden?), 1726.
    R   PrStB

1727

Besonders curieuses Gespräch im Vorhofe des Reichs der Todten zwischen zwey
    grossen . . . Dieben, Räubern und Mördern, nemlich Nicol Listen
    und Lips Tullianen . . . .
    Frankfurt, Leipzig and Nürnberg, 1727.
    HG   PrStB

1728

Curieuses drittes Gespräch im Vorhofe des Reichs der Todten zwischen zweyen
    Dieben, nemlich: Valentin Runchen (?) . . . und Hanss Gideon Perman-
    nen.
    Frankfurt, Leipzig and Nürnberg, 1728.
    PrStB
Der im Reiche derer Todten aufgerichtete Schauplatz unglücklicher Menschen,
    oder seltsame Lebens-Beschreibung solcher Personen, die durch ihr
    unartiges Leben ein trauriges Ende genommen, mit moralischen An-
    merckungen. . . .
    Leipzig, 1728.
    BM
Gespräche im Reiche der Todten unter den Münzen. Erste Entrevue.
    s.l., 1728.
    GöUB
Politisches Gespräch im Reich der Todten zwischen dem Eulogius Schneider und
    Luzifer.
    s.l., 1728.
    Zürich Zentralkatalog
Schultze, Peter. Preussischer Todes-Tempel worinnen Verstorbene Personen
    . . . miteinandern redend vorgestellt werden.
    s.l., 1728-29 (monthly).
    E   BonnUB

1729

Besonders=Curieuses Gespräch in dem Reich derer Todten, zwischen Zweyen
    . . . Ziegeuner=Spitzbuben Hemperla und Gabriel . . . . Hamburg, 1729.
    Herzog-August-Bibliothek Wolfenbüttel

Besonders curieuses Gespräch Im Reich der Todten / Zwischen zweyen im Reich
    der Lebendigen hochberühmten Männern, Christian Thomasio, . . .
    und August Hermann Francken / . . . .
    s. l. , 1729.
    GöUB   LpzUB
Curieus- und extraordinaires Gespräch in dem Reiche derer Todten . . . zwischen
    . . . dem General-Feld-Marschall Jacob Heinrich, Grafen von Flem-
    ming, und dem Rath und Cantzler Georgio, Grafen von Werther.
    Frankfurt, 1729.
    R   PrStB   LpzUB
Gespräche im Reiche der Todten zwischen Dem Hochberühmten Wittenbergischen
    General-Superintendenten und Professore Theologiae D. Gottlieb
    Wernsdorffen und dem gleichfalls Weltkundigen Perlebergischen In-
    spectore und Pastore Gottfried Arnolden, Darinnen beyder Männer
    merckwürdiger Lebens=Lauff / nebst anderer curieusen Particulari-
    täten anzutreffen.
    Freystadt, 1729.
    GöUB
[Gleichmann, Johann Zacharias]. Curieus Gespräche in dem Reiche derer Todten,
    zwischen den 2. Thüringischen Grafen Ludwig dem Springer, und Lud-
    wig von Gleichen.
    Frankfurt and Leipzig, 1729.
    R   PrStB
[Gleichmann, Johann Zacharias]. Gespräch im Reiche der Todten zwischen
    Roeßner und Huß.
    Leipzig and Frankfurt, 1729.
    R

                            1730

Ausserordentliches Gespräche im Reiche derer Todten zwischen Gottfried Wilhelm
    Leibnitzen und . . . Johann Franciscus Buddeo . . . . 1. und 2. Theil.
    s. l. , 1730.
    R   PrStB
Ausserordentliches Gespräch im Reiche derer Todten, zwischen der Königinn von
    Pohlen . . . Christiana Eberhardina und der Königinn von Dennemarck
    Louysa.
    s. l. , 1730.
    PrStB
Curieuses Gespräch im Reiche derer Todten zwischen zweyer k. Pohln. und
    Churfl. Sächsischer . . . Feld-Marschalle . . . Heinrich dem VI und
    Hans Adam von Schöningen.
    s. l. , 1730.
    PrStB
Curiöses Gespräch zwischen dem bekannten Autor der bezauberten Welt und dem
    ehemaligen Prediger in Holland, Balthasar Beckern, der beinahe wenig
    vom Teufel geglaubet, und zwischen dem in ganz Teutschland berühm-

ten Theologo Christian Scrievern, der einen Menschen zurecht ge-
bracht so einen Pakt mit dem Teufel gemacht, darinnen nebst ihren
Lebensbeschreibungen von allerhand denkwürdigen Sachen als Engeln,
Erscheinungen der Geister, dem Teufel, Zauberern, verschiedenen
Sprüchen der Heiligen Schrifft, so davon handeln, vornehmlich aber
von der Frage gehandelt wird, ob es Menschen gebe, die einen Pakt
mit dem Teufel gemacht hätten und was dieser sonst anhängig.
Frankfurt and Leipzig, 1730.
Leipzig and Braunschweig, 1731-34.
D   R   PrStB   LpzUB   HG
Historisches Jubel=Gespräch in dem Reiche derer Todten, zwischen D. Martin
Luthern und Johann Tetzeln. Worinnen beyder Personen gantz sonder-
barer Lebens=Wandel, wie auch die Geschichte der Reformation und
Ablas=Krames, nebst vielen andern Realien, kurtz deutlich und unge-
heuchelt beschrieben ist, Mit Kupffern.
Hamburg, 1730.
Continuation oder Fortsetzung des [historischen Jubel=Gespräches]
. . . In welchem die völlige Geschicht der Reformation Lutheri, nebst
denen sonderbaren Fatis des Tetzels / kurtz / deutlich und ungeheu-
chelt ist.
Hamburg, 1730.
GöUB

1731

Curieuses Gespräch im Reiche der Todten, zwischen Zweyen grossen Philosophis
. . . Rüdigern . . . und . . . Cartesio.
s.l., 1731.
PrStB
Curieuses Gespräch im Reiche derer Todten, zwischen . . . Johann Friedrich
Mayern . . . und Johann Wilhelm Petersen.
s.l., 1731.
R   PrStB
Curiöses Gespräche in dem Reiche derer Todten, zwischen der Contusche und
Adrienne.
s.l., 1731.
Ros
Gespräch im Reiche der Todten zwischen Pater Girard und Pater la Chaise.
2 Theile.
Cöln, 1731.
H
Gespräch im Reiche derer Todten, zwischen zweyer ehemaligen Staats=Leuten,
von dem Fall eines Ministers im Reich der Lebendigen . . . .
s.l., 1731.
PrStB
Ost=Indisches Gespräch in dem Reiche der Todten zwischen Bartholomäo Ziegen-
balg königl. dänischen Missionario . . . und Johann Cocceo, einem

holländischen Schiff=Prediger.
Frankfurt, 1731.
PrStB

1732

Besonderes Gespräche In dem Reiche derer Todten, Zwischen D. Martin Luthern
Und Einem den 15. Junii 1732 zu Altenburg verstorbenen Saltzburgi-
schen Emigranten Hannß Mosegger genannt. Darinnen gantz gründlich
und nach allen Umständen beschrieben wird, wann, wie, und wodurch
die Saltzburger zu der Erkantniß der Evangelischen Religion gekommen, was sie um derselben willen vor Verfolgungen ausgestanden, wie
sie von Hauß und Hof verjagt, was sie in ihrer Durchreise in Evangel.
Städten vor besondere Güte und Wohlthaten genossen, und wie sie endlich im Pohlnischen Preussen ankommen, und mit Hauß und Hof, Acker
und Vieh wiederum reichlich beschencket und versorget worden.
Berlin, 1732.
HJ   R   LpzUB   PrStB
Curieuses Gespräche im Reiche derer Todten zwischen zweyen Durchl. . . .
Hertzogen, als nehmlich Hertzog Moritz Wilhelm von Merseburg,
und Hertzog August Wilhelm von Braunschweig=Wolfenbüttel . . . .
s.l., 1732.
Herzog-August-Bibliothek Wolfenbüttel
Gespräche im Reiche der Todten zwischen Christian Gerbern und Johann Daniel
Schwerdtnern . . . . 2 Thle.
s.l., 1732.
Georgi
Gespräch im Reich der Todten zwischen zweyen Franckfurther gewesenen bürger-
lichen Ober-Offiziers, Capitain Henrici und Lieutenant Schmeltzer,
durch einen . . . Geist in das Reich der Lebendigen an den halb-ehr-
würdigen Hector Diez, Ritter zum rothen Pantoffel und in seinen Ge-
dancken vocirten Hof-Predigern zu guten Leuten bey Franckfurth . . .
übersandt von seinem . . . Patronen und Ordens-Herrn.
[Frankfurt], 1732.
Stadt-Bibliothek Frankfurt
Curieuses Gespräche Im Reiche der Todten Zwischen Frau Catharina Lutherin
gebohrne von Bohra Des unsterblichen Mannes GOttes Herrn D. Martin
Luthers Ehefrau, Und zwischen Frau Bernardin Herrn Bartholomäi
Bernard von Veldkirchen Des ersten verheyratheten Evangelischen
Predigers Eheliebste Darinnen beyder Weltgeprießenen Frauen beson-
dere Lebens Geschichte nebst verschiedenen Denckwürdigkeiten die
Nachkommenschafft Lutheri betreffend auf eine anmuthige Art beschrie-
ben werden.
Frankfurt and Leipzig, 1732.
HJ   R

Gespräche im Reiche derer Todten, zwischen . . . Johann Arndten . . . und D.
Philipp Jacob Spenern / . . . Darinnen die Lebensgeschichte des Welt-
bekannten Johann Arndts ingleichen verschiedenes von denen Streitigkeiten wegen seines wahren Christenthums angeführet, auch von andern
seinen Büchern gehandelt wird. 3 Thle.
s. l., 1733.
LpzUB

Gespräche im Reiche der Todten zwischen . . . Ludewig XIV und Francisco Ludo-
vico . . . die jetzigen . . . Pohinischen Conjuncturen betreffend.
s. l., 1733.
LpzUB

Gespräche im Reiche derer Todten, zwischen Zweyen grossen Königen unserer
Zeit, Nehmlich Dem Könige von Pohlen / und Chur=Fürsten zu Sachsen / Friedrich August / Und Dem Könige von Sardinien / und Hertzoge
von Savoyen / Victor Amadeo, Darinnen Beyder Herren ausserordent-
liche Lebens=Geschichte und Helden=Thaten . . . beschrieben werden.
s. l., 1733.
LpzUB   R

Entrevue Oder Gespräche In dem Reiche derer Todten, Zwischen Sr. Königl. Maj.
in Pohlen und Churfl. Durchl. zu Sachsen Friderico Augusto, Und Sr.
Kön. Maj. von Engeland und Churfl. Durchl. zu Hannover Georgio I.
Worinnen beyder vortrefflicher Monarchen, insonderheit aber Königs
Augusti Helden=Thaten und besondere Lebens=Geschichte unpartheyisch
beschrieben.
Frankfurt, 1733.
HJ   R

Gespräch im Reiche derer Todten zwischen . . . General=Feldt=Marschall Hertzog
Frantz Heinrich von Luxemburg und Doct. Johann Fausten . . . Der
bösen, gottlosen sichern Welt zur Warnung auffgestellt und gedruckt.
Leipzig, 1733.
R   HG   LpzUB

Curieuse Gespräche im Reiche derer Todten zwischen Zweyen Feld=Marschallen /
Dem Frantzösischen Hertzog von Berwyck, Der bey Philippsburg von
einer Falconet Kugel geblieben, Und dem Kayserlichen Feld=Marschall
Graf Mercy, Der im letzten Treffen in Italien erlegt worden, Darin-
nen beyde Herren von dem itzigen Kriege und andern denckwürdige
Sachen discoursiren. Erster Theil.
s. l., 1734.
GöUB

Gespräche im Reiche der Todten über die jetzigen Conjuncturen in Pohlen, Zwi-
schen dem General=Feldmarschall Flemming und General Kyau.
Frankfurt and Leipzig, 1734.
R

Gespräch im Reich der Todten, zwischen zweyer weltberuffenen Männern. Da der
erste: Herzog von Berwick / sich . . . auf dem Schauplatz dess Kriegs,
der andere: Christianus Democritus / sich im Feder-Krieg . . . be-
rühmt gemacht . . . .
Cosmopoli, 1734.
BasUB

1735

Ausserordentliches Gespräch im Reiche der Todten zwischen dem ersten Menschen
Adam und Joseph dem Pfleg=Vatter des Herrn Christi; Darinnen be-
sonders von dem grossen Werck der Schöpffung, und vielen Theologi-
schen, Philologischen und Physicalischen Sachen auf eine anmuthige
Art geredet wird. Erster Theil.
Frankfurt and Leipzig, 1735. (Between 1735 and 1737 fourteen parts
of this series were published.)
PrStB   HG   H   E   R   Staatsbibliothek München
[Faßmann, David]. Die neu=entdeckten Elisäischen Felder und was sich in denen-
selben sonderbares zugetragen . . . .
Parts 1-4 Frankfurt and Leipzig, 1735-1740;
Part 5 Frankfurt, Leipzig and Rudolstadt, 1742.
E
Gespräch in dem sogenannten Reich der Todten; zwischen dem vor Philippsburg
erschossenen Duc de Berwick und dem in der Schlacht bei Parma
gleichfalls gebliebenen Grafen von Mercy. Worinnen deren Leben und
merckwürdige Thaten . . . erzehlet werden. Nebst einem nöthigen
Vorbericht . . . .
Frankfurt, 1735.
MbgUB
[Gleichmann, Johann Zacharias?]. Gespräche In dem Reiche derer Todten Zwi-
schen Zweyen grossen Kriegen Helden, dem Durchlauchtigsten Prin-
tzen Ludewig von Würtemberg Ihro Kayserl. Majest. Feld Marschall,
der bey der letzten Action mit denen Frantzosen bey Guastalla auf dem
Bette der Ehren geblieben, und Ihro Excell. dem Königl. Pohlnischen
und Churfürstl Sächß. General Feld=Marschal etc. Christoph Heinrich
Grafen von Wackerbarth, darinnen dieser beyder Herren besondere
Lebens-Geschichte auf eine anmuthige Art vorgetragen werden.
s. l., 1735.
HJ
Gespräch in dem sogenannten Reich der Todten, zwischen Georg I., König von
Großbrittanien . . . und August II., König von Polen.
Frankfurt, 1735.
HG

1736

["Judgement scene"], Die mühsame Bemerckerin derer Menschlichen Handlungen, Stück 27 (Dantzig, 1736).

Christfels, P. E. Gespräch (zweytes, drittes) in dem Reiche der Todten über die
Bibel und Talmud, zwischen dem seeligen Herrn Doctor Luther und
. . . R. Salomon Jarchi . . . zusammen getragen von einem bekandten
Gerzedek P. E. C. und mit einer Vorrede versehen von Herrn Johann
Helwig Engerer.
Schwalbach, 1737-1739.
H   PrStB   BM
Kuriöses Gespräch zwischen dem Herzog von Würtemberg, Eberhard Ludwig und
Karl Alexander.
Frankfurt and Leipzig, 1737
D   R

[Knorr, Georg Wolfgang]. Historische Künstler-Belustigung oder Gespräch In
dem Reiche derer Todten, zwischen denen beeden Welt=bekannten
Künstlern Albrecht Dürer und Raphael de Vrbino, Worinnen deren
Geburt, Leben, Historische Begebenheiten, Verrichtungen und Tod,
mit kurtzen Anmerckungen, zur Erkenntnuß ihrer Wercke, nebst
ihren wahren und eigentlichen Portraits, nach deren beiten Stucken
accurat vorgestellet werden. Erstes Stuck.
Nürnberg, 1738.
HJ
Merckwürdige Staats-Assemblée In Dem Reiche derer Todten, Zwischen einem
gantz besondern Klee-Blat; Oder Dreyen unartigen Staats-Ministern,
Nemlich Dem Duc de Ripperda, dem Grafen von Hoymb, Und dem
Juden Süsz-Oppenheimer . . . .
Amsterdam, 1738.
FdF

Curieuse Gespräche im Reiche derer Todten /Zwischen dem Heldenmüthigen
Carolo dem XII, Könige von Schweden . . . Und . . . Friderico IV.
Hertzoge zu Hollstein=Gottorp, . . . Insgleichen dessen Sohne Carolo
Friderico . . . Worinne dieser dreyen hohen Personen Helden=Thaten
. . . enthalten.
s.l., 1739.
LpzUB
Gespräche zwischen Johann Christian Günthern aus Schlesien In dem Reiche der
Todten / Und einem Ungenannten In dem Reiche der Lebendigen: In
welchem Beyde des Erstern 1738 zu Breslau gedruckten Lebenslauf
beurtheilen; Und bey dieser Gelegenheit ihre Gedanken über einige
itztlebende deutsche Dichter und Dichterinnen eröfnen. Nebst eine
Zueignungsschrift an Seine Hochedeln, den Herrn D. Steinbach in

Breslau. Das erste Stück.
s. l., 1739.
GöUB
Gespräche im Reiche der Todten zwischen Carl XII. König von Schweden, und
August II. König von Pohlen. 2 Thle.
Berlin, 1739-42.
H
Gespräche im Reiche derer Todten zwischen dem Knees Alexi Dolgorucki, Ehe-
mahligen Rußischen Reichs=Cantzler, . . . Und seinem Sohne Knees
Johann Dolgorucki, Welcher am 6. Nov. 1739. zu Novogrod schwerer
Verbrechen halber, mit dem Rade bestraffet, und ihme sodann der
Kopf abgehauen worden, Insgleichen seinen Brüdern . . . , Welchen
beyden nebst ihren Vatter . . . gleichfalls . . . wegen des Lasters
beleidigter Majestät, und anderer grossen Verbrechen halber . . .
die Köpffe abgeschlagen worden; . . . Leben und Uebelthaten . . .
s. l. & a.
LpzUB
Gespräche im Reiche der Todten zwischen Telemach und Robinson Crusoe. 2 Thle.
Frankfurt and Leipzig, 1739. 1740.
H

1740

Gespräche im Reiche der Todten zwischen Friedrich Wilhelm, König in Preussen
und Piasto . . . . 2 Thle.
Altona, 1740.
R   H
Preußisches Militairisches Todten=Gespräch vom General bis zum Profoß. Mit
Poetischer Feder entworffen.
s. l., 1740.
GöUB
Merckwürdiges Gespräch im Reiche der Todten zwischen den ersten Erfindern
der Buchdrucker=Kunst, worinne von dem Ursprung / Fortgang /
und übrigen Schicksalen derselben gehandelt, und insbesondere der
Stadt Mayntz der Ruhm von der Erfindung solcher Kunst vindiciret
wird: in dem Dritten Buchdrucker=Jubilaeo der curiösen Welt nebst
einigen remarquablen Neuigkeiten aus dem Reiche der Lebendigen
mitgetheilet.
Erfurt, 1740.
GöUB   E
Gespräche im Reiche der Todten zwischen Leopold I Römischen Kaiser und Peter I.
Russischen Kaiser.
Frankfurt, 1740.
H

Gespräche im Reiche der Todten zwischen der Russischen Kaiserin Anna Iwanowna und Pabst Clemens XII. 2 Thle.
> Berlin, 1741.
> R   H

Gespräch im so genannten Reiche der Todten, zwischen Friedrich Wilhelm, Könige in Preussen und Churfürsten von Brandenburg . . . und Carl, Landgrafen zu Hessen=Cassell etc. Darinnen beyder . . . Ruhm=volles Leben und Helden=Thaten samt andern dahin gehörigen merckwürdigen Umständen, aus zuverläßigen Nachrichten, glaubwürdig erzehlet werden.
> Frankfurt, 1741.
> MbgUB

Gleichmann, Johann Zacharias. Curiöses Gespräch im Reiche der Todten, zwischen der Päbstin Johanna, und dem berühmten Friderico Spanhemio, welcher die Wahrheit der Historie von dieser Päbstinn in einem gelehrten Tractat nachdrücklich behauptet hat.
> Frankfurt and Leipzig, 1741. ²1744.
> NsZk   M   PrStB   R

Schlegel, Johann Elias. "Democritus. Ein Todtengespräche." Belustigungen des Verstandes und des Witzes, I (Leipzig, 1741), 101-126.
> JHU   E   R

Auserlesenes Gespräch in dem so genannten Reiche der Todten zwischen dem Königl. Preußischen General=Lieutenant der Cavallerie von der Schulenburg, und dem Königl. Ungarisch= und Böhmischen General Römer, den gegenwärtigen Krieg in Schlesien, Böhmen und Oesterreich betreffend.
> 1. Theil. Frankfurt and Leipzig, 1742.
> 2. und 3. Theil Frankfurt and Görlitz, 1742.
> PrStB   E   H   LpzUB

Gespräche im Reiche der Todten zwischen der Kaiserin Wilhelmina Amalie und Clemens XII. 4 Thle.
> Berlin, 1742.
> H

Gespräche im Reiche der Todten zwischen Ziska, dem Generalmajor von Werdeck und von Palland.
> Berlin, 1742.
> H

Gespräch im Reiche derer Todten zwischen der letzt=verstorbenen beyden grossen und Welt=berühmten Monarchen dem Könige Augusto II. von Pohlen und dem Könige Fridr. Wilhelmen von Preussen. Darinnen beederseits höchst=curieuses und ausnehmend merckwürdiges Leben, samt andern damit connectirten Historischen Wahrheiten der neuern Zeit

aufrichtig erzehlet werden. I., II., III. Entrevue.
Frankfurt and Leipzig, ³1742.
LpzUB
[Gespräch zwischen] Karl VI. und Friedrich Wilhelm I.
Köln, 1742.
R
Gespräch, zwischen Socrates dem Ober=Aufseher in dem Reiche der Geister und
dem letzt=verstorbenen Römischen Kayser Carolus VI.
Frankfurt, 1742.
LpzUB

<u>1743</u>

Auserlesene Gespräche im Reiche derer Todten, zwischen . . . Churfürsten von
der Pfaltz, Carl Philipp, und . . . Fleury . . . Premier-Ministre
in Frankreich . . . .
Leipzig and Braunschweig, 1743.
NsZk
Neuere und anderweite Gespräche in dem Reiche derer Todten dritte Entrevüe
zwischen dem Churfürsten von der Pfaltz, Carl Philipp, und dem
Cardinal von Fleury . . . .
Berlin, 1743.
PrStB
Gespräche im Reiche der Todten zwischen dem Freyherrn von Kyau und dem Duc
de Roquelor. Entrevue 1 and 2.
Frankfurt and Straßburg, 1743.
PrStB   R
Der stillen Gesellschaft im Reiche derer Todten Besondere Anmerkungen über die
jetzigen Zeit= und Staats=Läuffte der Welt, Darinnen Was zur Historie,
Geographie, Genealogie und Heraldic gehöret, Nebst denen neuesten
Begebenheiten aufs sorgfältigste verhandelt wird, Wie auch einem An-
hange von unterschiedlichen gelehrten Sachen. . . .
Erfurt, 1743.
D

<u>1744</u>

Der durch die blutige Seeschlacht in dem Gewässer bei Toulon um sein eigenes
erlittenes Ungewitter in der Nordsee nach dem Reiche der Todten
eiligst fliehende Kronprätendent von Engeland, wie solcher am Fluß
Lethe den vortrefflichen Grafen von Khevenhüller antrifft, sich mit
ihm in ein Gespräch einlässet, darinnen sie beiderseits einander ihr
Leben erzählen, der Graf Khevenhüller endlich in die elysischen Felder transportiret, der junge Prätendent aber vom Schiffer Charon in
diese Welt wieder zurückgerissen wird, erstlich wo nicht eine Krone,
doch wenigstens einen Paßport vom Tode zu holen angenehmen Zeitvertreib mitgeteilt erste Entrevue.
Frankfurt and Leipzig, 1744.
D

"Todtengespräche. Timon. Pylades", Neue Beyträge zum Vergnügen des Verstan-
des und Witzes, I (1745), Stück 6, 527-536.
"Todtengespräche. Horaz. Orbil", Neue Beyträge zum Vergnügen des Verstandes
und Witzes, I (1745), Stück 5, 367-374.
GöUB
Neue Belustigungen des Gemüths. Auf das Jahr 1745. (Hamburg and Leipzig, 1745).
"Todtengespräche. Lucretia. Sappho. Cato", pp. 129-134; "Thais. Ein
Todtengespräche", pp. 236-239; "Ein Todtengespräch. Diogenes und
Alexander", pp. 338-343; "Merkur und Momus. Ein Todtengespräch",
pp. 508-513.
JHU
Gespräche im Reiche der Todten, Zwischen dem Freyherrn von Leibnitz und Mag.
Thümmig, über den gegenwärtigen Zustand der Weltweisheit . . . .
Leipzig, 1745.
LpzUB

Der Mahler der Sitten, I (Zürich, 1746), No. 43, "Gespräche der Todten, wider
die Unersättlichkeit der Länderbezwinger", 488-497.
Der Mahler der Sitten, II (Zürich, 1746), No. 49, "Todtengespräche zwischen
Romulus und Cartusche, wider die glücklichen Übelthäter", 196-206;
No. 75, "Todtengespräche zwischen Themistocles und Diogenes, von
der Vergnüglichkeit", 262-270; No. 82, "Todtengespräche zwischen
Julius Cäsar und Crispinus Hilarus, ob der größer sey, der das
menschliche Geschlecht fortpflanzet, oder der es verheeret", 347-360.
JHU
Das verwirrete und wieder beruhigte Reich der Todten. Eine Lucianische Satyre,
ohne Vorrede.
Cöln: Marteau 1746.
NsZK

[Gleichmann, Johann Zacharias]. Merkwürdige Staats- und Kaysergespräche im
Reiche der Todten. 3 Vol.
Erfurt, 1747-1751.
M   R
[Gespräch zwischen] Johann Adolf II. von Sachsen-Weissenfels und Johann Wil-
helm von Sachsen-Gotha.
Frankfurt and Leipzig, 1747.
R
Gespräche im Reiche derer Todten . . . Leopoldo, Fürsten von Anhalt=Dessau,
. . . und dem Königl. Frantzös. Marschall von Villars, Worinnen
beyder . . . Helden= Lebens= und Kriegs=Geschichte . . . mitgetheilt

wird. Entrevue 1 and 2.
Frankfurt and Leipzig, 1747.
Herzog-August-Bibliothek Wolfenbüttel

1748

Gespräche im Reiche der Todten zwischen Sim. Lord Lovat und Jacob Fiz-Roi.
2 Thle.
London (?), 1748.
H

1750

"Radamanthus: Oder Abbildung des Richterstuhls im Reiche der Todten", Das allegorische Bildercabinet oder anmuthige Sittenlehre durch Bilder, Erzählungen, Fabeln und Gleichniße. Stücke 14 and 15 (Lübeck, 1750).

1751

Freundschafftliche Unterredungen der Seelen David Faßmanns und Thomas
Hobbes', durch welche beyder Charakter moralisch zergliedert wer-
den . . . .
Wiesenthal and Malmesburg, 1751.
HG   K   Damberg
Gespräche im Reiche der Todten zwischen Broune und Holstein Beck. 3 Thle.
Frankfurt and Leipzig, 1751.
H

1752

Gespräche im Reiche der Todten zwischen Leopold Maximilian und Bonneval.
2 Thle.
s.l., 1752.
H
Merkwürdiges Gespräch im Reiche derer Todten zwischen Friderico . . . Könige
in Schweden und Landgrafen in Hessencassel und Christiano VI. gewesenen Könige in Dänemark und . . . höchstmerkwürdige Lebensgeschichte enthalten. Entrevue 1 and 2.
Frankfurt and Leipzig, 1752.
MbgUB
Sonderbar curieuses und sehr merckwürdiges Gespräch im Reiche der Todten
zwischen dem Weltberühmten Graf Moritz von Sachsen . . . und dem
auf dem Bette der Ehren in Italien verstorbenen Baron Johann Leopold von Bärenklau . . . mit unpartheyischer Feder aufgezeichnet von
einem Wahrheit liebenden.
Frankfurt and Leipzig, 1752.
MbgUB   R

Gespräche im Reiche der Todten zwischen Ludwig XIV. und Friedrich, König in
Schweden.
Braunschweig, 1753.
H

[Richter, Christoph Gottlieb?] . Extraordinaire Entrevue in dem Reich der Todten
zwischen zweyen Zeitungsschreibern, Herrn Johann Gottfried Groß
und Herrn Joseph Anton von Bandel.
s.l., 1753. (Eisenach, 1754?).
BonnUB   M   H

1754

Auserlesene Unterredungen abgeschiedener hoher Personen, Darinnen Monarchen,
Helden, hohe Bediente des Staats, grosse Gelehrte, geist= und weltli-
chen Standes, der alten, mitlern und neuern Zeit aufgeführet werden,
welche sich einander die merkwürdigsten Geschichte ihres Lebens und
was dahin einen Einflus hat erzelen, so daß man findet alles vor viele, und etwas vor alle aus denen bewärtesten Geschichtsschreibern
herausgezogen, und mit aufrichtiger Feder vorgetragen. 12 Stücke.
Erfurt, 1754-56.
GöUB

Gleichmann, Johann Zacharias. Merckwürdige und in der historischen Wahrheit
gegründete Ertzbischöffliche und Churfürstliche Gespräche in der
stillen Gesellschaft des Reichs der Todten, in welchen zuerst die Erz-
bischöffe und Churfürsten zu Maynz, Trier und Cölln, wie sie in ihren
Regirungen auf einander gefolget, auch alle weltliche Churfürsten,
nach der Successions- und Juris publici ordnung aufgeführet werden,
Und von ihnen alles Notable, so unter ihren Regirungen vorgefallen,
erzehlet wird; wobey zu Ende eines jeden Stückes auch das remarquab-
leste aus denen Reichen und Staaten der Welt mit vorkommet, und mit
einem vollständigen Register versehen.
Erfurt, 1754 (Title page.).
GöUB

Westphälische Bemühungen zur Aufnahme des Geschmaks und der Sitten (Lemgo,
1754), Stück 16, "Pluto, Merkur, einige Schatten", pp. 251-258; Stück 17,
"Todtengespräch. Vasman. Schwift.", pp. 332-338.
E

1755

Gespräche im Reiche der Todten zwischen Mahomed V. und Moriz Graf von Sach-
sen. 2 Thle.
Frankfurt and Leipzig, 1755.
H

"Gerichte in dem Felde der Wahrheit", Der Bienenstock. Eine Sittenschrift der
   Religion Vernunft und Tugend gewidmet, II (Hamburg and Leipzig,
   1756), 209-216.
   GöUB

[Faßmann der Jüngere, pseud.]. Gespräch zwischen den Königinnen von Polen
   und Preussen.
   s.l., 1757.
   Ros   K
Gespräche im Reiche der Todten, zwischen dem Königl. Preuss. General-Feld-
   Marschall Grafen von Schwerin und dem K. K. Oesterreichischen
   General Grafen Bathiani. Entrevue 1-4.
   Frankfurt and Leipzig, 1757.
   Kirchner
[Richter, Christoph Gottlieb]. Die Geschichte des jetzigen Kriegs zu unpartheyi-
   scher Erkenntniß seines Anfangs und Fortgangs in Gesprächen im
   Reiche der Todten vorgestellt. Erster Band. In Welchem die Historie
   von A. 1756 und A. 1757. in X. Stücken beschrieben ist. Nebst einer
   Vorrede von dem Gebrauche und der Absicht dieses Buchs, und einigen
   Zusätzen zu den darinne enthaltenen Nachrichten, von den vornehmsten
   Generals und andern hohen Officiers, die sich bey diesem Kriege einen
   Namen erworben, wie auch einem gedoppelten Register.
   Frankfurth and Leipzig, 1758. (Title page. The series was issued
   monthly from 1757 to 1763.)
   GöUB   R   E   WidL

Gespräche im Reiche der Todten zwischen dem . . . Pabst Benedict dem XIV und
   Kronprinz von Preussen August Wilhelm . . . politische Anmerkungen.
   Frankfurt and Leipzig, 1758.
   PrStB
Merkwürdiges Gespräch im Reiche der Todten zwischen dem königlich preuß. Ge-
   nerallieutenant von Winterfeld und dem Königl. polnischen und Chur-
   sächsische General . . . Grafen von Nostiz . . .
   Frankfurt and Leipzig, 1758.
   PrStB

[J. Ch. Rasche]. Vier Gespräche im Reiche der Todten zwischen Schwerin und
   Braun.
   s.l., 1758 (Frankfurt and Leipzig?)
   R   E   M

Gespräch im Reiche der Todten zwischen dem . . . kaiserlichkönigl. General
Joseph von Siskowiz und dem königlich. preuss. General und berühm-
testen Partheygänger Johann von Mayer darinne die Thaten beider Hel-
den . . . .
Frankfurt and Leipzig, 1759.
PrStB

Gespräch im Reiche der Todten, zwischen dem königl. preuß. General Major . . .
Johann von Mayr, und dem Feldherrn Franziscum von der Trenk . . .
Freiburg, 1759.
PrStB

Gespräch im Reiche der Todten zwischen dem Russischkaiserl. Generalfeldmar-
schal Steph. Födorowiz von Apraxin . . . und dem Königl. preuss.
Generalfeldmarschal Jacob von Keith . . . .
Frankfurt and Leipzig, 1759.
PrStB

Gespräch im Reich der Todten zwischen dem Urheber der Zusammenverschwörung
wider den König in Portugall Joseph de Mascarenhas, ehemaligen Herzog von Aveiro und Robert Franz Damieno, bekannten Königsmörder
in Frankreich.
Frankfurt and Leipzig, 1759.
H   PrStB

Neues Gespräch im Reiche der Todten zwischen einem Königs- und Prinzenmörder
Johann Castell von Paris . . . und Franz Gujon sonst Balthasar Guera-
ro den Mörder des Prinzen Wilhelm von Nassau des Großen . . . Le-
ben geschildert . . . blutige Portugiesische Historie.
Lisabon (?), 1759.
PrStB

"Todtengespräch über die Genügsamkeit", Der Bienenstock, III (Hamburg and
Leipzig, 1759), 369-373.
GöUB

Gespräche im Reiche der Todten zwischen dem portugiesischen Jesuiten Gab.
Malagrida und dem Mörder König Heinrichs III. Clement.
Ulm and Stettin, 1760.
H   Weller

Neues gemeinnütziges Magazin für die Freunde der nützlichen und schönen Wissen-
schaften und Künste, II (1760), "Todtengespräch zwischen Dion und
Celo", 130-134; "Todtengespräch. Achilles und Homerus", 551-554;
"Zweytes Todtengespräch. Rhadamanthus, Cato der Censor, und Scipio
der Africaner".
GöUB

Unglücklicher Zeitpunct . . . der Jesuiten in Portugall . . . Malagrida / Charnock.
s. l. , 1760.
LpzUB

Gespräch im Reiche der Todten zwischen dem gewesenen Urheber, Ältesten und
  Bischof . . . Nikolaus Ludwig Grafen von Zinzendorf . . . und dessen
  ehemaligen Freunde, dem berüchtigten Schwärmer Johann Dippel . . .
  worinnen beider seltene Handlungen und Begebenheiten . . . .
  s. l., 1760.
  Zweytes Gespräch . . . .
  Frankfurt, 1761.
  PrStB

1761

[Gespräch zwischen] Georg II. und dem Großmogul.
  Braunschweig and Leipzig, 1761.
  R
[Gespräch zwischen] Georg II. von England und Erbprinz August Wilhelm von
  Preussen.
  Frankfurt, 1761.
  R
Neues gemeinnütziges Magazin, III (1761), "Ein Todtengespräch, zwischen dem
  Menippus und Lycambas", 255-6; "Zweytes Gespräch. Hieron und
  Pindar", 383.
  GöUB
Neugebauer, Wilhelm Ehrenfried. Die Fabeln des Fuchses nebst einem Versuch
  in Todtengesprächen.
  Glogau, 1761.
  HJ   JHU

1762

Gespräch im Reiche derer Todten zwischen August dem Dritten von Sachsen . . .
  und Peter dem Dritten . . . .
  Frankfurt and Leipzig, 1762. (Also 1764?)
  LpzUB   R

1763

Bodmer, Johann Jakob. Gespräche im Elysium und am Acheron.
  s. l., 1763.
  Goedeke
Wegelin, Jacob. Religiose Gespräche der Todten.
  Lindau, Frankfurt and Leipzig, 1763.
  M   E   R

1764

Erstes Gespräch Im Reiche der Todten Zwischen dem Bürgermeister Riemann,
  dem Rathsvierherrn Ueben und dem Bürgersyndicus Eilhardt aus

Nordhausen.

Frankfurt and Leipzig, 1764. Cologne (?), 1764.

PrStB

Gespräch im Reiche der Todten zwischen Leopold und dem Grafen von Dessau und
dem Grafen von Brühl. Stück 1.

Frankfurt and Leipzig, 1764.

MbgUB

Gespräch im Reiche der Verstorbenen zwischen Seiner königlichen Hoheit Friedrich dem dritten, Churfürsten von Sachsen und Sr. Excellenz dem
Grafen von Brühl.

Frankfurt and Leipzig, 1764.

LpzUB   PrStB

1765

"Diogenes, Rabutin." Der Mann ohne Vorurtheil (Vienna, 1765), 605-610.

GöUB

[Matthaei, A. R. S.]. Kurzes Gespräch im Reich der Todten, zwischen Herrn
D. Heumann aus Göttingen, und dem gelehrten Proselyten Frommann,
aus Halle, wegen der Lehre des seel. D. Luthers vom Heil. Abend-
mahl.

Leipzig, 1765.

Stadtbibliothek Nürnberg   E   R

[Paulus, Gottlob Christoph]. Gespräch im Reich der Todten zwischen dem ehemaligen Giessischen Kanzler, D. Christoph Matthäus Pfaffen, und
dem vor einiger Zeit verstorbenen Göttingischen Gottesgelehrten D.
C. A. Heumann, worinnen nicht nur allein der Crypto-Calvinismus
des letzern geprüfet, . . . von Georgius Christophorus Philalethes.
[Stuttgart], 1765.

M   E

1766

"Todtengespräch zwischen Horaz und einem neuern Gelehrten", Unterhaltungen, I
(Hamburg, 1766), 246-257.

GöUB

"Octavia und Julia, ein Todtengespräche", Der Verbesserer, I (Vienna, 1766),
Stück 25, 195-202.

"Ninon von Lenclos, und Phillis, ein Todtengespräche", Der Verbesserer, II
(Vienna, 1767), Stück 12, 89-96.

1767

"Gespräch zwischen Rhadamanthos und Zween Schatten", Baierische Sammlungen
und Auszüge zum Unterricht und Vergnügen (Weinmonath, 1767),
pp. 47-55. (A reprint from Der Bienenstock.)

GöUB   E

154

"Ariadne und Sapho ein Gespräch", <u>Theresie</u> und <u>Eleonore</u>, II (Vienna, 1767),
340-344.
GöUB

<u>1770</u>

Gespräch vom Zustand der Heiligen im Himmel, zwischen den Schatten Luthers
und Mosheims.
Hamburg, 1770.
H

<u>1772</u>

Kretschmann, Karl Friedrich. "Gellert und Rabener", <u>Sämtliche</u> <u>Werke</u>, V
(Leipzig, 1789), 201-214.
GöUB

<u>1773</u>

Gespräch in dem Reiche der Todten, zwischen den beyden ehemaligen Grafen,
Johann Friedrich Struensee, und Enewole Brand, und zwischen dem
ehemaligen Dänischen Reichshofmeister Cornifitz Ulefeld, worinn
die Erhebung und der Fall derselben, und die Hinrichtung der ersten
beyden umständlich beschrieben ist.
Koppenhagen, 1773.
R   WidL   GöUB
Göckingk, Leopold Friedrich Günther von. "Demokrit und Heraklit. Ein Gespräche
im Reich der Schatten". Hannover, 1773. Reprinted in <u>Auswahl</u> <u>der</u>
<u>besten</u> <u>zerstreuten</u> <u>prosaischen</u> <u>Aufsäze</u> <u>der</u> <u>Deutschen</u>, II (Leipzig,
1780), 214-269.
Herzog-August-Bibliothek Wolfenbüttel   E   PrStB
Goethe, Johann Wolfgang. "Götter, Helden und Wieland".
Kehl, 1774.
Die Zusammenkunft im Reiche der Todten der Grafen Struensee und Brand, und
der Graf Cornifitz von Uhlfeld, nebst Anekdoten und der Lebensge-
schichte derselben.
Frankfurt and Leipzig, 1773.
Zürich <u>Zentralkatalog</u>

<u>1774</u>

Gespräche im Reiche der Todten, zwischen beeden jüngstverstorbenen Königen,
Ludwig dem XV, von Frankreich, und Karl Emanuel von Sardinien.
In welchem die wichtige Geschichte beeder Monarchen erzehlt wird.
Frankfurt and Leipzig, 1774.
BasUB   H   WidL
Gespräch im Reiche der Todten zwischen dem verstorbenen Erlanger Zeitungs-

schreiber Groß und dem Licentiaten Richter.
Estrada (Nürnberg ?), 1774.
Wel

Korn, Christoph Heinrich. Gespräch im Reiche der Todten, zwischen dem Pater
Angelo, einem Jesuiten, und dem Ritter von Moncada, einem ehemali-
gen Tempelherrn; worinn die Geschichte dieser beeden berühmten
Orden, und die Aufhebung derselben, nebst andern merkwürdigen Din-
gen kurz und unpartheyisch erzehlet wird.
s.l., 1774. Theile 1-5.
HJ   GöUB
_____. Gespräch im Reiche der Todten zwischen Tottleben und AliBey.
Ulm, 1774.
M   H

1775

Korn, Christoph Heinrich. Anhang zu dem Gespräch im Reiche der Todten, zwischen dem Pater Angelo . . . und dem Ritter von Moncada . . ; worinn
noch mehrere Merkwürdigkeiten, die sich nach Aufhebung der Gesellschaft Jesu ereignet haben, kurz und unpartheyisch erzählt werden.
s.l. (Ulm ?), 1775.
GöUB   HJ
_____. Neue Nachrichten aus dem Reiche der Todten. Oder Fortsetzung der
Gespräche zwischen dem Pater Angelo, einem Jesuiten, und dem Ritter von Moncada, einem Tempelherrn; worinn noch mehrere die Gesellschaft Jesu betreffende merkwürdige Umstände, nebst dem, was
weiter nach der Aufhebung derselben erfolgt, erzählt, und die Briefe
über das Mönchswesen geprüfet werden.
GöUB   HJ
_____. Gespräch im Reiche der Todten zwischen dem Stifter des Jesuiten=
Ordens Ignatius Lojola und dem letztverstorbenen Pabst Clemens XIV.
3 Stücke.
s.l. (Ulm ?), 1775.
E   H   HJ   Staatsbibliothek München

Fäsi, Johann Konrad. Todtengespräche über wichtige Begebenheiten der mittleren
und neueren Geschichte.
Leipzig, 1775.
H   M   LpzUB

Reiche, Karl Christoph. Gespräche zwischen Töllner, Abraham und Sokrates.
Berlin, 1775.
M

1776

Abendstunden in lehrreichen und anmuthigen Erzählungen. XIV (Breslau, 1776),
"Gespräch im Reich der Todten zwischen Alcibiades und Tymon, dem
Menschenfeinde", 117-125; "Gespräch im Reich der Todten zwischen

156

Olivier Cromwel und dem Cardinal Richelieu", 141-147; "Gespräch im
Reich der Todten zwischen Thamas Kouli=Kan, Könige in Persien; und
der Prinzeßinn Al= = = verwittweten Großfürstinn von R= = =", 160-170.
Goedeke   Ros   H
Gespräche im Reiche der Todten zwischen den Päbsten Benedict XIV. und Cle-
mens XIV. 2 Thle.
Nürnberg, 1776.
H
Gespräch, im Reiche der Todten, zwischen einem Finanzier und einem Kommer-
zienrathe, über das Kommerzium ihres Vaterlandes.
Frankfurt and Leipzig, 1776.
Bibliothek Bipontina Zweibrücken   H

1777

Fäsi, Johann Konrad. Unterredungen verstorbener Personen über wichtige Be-
gebenheiten der ältern, mittlern und neuern Geschichte.
Halle, 1777.
H   M   LpzUB

1778

Gespräche im Reiche der Todten zwischen dem baierischen Pombal Gr. B. dann
dem ehemaligen Beichtvater P. St. und dem geistlichen Raths Direk-
tor P. v. O. aus sichern Urkunden und Handschriften zusammenge-
tragen, so nach dem Vulcan entrißen worden.
s.l., 1778.
GöUB
Neuere Gespräche im Reiche der Todten zwischen dem Staatsminister. und Kam-
merpräsidenten Grafen v. Berchem dann dem geheimen Rath Frey-
herrn v. Ickstatt.
s.l., 1778.
GöUB
[Lehner, J. M.]. Gespräche im Reiche der Todten zwischen Benedict XIII. und
Clemens XII.
Schwalbach, 1778.
E   H
Zapf, Georg Wilhelm. Zusammenkunft im Reiche der Todten zwischen Maximilian III.
Churfürsten von Bayern und Ganganelli unter dem Namen Clemens XIV
römischen Pabste.
Augsburg, 1778.
Gradmann

1779

[Bauer, Johann Jacob?]. Gespräch im Reich der Todten zwischen dem Buchhändler Johann Jacob Bauer und Kaufmann L** von den vielerley Arten des

Buchhandels in ihrem rechten Gebrauch und Mißbrauch; und über die
Frage: Ob ein Buchhändler ein Gelehrter sein muß? da die Wissen-
schaften die höchste Stuffe erreicht haben sollen.
Nürnberg, 1779.
M   H   Stadtbibliothek Nürnberg
"Gespräch im Reiche der Todten, zum Nutz und Frommen der Lebendigen, zwi-
schen Herrn Lithophus, Herrn Maron und Herrn Friedorf", Hanaui-
sches Magazin, II (Hanau, 1779), Stücke 38 and 40, 303-320, 329-336.
GöUB
Wekhrlin, Wilhelm Ludwig. "Über den deutschen Geist", Chronologen, I (Frank-
furt and Leipzig, 1779), 38-48.

1780

Gespräch zwischen Voltaire und Hr. D. Bahrdten im Reiche der Todten in welchem
dieselben einander inre Begebenheiten erzählen.
[Mühlhausen], 1780.
R   JHU
"Mags wol gethan seyn, das Volk aus der Dummheit zu reissen?" Der schweizeri-
sche Sammler (Winterthür, 1780), pp. 184-208. (Dialogue between
popes Gregory VII and Leo X.)
GöUB
Seybold, David Christoph. Neue Gespräche im Reich der Todten. Nach Luciani-
schem Geschmack.
Hanau, Frankfurt and Leipzig, 1780.
E   M

Wieland, Christoph Martin. "Dialogen", Teutscher Merkur, IV (1780), 67-75;
122-138.
JHU

1781

Entnersfeldt, E. F. F. Gespräch im Reiche der Todten zwischen Maria Theresia,
Frantz I und dem König von Portugal.
Vienna, 1781.
Holzmann-Bohatta   E
Gespräche im Reiche der Todten zwischen Cromwell, Penn, Heinsius und Sully.
Amsterdam, 1781.
H
Gespräche im Reiche der Todten zwischen Kaiserinnen Maria Theresia und Elisa-
beth.
Ulm and Stettin, 1781.
H

Braun, Johann Adam. Pater Martin Kochems hypochondrische Stunden im Reich
 der Todten. (Dialogue between Martin Kochem, Abraham a Santa
 Clara and Pater Pfyffer.)
 s.l., 1782.
 Goedeke

Gespräch im Reiche der Todten zwischen dem Antiquar und Sprachmeister,
 Adolpf Friedrich Kritzinger, und dem Antiquar Petschke in der Ritter-
 strasse. Halle. Auf Kosten des Verfassers. 1782. In: Schletter,
 Hermann Thomas. Platner und Wezel. Kriegsscenen aus der Leipziger
 Literaturgeschichte 1781/82.
 Leipzig, 1846.
 LpzUB

Gespräch im Reiche der Todten zwischen D. Ernst Platner und Johann Karl Wezel
 über die in ihrem Leben mit einander geführten Streitigkeiten. Halle,
 1782. In: Platner und Wezel.
 LpzUB

Gespräch im Reiche der Todten zwischen den Leipziger Buchhändlern Adam Friedrich Böhme und Karl Friedrich Schneider, die Platner= und Wezelschen Streitschriften betreffend. Halle, 1782. In: Platner und Wezel.
 LpzUB

Meißner, August Gottlieb. Lope di Vega, Leßing und Pastor Richter. Eine Anek-
 dote aus der Unterwelt.
 Leipzig, 1782.
 R GöUB

Wieland, Christoph Martin. "Phaon. Ein Dialog im Elysium", Teutscher Merkur,
 I (1782), 55-66.
 JHU

Gaum, Johann Ferdinand. Gregor VII, Clemens XIV und Luther. Ein Gespräch im
 Reiche der Todten. 3 Stücke.
 Ulm, Stettin (?), 1783.
 Gradmann

[Merck, Johann Heinrich]. "Die schöne und die häßliche Seele. Scenen im Elysium", Teutscher Merkur, I (1783), 29-49; 252-262.
 JHU

Unterhaltungen im Todtenreiche, eine interessante Piece.
 Neustadt, 1783.
 H

Gespräch zwischen Peter, Julius II und seinem Schutzgeiste.
 Frankfurt and Leipzig, 1784.
 LpzUB

[Meißner, August Gottlieb ?]. "Dialog, wie K. Ludewig XIV. und Fenelon ihn
    gehalten haben könten", Deutsches Museum, VI (1784), 417-420.
    JHU

1785

Claudius, Georg Karl. "Die Schatten. Erster und zweyter Transport", Taschen-
    buch für das Verdauungsgesellschaft von 1785. Spashausen (?), 69-89.
    M
Kretschmann, Karl Friedrich. "Basannia und Ikaste. Ein Todtengespräch",
    Für Ältere und Neuere Lectüre, III (Leipzig, 1785), 32-42.
    GöUB

1786

Gespräch im Reich der Todten zwischen Johann Melchior Goeze weyland Pastor
    zu St. Catharinen und Scholarchen in Hamburg und Dessen beyden
    Collegen Alberti und Friederici, die lange vor ihm den Weg wandel-
    ten. Altona, 1786. (Page 7 of this piece mentions "das 2te Gespräch
    Goeze, Leßing und Mendelssohn".)
    Staatsbibliothek Bremen
"Gespräch im Reiche der Schatten, zwischen Klotz, Lessing und einem Land-
    priester", Journal aller Journale, I (Hamburg, 1786), 362-372.
    GöUB
Das Reich der Todten, enthaltend politische Gespräche der Todten, politische
    Reden nebst geheimen Briefwechsel zwischen den Lebendigen und den
    Todten. s.l. [Neuwied], 1786-1810. (= "Neuwieder Gespräche", also
    published in several editions.)
    Kirchner   HG   R
Richter, Joseph. König Friedrich am Höllenfluß. Ein Scene aus der Unterwelt,
    der Wahrheit zum Besten auf die Oberwelt gebracht von einem Unter-
    irdischen Passagier.
    Dantzig, 1786.
    August Sauer
Schröckh, Samuel Jacob. Friedrich im Elysium.
    s.l., 1786, [2]1790 (Leipzig ?).
    Holzmann-Bohatta   H   M
Wekhrlin, Wilhelm Ludwig. "Der Schatten des Schach=Lolo vor seinem Richter",
    Das graue Ungeheur, IX (1786), 133-152. "Zweyter Theil", X (1787),
    154-285.
    JHU

1787

Gaum, Johann Ferdinand. Gespräch im Reiche der Todten zwischen Maria There-
    sia und Friedrich, dem Zweyten, worinnen dieser hohen Personen
    Leben und merkwürdige Thaten bis ihrem Tode unpartheiyisch erzählt

werden. Erstes und zweytes Stück. Mexico [Ulm], 1787. 3. und 4.
    Stück, Mexico, 1787. 5. Stück, s. l. & a.
    GöUB   R

_____. Leo X und Adrian VI. Eine Unterredung über das Wiederaufleben der
    Rechte . . . der hohen röm.=katholischen Geistlichkeit . . . .
    Tripoli [Ulm], 1787.
    Gradmann

Lessing, Mendelsohn, Risbeck, Goeze, ein Todengespraech.
    Braunschweig, Berlin, Arau and Hamburg, 1787.
    Goedeke

Schröckh, Samuel Jacob. Friedrich der Große im Reiche der Schatten. Selbst-
    geständniß.
    Nürnberg, 1787.
    Holzmann-Bohatta   H

Seybold, David Christoph. "Pluto, Hannibal, Alexander, Scipio, Epaminondas,
    Condé, Turenne, Marschal von Sachsen" and "Pluto, Asträa, Viele
    stumme Personen", Deutsches Museum, II (1787), 7-14.
    JHU

"Todtengespräch. Charon, drei Schatten", Deutsches Museum, II (1787), 101-104.
    JHU

Zusammenkünfte in den elysäischen Feldern. Zwischen letzt verstorbenen hohen
    Häuptern, Fürsten, Kriegshelden, Gelehrten und andern berühmten
    Männern. Ein Denkmal des 18. Jahrhunderts.
    s.l., 1787.
    August Sauer

1788

"Carl. Ferdinand. Ein Geist. Eine Sibylle. Helias. Maximilian. — Ein Todenge-
    spräch", Neue Litteratur und Völkerkunde, II (Dessau and Leipzig,
    1788), 38-50.
    GöUB

Wieland, Christoph Martin. "Peregrin und Lucian. Ein Dialog im Elysium",
    Teutscher Merkur, II (1788), 176-190.

1789

[Geiger, Carl Ignaz]. Friderich II. als Schriftsteller im Elisium. Ein dramma-
    tisches Gemälde.
    Constantinopel [Augsburg], 1789.
    H   Holzmann-Bohatta   M

Heinrich der Große, Rousseau, Foulon, Bertier und Friedrich der Große.
    Essendischen Nachrichten, 1789.
    D

Bartholoneidis, L. (?). Gespräche Zwischen Kaiser Joseph II und Mathias
      Corvinus, Im Reiche der Todten.
      Neushol., 1790.
      E
"Friedrich der Zweite, Voltaire und Wolf; ein Todtengespräch" and "Friedrich
      der Zweite und Lessing; ein Todtengespräch", Neues deutsches Museum,
      III (Leipzig, 1790), 749-757, 1048-1052.
      GöUB
Gespräch im Reiche der Todten zwischen Elliot und Laudon.
      Leipzig, 1790.
      H
Klein, Ernst Ferdinand. "Ist es Schuldigkeit oder Gnade, wenn ein Fürst sein
      Land wohl regiert?", Berlinische Monatsschrift, XV (Berlin, 1790),
      304-328. (Dialogue among Charon, a professor and a prince.)
      GöUB
Schröckh, Samuel Jacob. Joseph II in Elysium.
      s.l., 1790.
      M

Plaudereyen aus der Unterwelt. Einige Partikel aus Meister Lucians Schnapsack.
      Niesenhofen (?), 1791.
      E   R

"Diogenes und die Sansculottes" and "Mahumet und le Pelletier", Magazin der
      Kunst und Literatur, II (1793), 32-44.
      JHU
Friedrich [II., König von Preußen] und Mirabeau. Dialog in Elysium.
      Leipzig, 1793.
      H
Gaum, Johann Ferdinand. Maria Stuart und Maria Antoinette.
      s.l., 1793.
      Gradmann
Gespräch in Reich der Todten zwischen Ludwig XVI. Leopold II. und Gustav III.
      Samt dem Portrait des Königs von Frankreich.
      Augsburg, 1793.
      PrStB   LpzUB

Gaum, Johann Ferdinand. Brutus und Corday. Eine Unterredung.
      s.l., 1794.
      Gradmann

Bodmer, Johann Jakob. "Claudius Tacitus. Tiberius", Erholungen, III (Leipzig,
    1798), 191-204.
    GöUB

Gespräch im Reiche der Todten zwischen einer Zehntgarbe und einem Bodenzins-
    mäs.
    s.l., 1798.
    BasUB

Politische Gespräche im Reich der Todten. Stück 1. Gespräch im Reich der
    Todten zwischen einem Inquisitoren von 1749 und dem Präsidenten
    der ehemaligen Kornkammer in Bern . . .
    s.l., 1798.
    BasUB

Gespräch im Reiche der Todten zwischen Karl Theodor, Kurfürsten von Pfalz-
    baiern und Max Joseph, seinem Regierungsvorfahrer.
    s.l., 1799.
    Tübingen UB

Werdmüller, J. H. Gespräch im Reiche der Todten, zwischen Grenadierhaupt-
    mann Leonhard Denzler . . . und Hauptmann Heinrick Freyenmuth
    . . . .
    Zürich, 1799.
    Zürich Zentralkatalog   E

Gespräch im Reiche der Todten zwischen Pius VI, Papst, Joubert, Feldherrn
    der Franzosen, Hotze, Feldherrn der Oestreicher, Voltaire, und
    einem Nachdrucker. Worinn unter andern auch Nachricht gegeben
    wird, daß der jüngste Tag der richtigsten Ausrechnung nach, erst
    auf den 7. Sept. 1801 fällt.
    s.l., 1800.
    PrStB

Wieland, Christoph Martin. "Agathon und Hippias, ein Gespräch im Elysium",
    Attisches Museum, III (Lucerne, 1800), 269-295.
    JHU

Gespräch im Reich der Todten zwischen den beiden Comitialgesandten Freiherrn
    von Strauß und Freiherrn von Gemmingen über die neue kurpfälzische
    Substitution.
    s.l., 1801.
    GöUB

Falk, Johann Daniel. "Die Dichterwaage. Nach Aristophanes", Elysium und Tartarus (9 Feb., 1806); "Doktor Luther und Nelson in Elysium", Elysium und Tartarus (19 Mar., 1806); "Gespräch im Reich der Todten, zwischen Keith, Schwerin, Winterfeld, Ziethen und Friedrich dem Großen", Elysium und Tartarus (21 Sept., 1806).
Allen GöUB

Gespräche im Reiche der Todten von der Mutter Bojaria, ihrem Sohn Maximilian Emanuel, mit ihrer Tochter Austria, nebst einem angehängten Gedicht und einer poetischen Unterredung der vorzüglichsten Regenten in Europa. Verf. von einem königl. bair. Patrioten.
s.l., 1806.
LpzUB

Grillparzer, Franz. "Todtengespräch. Friedrich der Große, Voltaire, Prinz Louis von Preußen, Prinz von Braunschweig", Sämtliche Werke II, 6 (Vienna, 1923), 3-5.
GöUB

Lateinische und deutsche Gespräche im Reiche der Todten und Briefe, nach versch. Erläuter.
Prag, 1806.
H

Johann Joachim Perinet. Der weyland Casperl aus der Leopoldstadt im Reiche der Todten. Ein Gespräch in Knittelversen.
Vienna, 1806.
Goedeke

_____. Laroches Todtenfeyer oder Des sog. Kasperls Gespräch am jenseitigen Ufer des Styx mit dem Schatten eines seiner Directeure. In Knittelreimen.
s.l., 1806.
Gugitz

1807

Gespräch im Reiche der Todten zwischen Friedrich dem Großen, König von Preußen; Maria Theresia, Kaiserin von Oestreich; Catharina der Zweyten, Kaiserin von Rußland; Carl Wilhelm Ferdinand, Herzog von Braunschweig; Franz Friedrich Anton, Herzog von Coburg; und Prinz Louis.
s.l., 1807.
PrStB

Gespräch über den k. k. Hofschauspieler Herrn [Josef] Weidmann im Reiche der Todten, und Bartholomäus Zitterbarths, gewesenen Theaterunternehmer an der Wien, Ankunft im Elisium in Knittelreimen.
[Vienna ?], 1807. Facsimile reprint, Vienna, 1928.
PrStB

1808

Gespräch von sechs hingerichteten Räubern und Dieben.
      Meißen, 1808.
      R

1809

Gespräche im Reiche der Todten zwischen Friedrich II und Salomo . . . über alle
      Gegenstände der Welt.
      Ratibor, 1809.
      HG

1833

Dramatisches Gespräch im Reiche der Todten, zwischen Schiller, Wieland, Iff-
      land, Kotzebue und Göthe. In vier Abtheilungen. Quedlinburg und
      Leipzig. Druck und Verlag von Gottfr. Basse. 1833. Von * * * S * *.
      E

1841

Grillparzer, Franz. "Friedrich der Große und Lessing. Ein Gespräch im Ely-
      sium". Sämtliche Werke, I, 13 (Vienna, 1930), 134-139.
      JHU

1905

Mauthner, Fritz. Todtengespräche.
      München, 1905.
      E

1931

Ernst, Paul. Erdachte Gespräche.
      München, 1931.
      Kosch

Undated Material

"Friedrich der Große, Prinz Louis Ferdinand und General von Schmettau", Der
      Telegraph. Ein Journal der neuesten Kriegs-Begebenheiten. (After
      1806.)
      R
Geheime Conference Vornehmer Persohnen In dem Reiche derer Todten. Erste
      Entrevuë zwischen Jacobo Grami Dem unglückseeligen Marggrafen
      von Montrose und S. Previl, Gewesenen Gouverneur zu Arras, In

welcher Ihr geführtes Leben und die ihnen darinnen passirten Fatali-
täten enthalten, worbey auch vom Hoff=Leben, und was zu einen Hoff-
mann gehöret, ingleichen was eine wahre Ehre sey, und wodurch man
zu rühmlicher Ehre gelangen kan, discouriret wird.
Freyburg and Leipzig, s. a.
HJ

"Ein Gespräch zwischen dem Czaar, dem Pabst Pius VI., Kant, Klopstock und
dem weisen Tzee", <u>Koblenzer Zeitung</u>, ed. Franz von Lassaulx.
(After 1800 ?)
D

Gespräch im Reiche der Todten, Allen artigen Mädgen und hübschen Büfgen zum
Zeitvertreib, Nutz und Nachsinnen entworffenes, zwischen Adam und
Eva, unsern ersten Eltern, und einem neumodischen Galanthomme.
s. l. & a. (Leipzig, 1758 ?).
HG

Gespräche im Reiche der Todten zwischen 36 verschiedenen merkwürdigen Per-
sonen der neuern Zeit. 2 Thle.
Regensburg, s. a.
Freie Universität Berlin   HG

Gespräche im Reiche der Todten zwischen zweien in Breslau wohlbekannten Per-
sonen, nämlich dem Unterofficier Ell und dem Kirchendiener Müller.
Breslau, s. a.
Kayser

Gespräch im Reiche der Todten zwischen Maria Theresia, Friedrich dem II und
einem Brabanter.
Bibliothek Vernhagen

Günther, Georg. Gespräche in dem Reiche der Todten zwischen Abraham und dem
reichen Manne.
D

DAVID CHRISTOPH SEYBOLD'S "GOTTSCHED UND KLOTZ."

From: <u>Neue</u> Gespräche <u>im</u> Reich <u>der</u> Todten. <u>Nach</u> <u>Lucianischem</u> Geschmack. (Hanau, Frankfurt and Leipzig, 1780), pp. 10-14.

GOTTSCHED UND KLOTZ.

GOTTSCHED.

     Bist mir bald nachgefolgt, Bruder Klotz.

KLOTZ.

     Euer Hochedelgebohrne Magnificenz
thun mir zu viel Ehre an, daß Sie mich
Ihren Bruder nennen.

GOTTSCHED.

     Sez' das bey Seite! Wir sind doch   5
Brüder. Denn wir haben gleiches Schicksal
gehabt. Wir saßen beyde auf papiernen
Thronen, und beyden sind sie von unsern
Feinden zu Asche verbrannt worden, und
nichts von dem erschlichenen Ruhme ist uns   10
übrig geblieben, als dir einiges Verdienst
um das Studium der Alten, und mir um
die teutsche Sprache.

KLOTZ.

     Leider! Die neu ankommenden Schrift=
steller sagen aus, mein Name werde kaum   15
noch genennet. Wart', Leßing! und
wart', Herder, und du vollends, Nicolai!
kommt nur einmal herab! Ich will euch
versohlen.

GOTTSCHED.

Ich habe den Schweitzern, die mich   20
dethronisirten, verziehen. Verzeih' du auch.

KLOTZ.

Ich kanns nicht so gleich. Einen Mann,
den Könige und Fürsten so sehr ehrten! - -
„O du! um den zwey Könige gestritten!"
sang einmal der Dichter der güldenen Aue   25
und der -- Juden -- und dem sie Schau=
münzen schickten.

GOTTSCHED.

Hab' ich nicht auch eine Dose von der
Kayserinn erhalten?

KLOTZ.

Aber wo hast du sie einmal stehen lassen?   30

GOTTSCHED.

Und wo ist das Dreysigdukatenstück
vom Könige in Dännemark hingekommen,
das du für die Dedikation des Saxo erhiel=
test? Hm! sags einmal!

KLOTZ.

Hätten nur mehrere Fürsten sich so ein-   35
gestellt! Man brauchte immer ein Stück=
chen Geld, um Wein zu trinken.

GOTTSCHED.

Was hilfts? izt brauchst du keins mehr.
Wie schmeckt dir das Wasser aus dem Styx?

KLOTZ.

Wie Leßings antiquarische Briefe,   40
oder Nicolais Vorrede zum achten Bande
der Bibliotheck.
Heu non regna vini −

168

Aber sag' mir einmal, sind schon die Wich=
männer, oder Wilke, oder sonst ein   45
Schriftsteller angekommen, den ich abkla=
wastert habe? 's ist mir doch nicht ganz
wohl bey der Sache.

GOTTSCHED.

      Wilke ist da! Will dir schon gegen
diesen beystehen, wenn du mich gegen Bod=   50
mer und Breitinger schützest.

KLOTZ.

      Gieb mir die Hand drauf. Izt ists mir
leichter ums Herz, weil ich einen baum=
startken RIESEN zum Sekondanten
          habe.   55

LIST OF WORKS CONSULTED

Allen, Richard J. "Johann Daniel Falk and the Theory of Characteristic Art". MLN, LXXXVI (1971), 345-377.

_____. Johann Daniel Falk and the Traditions of German Satire. Johns Hopkins University Dissertation, 1969.

Allgemeine deutsche Biographie. 56 vols. Leipzig and München, 1875-1912.

Almanach der deutschen Musen. Leipzig, 1770-1781.

Der Alte Deutsche. Hamburg, 1730.

Aristophanes. Benjamin Bickley Rogers, trans. Vol. 2. London, 1924.

Ausführliche und kritische Nachrichten von den besten und merkwürdigsten Schriften unsrer Zeit nebst andern zur Gelehrtheit gehörigen Sachen. Stück 1. Lindau, Frankfurt and Leipzig, 1763.

Ayrault, Roger. "Une 'Farce' de Goethe dans ses années de Sturm und Drang: 'Götter, Helden und Wieland'", EG, XX (1965), 161-171.

Baechtold, Jakob. Geschichte der deutschen Literatur in der Schweiz. Frauenfeld, ^{2}1919.

Bahrdt, Carl Friedrich. Geschichte seines Lebens, seiner Meinungen und Schicksale. Berlin, [1922].

Bantel, Oskar. Christoph Martin Wieland und die griechische Antike. Tübingen Dissertation, 1953.

Barthel, Marga. Das "Gespräch" bei Wieland. Untersuchungen über Wesen und Form seiner Dichtung. Frankfurt, 1939.

Bellinger, Alfred R. "Lucian's Dramatic Technique", YCS, I (1928), 3-40.

Beutler, J. H. Ch. and J. Ch. T. Guts-Muths. Allgemeines Sachregister über die wichtigsten deutschen Zeit- und Wochenschriften, voran als Einleitung ein raisonnirendes litterarisches Verzeichniß aller in diesem Jahrhundert bis jetzt erschienenen periodischen Blätter . . . . Leipzig, 1790.

170

Böttiger, Karl August. Literarische Zustände und Zeitgenossen. Leipzig, 1838.

Boyce, Benjamin. "News from Hell, Satiric Communications with the Nether World in English Writing of the Seventeenth and Eighteenth Centuries", PMLA, LVIII (1943), 402-437.

Bräuning-Oktavio, Hermann. J. H. Merck als Mitarbeiter an Wielands "Teutschen Merkur" in den Jahren 1773 bis 1791. Braunschweig, 1913.

Carré, J.-R. La Philosophie de Fontenelle, ou le sourire de la raison. Paris, 1932.

Clark, William Harrington, Jr. Christoph Martin Wieland and the Legacy of Greece: Aspects of his Relation to Greek Culture. Columbia University Dissertation, 1954.

Cosentini, John W. Fontenelle's Art of Dialogue. New York, 1952.

Croiset, Maurice. Essai sur la vie et les oeuvres de Lucien. Paris, 1882.

Currie, Pamela. "Moral Weeklies and the Reading Public in Germany, 1711-1750", Oxford German Studies, III (1968), 69-86.

Damberg, Wilhelm. Die politische Aussage in den Totengesprächen David Fassmanns, ein Beitrag zur Frühgeschichte der politischen Zeitschrift. Münster Dissertation, 1952.

d'Ester, Karl. Das politische Elysium oder Die Gespräche der Todten am Rhein. 2 vols. Neuwied, 1936-37.

Deutsche Bibliothek der schönen Wissenschaften. Halle, 1767-1771.

Diesch, Carl. Bibliographie der Germanistischen Zeitschriften. Leipzig, 1927.

Distel, Thomas. "Die erste Verdeutschung des 12. Lukianischen Totengesprächs nach einer urtextlichen Handschrift von J. Reuchlin (1495) und verwandtes aus der Folgezeit", Zeitschrift für vergleichende Literaturgeschichte, Neue Folge 8 (1895), 408-417.

Ebeling, Friedrich Wilhelm. Geschichte der komischen Literatur in Deutschland. 3 vols. Leipzig, 1765-69.

Egilsrud, Johan Storjohann. Les discours des morts dans les littératures française, allemande et anglaise (1644-1789). Paris, 1934.

Der Einsiedler. Königsberg, 1740-41.

Faber du Faur, Curt von. German Baroque Literature. A Catalogue of the Collection in the Yale University Library. New Haven, 1958.

La Mothe-Fénelon, François de Salignac de. Dialogues des morts composez pour l'education d'un prince. Paris, 1712.

Fischer-Lamberg, Hanna. "Eine Quellenstudie zu Götter, Helden und Wieland", Beiträge zur Goetheforschung, XVI (1959), 139-142.

Flögel, Carl Friedrich. Geschichte der komischen Litteratur. 4 vols. Liegnitz and Leipzig, 1784-87.

Fontenelle, Bernard Le Bouyer de. Nouveaux dialogues des morts. Paris, 1683.

_____. Gespräche der Todten und Plutons Urtheil über dieselben; zum erstenmahl ins Teutsche übersetzt, und mit einer Vorrede, von Gesprächen überhaupt, versehen von Johann Christoph Gottsched. Leipzig, 1727.

Förster, Richard. "Lucian in der Renaissance", Archiv für Literaturgeschichte, XIV (1886), 337-363.

Frederick II., King of Prussia. Oeuvres posthumes de Fréderic II, Roi de Prusse. Vol. 7. Berlin, 1788.

Geigenmüller, Paul. "Lucian und Wieland", Neue Jahrbücher für Wissenschaft und Jugendbildung, III (1927), 35-47.

Gemeinhardt, L. E. "The Dramatic Structure of Goethe's 'Götter, Helden und Wieland' ", JEGP, XLI (1942), 345-348.

Gewerstock, Olga. Lucian und Hutten. Zur Geschichte des Dialogs im 16. Jahrhundert. Berlin, 1924.

Goedeke, Karl. Grundriss zur Geschichte der deutschen Dichtung. 13 vols. Dresden, ^{2}1884-1953.

_____. Grundriss zur Geschichte der deutschen Dichtung. Continued by E. Goetze. Vol. IV, 1-4. Dresden, ^{3}1910-1916.

Goethe, Johann Wolfgang. Goethes Briefe. 4 vols. Hamburg, 1962-67.

_____. Werke. I, Vol. 36. Weimar, 1907.

_____. Sämtliche Werke. Vol. 24. Stuttgart and Berlin, 1902.

Gottsched, Johann Christoph. Die Deutsche Schaubühne, nach den Regeln und Exampeln der Alten . . . . Leipzig, 1746-50.

Gradmann, Johann Jakob. Das gelehrte Schwaben, oder Lexikon der jetzt lebenden Schwäbischen Schriftsteller. Ravensberg, 1803.

Grillparzer, Franz. Werke. Erinnerungsblätter 1822-1841. Vol. 6. Vienna, 1924.

Grimm, Jacob and Wilhelm, et al. Deutsches Wörterbuch. 16 vols. Leipzig, 1854-1960.

Gugitz, Gustav. "Joachim Perinet. Ein Beitrag zur Wiener Theatergeschichte", Jahrbuch der Grillparzer-Gesellschaft, XIV (1904), 170-223.

Hayn, Hugo and Alfred N. Gotendorf. Bibliotheca Germanorum erotica et curiosa. 9 vols. München, 1912-1929.

Hazard, Paul. La Crise de la conscience européenne (1680-1715). Vol. 1. Paris, 1935.

Heidegger, Gotthard. Mythoscopia Romantica: oder Discours von den so benannten Romans . . . . Zürich, 1698.

Heinsius, Wilhelm. Allgemeines Bücher-Lexikon oder Vollständiges alphabetisches Verzeichnis aller von 1700-1892 erschienenen Bücher. 19 vols. Leipzig, 1812-1894.

Helm, Rudolf. Lucian und Menipp. Leipzig and Berlin, 1906.

Hettner, Hermann. Literaturgeschichte des achtzehnten Jahrhunderts. Braunschweig, 1893.

Hildebrand, Sune. Die Discourse der Mahlern, Zürich 1721-23, und Der Mahler der Sitten, Zürich 1745, sprachlich verglichen, ein Beitrag zur Geschichte der neuhochdeutschen Schriftsprache in der Schweiz. Upsala Dissertation, 1909.

Hirzel, Rudolf. Der Dialog. Ein literarhistorischer Versuch. 2 vols. Leipzig, 1895.

Holzmann, Michael and Hanns Bohatta. Deutsches Anonymen-Lexikon. Aus den Quellen bearbeitet. 7 vols. Weimar, 1902-1928.

_____. Deutsches Pseudonymen-Lexikon. Vienna, 1906.

Jöcher, Christian Gottlieb. Allgemeines Gelehrten-Lexikon. 11 vols. Leipzig, 1750-1819, 1897.

Jördens, Karl Heinrich. Lexikon deutscher Dichter und Prosaisten. 6 vols. Leipzig, 1806-1811.

Kaschmieder, Käthe. David Faßmanns "Gespräche im Reiche der Toten" (1718-1740). Ein Beitrag zur deutschen Geistes- und Kulturgeschichte des achtzehnten Jahrhunderts. Breslau, 1934.

Kawczyński, Max. Studien zur Literaturgeschichte des XVIII. Jahrhunderts, Moralische Wochenschriften. Leipzig, 1880.

Keener, Frederick Michael. Shades of Lucian: British Dialogues of the Dead in the Eighteenth Century. Columbia University Dissertation, 1965.

Kirchner, Joachim. Bibliographie der Zeitschriften des deutschen Sprachgebietes bis 1900. Vol. 1. Stuttgart, 1969.

_____. Das deutsche Zeitschriftwesen, seine Geschichte und seine Probleme. Leipzig, 1942.

_____. Die Grundlagen des deutschen Zeitschriftwesens mit einer Gesamtbibliographie der deutschen Zeitschriften bis zum Jahre 1790. 2 vols. Leipzig, 1931.

Kleines österreichisches Literaturlexikon. H. Giebisch et al. edd. Vienna, 1948.

Klotz, Christian Adolf. Über das Studium des Alterthums reviewed in the Allgemeine deutsche Bibliothek, VIII (Berlin and Stettin, 1768).

Kosch, Wilhelm. Deutsches Literatur-Lexikon. Biographisches und bibliographisches Handbuch. 4 vols. Bern, [2]1949-1958.

Kurth, Lieselotte E. "Formen der Romankritik im achtzehnten Jahrhundert", MLN, LXXXIII (1968), 655-693.

_____. "Wilhelm Ehrenfried Neugebauer − Der teutsche Don Quichotte", Jahrbuch der deutschen Schillergesellschaft, IX (1965), 106-130.

_____. Die zweite Wirklichkeit. Studien zum Roman des achtzehnten Jahrhunderts. Chapel Hill, 1969.

Lachmanski, Hugo. Die deutschen Frauenzeitschriften des achtzehnten Jahrhunderts. Berlin Dissertation, 1900.

Lazarowicz, Klaus. Verkehrte Welt. Vorstudien zu einer Geschichte der deutschen Satire. Tübingen, 1963.

Lindenberg, Ludwig. Leben und Schriften David Fassmanns (1683-1766) mit besonderer Berücksichtigung seiner Totengespräche. Berlin, 1937.

Lucian. A. M. Harmon et al. trans. 8 vols. London and New York, 1921ff.

174

Lyttleton, George Lord. Dialogues of the Dead. London, 1760.

_____. Gespräche der Verstorbenen, eine Englische Schrift von [J. G. H.] Oelrichs. Stettin, Berlin and Leipzig, 1761.

Maltzahn, Wendelin von. Deutscher Bücherschatz des 16., 17. und 18. bis in die Mitte des 19. Jahrhunderts. Jena and Frankfurt, 1875-1882.

Martens, Wolfgang. Die Botschaft der Tugend. Die Aufklärung im Spiegel der deutschen Moralischen Wochenschriften. Stuttgart, 1968.

Merker, Paul and Wolfgang Stammler. Reallexikon der deutschen Literaturgeschichte. 4 vols. Berlin, 1925-1931.

Meusel, J. G. and G. C. Hamburger. Das gelehrte Teutschland; oder Lexikon der jetzt lebenden teutschen Schriftsteller. 23 vols. Lemgo, 1796-1834.

_____. Lexikon der vom Jahr 1750 bis 1800 verstorbenen teutschen Schriftsteller. 15 vols. Leipzig, 1802-1816.

Nadler, Josef. Franz Grillparzer. Vienna, 1962.

_____. Literaturgeschichte Österreichs. Linz, 1948.

Neukirch, Johann George. Anfangs=Gründe zur reinen teutschen Poesie Itziger Zeit / Welche der Studierende Jugend zum Besten und zum Gebrauch seines Auditorii in zulänglichen Regeln und deutlichen Exempeln entworffen. Halle im Magdeb., 1724.

Niemann, Gottfried. Die Dialogliteratur der Reformationszeit nach ihrer Entstehung und Entwicklung. Leipzig, 1905.

Der Nordische Aufseher. 3 vols. Copenhagen and Leipzig, 1759-1761.

Osborn, Max. Die Teufelliteratur des XVI. Jahrhunderts. Berlin, 1893.

Paulson, Ronald. The Fictions of Satire. Baltimore, 1967.

The Dialogues of Plato. B. Jowett, trans. 4 vols. Oxford, [4]1967.

Prutz, Robert. Geschichte des deutschen Journalismus. 2 vols. Hannover, 1845.

Radermacher, Ludwig. Das Jenseits im Mythos der Hellenen. Untersuchungen über antiken Jenseitsglauben. Bonn, 1903.

Raßmann, Friedrich. Literarisches Handwörterbuch der verstorbenen deutschen Dichter. Leipzig, 1826.

Rentsch, Johannes. Das Totengespräch in der Literatur. Lucianstudien II. Wissenschaftliche Beilage zu dem Programme des Königlichen Gymnasiums zu Plauen. Plauen, 1895.

Rosenbaum, Richard. Review of Johannes Rentsch's Lucianstudien. Euphorion, V (1898), 126-134.

Salomon, Ludwig. Geschichte des deutschen Zeitungswesens, von den ersten Anfängen bis zur Wiederaufrichtung des Deutschen Reiches. Oldenburg and Leipzig, 1900-1906.

Scenna, Anthony. The Treatment of Ancient Legend and History in Bodmer. New York, 1937.

Schade, Oskar, ed. Satiren und Pasquille aus der Reformationszeit. 2 vols. Hannover, 1856.

Scheibe, Siegfried. "Zur Druck- und Wirkungsgeschichte der 'Belustigungen des Verstandes und des Witzes'. Philologische Befunde. Forschungen und Fortschritte, XXXIX, 4 (1965), 119-123.

Schletter, Hermann Thomas. Platner und Wezel. Kriegsscenen aus der Leipziger Literaturgeschichte 1781/82. Leipzig, 1846.

Schmidt, Erich. "Zu 'Götter, Helden und Wieland'", GJb, I (1880), 378-379.

Schöffler, Herbert. Das literarische Zürich 1700-1750. Frauenfeld and Leipzig, 1925.

Schubart, C. F. D. Des Patrioten gesammelte Schriften und Schicksale. 8 vols. Stuttgart, 1839-1840.

Schüling, Hermann. Bibliographischer Wegweiser zu dem in Deutschland erschienenen Schriftum des 17. Jahrhunderts. Giessen, 1964.

Schwartz, Jacques. Biographie de Lucien de Samosate. Bruxelles-Berchem, 1965.

Semenjuk, Natalija. "Einige Probleme der sprachgeschichtlichen Untersuchung der deutschen periodischen Literatur des achtzehnten Jahrhunderts", Forschungen und Fortschritte, XXXVIII, 6 (1964), 178-182.

Semler, Johann Salomo. Gedanken von Uebereinkommung der Romane mit den Legenden. Halle, [1749].

Sengle, Friedrich. Wieland. Stuttgart, 1949.

Seuffert, Bernhard. "Der junge Goethe und Wieland", Zeitschrift für deutsches Altertum, XXVI (1882), 252-287.

Seybold, David Christoph. Reizenstein oder die Geschichte eines deutschen Officiers. 2 vols. Leipzig, 1778-79.

Stain, Hanns. Das Leben David Fassmanns. Dissertation Vienna, 1908.

Steinberger, Julius. Lucians Einfluß auf Wieland. Göttingen Dissertation, 1902.

Sterne, Laurence. A Sentimental Journey through France and Italy by Mr. Yorick.
Gardner D. Stout, Jr., ed. Berkeley and Los Angeles, 1967.

Stötzner, P. "Der Satiriker Trajano Boccalini und sein Einfluß auf die deutsche
Litteratur", Archiv für das Studium der neueren Sprachen und Littera-
turen, CIII, 53 (1899), 107-147.

Der teutsche Merkur. Weimar, 1773-1810.

Thompson, Lawrence S. "German Translations of the Classics between 1450 and
1550", JEGP, XLII (1943), 343-363.

Trenck, Friedrich Freiherr von der. P. Pavian, Voltaire und Ich in der Unterwelt. Berlin and Leipzig, 1784.

Ulbrich, Franz. Die Belustigungen des Verstandes und des Witzes. Ein Beitrag
zur Journalistik des achtzehnten Jahrhunderts. Leipzig, 1911.

Valdés, Alfonso. Dialogo de Mercurio y Caron, ed. Jose F. Montesinos. Madrid,
1929.

_____. Discovrs Vber Kayser Carolen den Fünfften mit dem König aus Franck-
reich Francisco Valesio . . . . Amberg, 1609.

Van Abbé, Derek Maurice. Christoph Martin Wieland (1733-1813). A Literary
Biography. London, 1961.

Vermischte, mehrenteils historische gelehrte Abhandlungen, von verschiedenen
Verfassern. Rostock, 1967.

Die Vernünftigen Tadlerinnen. Leipzig, 1725-26.

Vetter, Theodor. Zürich als Vermittlerin englischer Literatur im achtzehnten
Jahrhundert. Zürich, 1891.

Wahl, Hans. Geschichte des Teutschen Merkurs. Berlin, 1914.

Waniek, Gustav. Gottsched und die deutsche Literatur seiner Zeit. Leipzig, 1897.

[Wegelin, Jacob]. Die letzten Gespräche Socrates und seiner Freunde. Von W* * *.
Zürich, 1760.

Weller, Emil. Annalen der Poetischen National-Literatur der Deutschen im XVI. und XVII. Jahrhundert. 2 vols. Freiburg, 1862.

_____. Die ersten deutschen Zeitungen. Tübingen, 1872.

_____. Lexicon Pseudonymorum. Wörterbuch der Pseudonymen aller Zeiten und Völker oder Verzeichnis jener Autoren, die sich falscher Namen bedienten. Regensburg, [2]1886.

_____. Repetorium typographicum. Die deutsche Literatur im ersten Viertel des sechzehnten Jahrhunderts. Nordlingen, 1864.

Westphälische Bemühungen zur Aufnahme des Geschmaks und der Sitten. Lemgo, 1753-55.

Wieland, Christoph Martin. Gesammelte Schriften, ed. Wilhelm Kurrelmeyer. Abteilung I, 15 vols. Berlin, 1909ff.

_____. Werke. Vol. 28. Berlin, 1879.

Wilkinson, Elizabeth Mary. Johann Elias Schlegel. A German Pioneer in Aesthetics. Oxford, 1945.

Witkowski, Georg. Geschichte des literarischen Lebens in Leipzig. Leipzig and Berlin, 1909.

Wurzbach, Constant von. Biographisches Lexikon des Kaiserthums Oesterreich. Vienna, 1883.

Zeitler, Julius. Goethe=Handbuch. 3 vols. Stuttgart, 1916.

Zenker, E. V. Geschichte der Wiener Journalistik, von den Anfängen bis zum Jahre 1848. Ein Beitrag zur deutschen Culturgeschichte. Mit einem bibliographischen Anhang. Vienna and Leipzig, 1892.

INDEX

This index includes authors from classic and modern literatures. Political figures are not listed unless they happen also to be authors of interest to belles lettres. A few citations are made from the Notes following each chapter and are indicated by the sign "(n.)".

Ablancourt, Nicolas Perrot d', 50, 87.
Aeschylus, 118, 120.
Aesop, 90.
Agathon, 92-93, 94, 95.
Albrecht, Johann Georg, 108.
Anacreon, 90.
Aristippus, 93-94, 95.
Aristophanes, 62-63, 108, 118-119.
Aristotle, 106.
Arnold, Gottfried, 32.
Bahrdt, Carl Friedrich, 109.
Beaumont, Francis, 120.
Becker, Wilhelm Gottlieb, 70, 80.
Bekker, Balthasar, 33.
Boccalini, Trajano, 24.
Bock, Friedrich Samuel, 51.
Bodmer, Johann Jakob, 48-50, 51-52, 58 (n.), 70, 74, 76, 77-81, 83, 84, 86, 129, 130, 131.
Böttiger, Karl August, 87.
Bohse-Talander, August, 50.
Boileau, Nicolas, 52.
Brant, Sebastian, 125 (n.).
Brenner, Anton Jakob, 117.
Brockes, Barthold Heinrich, 37, 105.
Bucholtz, Andreas Heinrich, 52.
Burke, Edmund, 95.
Caesar, Gaius Julius, 79, 80, 81.
Calderón de la Barca, Pedro, 120.
Cato "Censorius", Marcus Porcius, 81.
Cato Uticensis, Marcus Porcius, 78-79.
Cicero, 79, 81.
Claudius, Georg Karl, 12, 112-115.
Corneille, Pierre, 120.
Cramer, Johann Andreas, 55.
Crébillon (= Prosper Jolyot), 59 (n.), 120.
Dacier, Anne, 14.

Dante, 24.

Democritus, 21, 47, 62-63, 83, 108.

Diderot, Denis, 66-67.

Dyk, Johann Gottfried, 114.

Edzardus, Sebastian, 32, 33, 34.

Epicurus, 115.

Erasmus, 22, 24, 77.

Ernst, Paul, 130.

Euripides, 107, 118, 120.

Fäsi, Johann Konrad, 14-15, 20, 74, 83-84.

Falk, Johann Daniel, 118-119.

Faßmann, David, 11, 13, 15, 20, 21, 24, 27-40, 42 (n.), 43 (n.), 47, 50, 51,
    64-65, 73-74, 81, 84, 103-104, 109, 129, 130.

"Faßmann der Jüngere", 35-36.

Fénelon, François de Salignac de La Mothe, 11, 20, 27-28, 55, 66, 73, 111, 130.

Fielding, Henry, 16.

Fletcher, John, 120.

Fontenelle, Bernard Le Bouyer de, 11, 20, 27-28, 30, 31, 38, 49, 50, 51, 55,
    73, 74, 75, 78, 80, 84, 86, 130.

Francke, August Hermann, 32.

Frederick II, King of Prussia, 14, 19, 38, 39, 40, 44 (n.), 45 (n.), 66, 115-116,
    121-123.

Gaum, Johann Ferdinand, 39.

Geiger, Carl Ignaz, 115-117.

Gellert, Christian Fürchtegott, 21, 36-37, 71 (n.), 82, 121.

Gessner, Salomon, 87.

Gibbon, Edward, 122.

Gleichmann, Johann Zacharias, 34, 36-37, 39, 130.

Göckingk, Leopold Friedrich Günther von, 21, 83.

Goethe, Johann Wolfgang, 21, 29, 45 (n.), 86, 95, 97, 107-109, 119-121, 122-123,
    129, 130.

Gottsched, Johann Christoph, 18 (n.), 31, 50-51, 52, 53, 55, 62, 63, 71 (n.), 85,
    86, 104-105, 129, 130.

Gottschedin, Louise Adelgunde Victoria, 105.

Grillparzer, Franz, 19, 121-124, 129, 130.

Günther, Johann Christian, 103-105, 114.

Hagedorn, Friedrich von, 37, 71 (n.).

Haller, Albrecht von, 105.

Hamann, Johann Georg (the elder), 51.

Harsdörffer, Georg Philipp, 23.

Heidegger, Gotthard, 52.

Henrici-Picander, Christian Friedrich, 104.

Herder, Johann Gottfried, 85.

Heß, Jonas Ludwig, 70.

Hippias, 94.

Hobbes, Thomas, 103.

Hofmann von Hofmannswaldau, Christian, 49, 53.

Shakespeare, William, 108, 120, 122.
"Silvander" (= Heinrich Christian von Brocke?), 37.
Sonnenfels, Joseph von, 52, 56.
Sophocles, 120.
Steinauer, Johann Wilhelm, 103-105.
Steinbach, Christoph Ernst, 103-105.
Sterne, Laurence, 9, 131.
Stoppe, Daniel, 75, 104.
Swift, Jonathan, 64-65.
Tacitus, 66.
Talander, s. Bohse-Talander
Tentzel, Wilhelm Ernst, 29.
Thomasius, Christian, 29, 32.
Tonder, Moritz Flavius Trenk von, 21, 39-40.
Trenck, Friedrich Freiherr von der, 18 (n.).
Triller, Daniel Wilhelm, 37.
Uz, Johann Peter, 71 (n.), 119.
Valdés, Alfonso de, 24.
Virgil, 115-116.
Voltaire, 18 (n.), 34, 66, 109, 111, 115-116, 121.
Waser, Johann Heinrich, 87.
Wegelin, Jacob, 74, 77.
Weidmann, Josef, 117.
Weiße, Christian Felix, 114.
Wekhrlin, Wilhelm Ludwig, 66.
Wezel, Johann Karl, 110-111.
Wieland, Christoph Martin, 14, 19-20, 29, 74, 84, 86-97, 107-109, 112, 114,
        119-120, 129, 130, 131.
Willebrandt, Johann Peter, 52.
Wolff, Christian, 66.
Zäunemannin, Sidonia Hedwig, 105.
Zimmermann, Johann Georg, 86.
Zitterbarth, Bartholomäus, 117.

EDITOR'S NOTE

Most scholars who use the libraries must have had the experience I very often had after reading a sound work of scholarship: one wishes then that a few remarks about the author were included in the text. The modern publisher generally supplies some such information on the dust-wrappers, but when it is discarded we have no information left. Looking through bibliographies or publications of learned societies is generally too time-consuming, and thus a person whose knowledge we have come to admire and whose presentation made us eager for more personal details is lost to us entirely.

To overcome this bothersome weakness of objectivity, the "German Studies in America" bring always a few remarks on the subject and the author which will at least give a first idea of the person behind all the labor that goes into scholarly work.

Dr. John Rutledge was good enough to supply a short outline of his life. In so objective a study as his nothing should be more appropriate than adding his own objective summary. Here it is:

ABOUT THE AUTHOR

Don John Rutledge, Jr., was born on November 16, 1944, in Fayetteville, Tennessee; social ties with German families in Huntsville, Alabama, awakened his interest in the German language and literature. Pursuit of this interest led to a Bachelor of Arts degree with a major in German from The George Washington University in 1966.

Thanks to a Gilman Fellowship, Mr. Rutledge was able to begin graduate study at The Johns Hopkins University, where he received the Master of Arts degree in 1967. At Hopkins he worked as a research assistant for Dr. Lieselotte E. Kurth and taught elementary and intermediate German and a course in Modern German Short Fiction.

A fellowship from the Deutsche Akademische Austauschdienst (1969-70) enabled the author to do extensive research on his dissertation in Germany, principally at the university library in Göttingen. After returning from Germany he and the former Joyce Anne Simpkins, then a student of German literature at The Johns Hopkins University, were married at Mount Calvary Episcopal Church, Baltimore. In May, 1971, he was appointed to the position of Instructor, later Assistant Professor, at Southeastern Massachusetts University, North Dartmouth, Massachusetts, where he has taught until the present. The dissertation, the basis for this book, was completed in January, 1972, under the guidance of Professors Lieselotte E. Kurth and Harold Jantz.